We acknowledge the Traditional Owners
of the lands on which these recipes
were shaped, these stories were shared,
and this book was written and made.
We pay our respects to all Aboriginal
and Torres Strait Islander Elders,
past and present.

The *Baker's* Book

FAVOURITE RECIPES
AND KITCHEN WISDOM BY
AUSTRALIAN BAKERS YOU LOVE

Edited by **Ruby Goss**
Foreword by **Natalie Paull**

Art by **Beci Orpin**
Photography by **Rochelle Eagle**
Styling by **Lee Blaylock**

murdoch books
Sydney | London

Foreword

by Natalie Paull

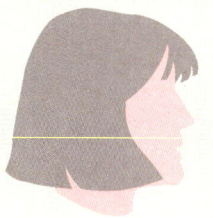

founder of beloved former Melbourne cake house Beatrix, author of *Beatrix Bakes* and *Beatrix Bakes: Another Slice*

We love to bake.

We give you what our hands and ovens have wrought because we want you to feel good. We are telling you we love you.

From scratch doesn't capture the complexity of turning ingredients into new structures. The transfiguration. Our hands feel if moisture needs adjusting. We forge butter and flour into a million layers (actually 729 for the perfectly laminated puff pastry) and give yeast the ideal environment and time to ferment. We watch caramel with acute eyes and noses. We have superhuman abilities to cut precise amounts of butter or intuit temperatures, nurturing and sensing, innately knowing the timing for the next step – three seconds? Best to wait ten. And then it will be ready. All our senses are at work – listening for the right slapping sound of the beating batter, looking at the colour of the cookie as it bakes. We choreograph cream and crunch, and we compute ratios – art, craft and chemistry, deliciously blurred.

Some of us are the young bakers and cakers plying our repetitive craft in small kitchens with undependable ovens, no coolroom (but fingers crossed, one day ...) and inadequate work surfaces. Every gram of ingredient and ounce of labour measured to eke out another day of baking (enough to make a future).

Others of us are tenacious elders who have built businesses from our own bootstrapped beginnings into a boundless array of baked goods (blessed now with coolrooms!), zeal as intact as the day we weighed that first kilo of flour.

> We use the hand-me-down recipes of our heritages and, with our tinkerings, carry them through the portal into a new day

We bake along a scale: simple to complex. No matter where we land, we are in the business of construction. We are wholly anti-deconstruction. We *have* to, *must* build a structure to carry our flavours. What we craft cannot be broken into parts on a fancy white plate. Our baking maybe won't ever see a plate. More likely it will be consumed from a box or paper bag that someone holds close to their chin as a drift of caramel-hued flakes settles onto lips, lapels and lap. An eyes-closed moment of joy coursing from mouth to heart.

We are the early risers. We are the ones who turn ovens on in blistering summer heatwaves and and work in t-shirts in the depth of winter, relishing the warming nature of our tasks. We are quasi nocturnal and switch on retina-searing fluorescents in our bake spaces in that plush, inky darkness that comes right before the dawn. Our doughs rise with the sun's rise. Without the passion, would we still rise? Yes. Yes! That is our nature.

We forage in the savoury sections, encasing vegetables in buttery crusts with as much ease as a ripe peach or tart apple. We borrow salt and squeezes of lemon to bring balance and zing.

And just before the final recipe is sent or the countertop full, we have a moment of proud repose (sometimes regretful critique). A moment to take in the bake. A moment before the preparation for the next new recipe or full countertop begins.

Of course we are people pleasing. It's not a toxic trait but pure want – for you to have a slice of something to counter any woes. Perhaps even to bake it for yourself. Our cakes are beside you to mark a momentous moment or a mere morning. We are the ones who teach our craft to eager new hands and minds. We write our recipes impeccably and share them in books, online and betwixt our peers so knowledge is transformed into a precious gift.

We use the hand-me-down recipes of our heritages and, with our tinkerings, carry them through the portal into a new day, into our current kitchen. And we hope that our recipes will be carried through a future portal, one day, when we will no longer be.

Would you like a piece of what we've baked for you?

Nat x

Dark chocolate, orange and almond crumb-kies

Natalie Paull

MAKES 6
SPECIAL EQUIPMENT six 8–9 cm (3¼–3½ inch) egg rings (see note), stand mixer with paddle attachment (optional)

90 g (3¼ oz) raw almonds
100 g (3½ oz) cake flour
85 g (3 oz) unsalted butter, cold and diced, plus extra for greasing
45 g (1½ oz) light brown sugar
35 g (1¼ oz) quality dark chocolate, 70%, chopped into pea-sized chunks, or chocolate chips
20 g (¾ oz) polenta (cornmeal)
finely grated zest of 1 orange
½ teaspoon vanilla bean paste
¼ teaspoon baking powder
⅛ teaspoon fine sea salt

Inspired by the leftover cooked crumble bits from a tray of crumble pies at Beatrix Bakes (my favourite baker-treat snack!), these are the best of both buttery worlds. They are adaptrixable to almost infinite combinations of chocolates and nuts (I've used almonds here, but they're equally good with hazelnuts – toast them first, then rub their skins off and chop them into chunks). Consider them simple cookies to snack on while you choose your first bake.

Preheat the oven to 150°C/300°F fan-forced (170°C/350°F conventional).
Roughly chop the almonds into chunky bits – halves and quarters. Spread them on a baking tray and toast in the oven for 15 minutes until barely browned. Refrigerate for a few minutes to cool quickly.
Combine the almonds and the remaining ingredients in the bowl of a stand mixer with the paddle attachment and mix on low speed for 2–5 minutes. You can also do this by hand. The mixture will evolve through powdery white flour with large butter lumps to clumps of crumble that hold together with a light squeeze. If the dough goes further and forms a ball, stop mixing and tease it back out into crumbly boulders.
Line a shallow baking tray with baking paper. Melt about 1 teaspoon of extra butter and liberally brush the insides of six 8–9 cm (3¼–3½ inch) egg rings and place well apart on the baking tray. Divide the dough evenly between the rings (about 60 g/2¼ oz each), then press it lightly so it meets the ring edges without compromising the crumbly vibe.
Bake for 30 minutes until evenly tan from edge to centre. As soon as the crumb-kies come out of the oven, carefully run a sharp knife around the inside edge of the egg rings and lift the rings off.
Eat while warm. They will keep in an airtight container at room temperature for 1 week.

If you don't have egg rings, make a little collar out of foil! I fold a piece of foil over and over to around 2.5 cm (1 inch). Take the two ends and make a teardrop shape. Fold over a few times to seal the ends, then reshape to a circle and grease.

Contents by Chapter

14 Introduction
16 Before you begin

SMALL PLEASURES

25 Marshmallow brownies, Orlando Artavilla
28 Chocolate rye tahini cookies, Gad Assayag
32 Strawberry and matcha maritozzi, Ryan and Seren Chu
39 Miss Trixie's honey joy slice, Alice Bennett
42 Pistachio amaretti, Marianna Di Bartolo
47 Burnt butter and pecan cakes, Charlie Duffy
51 Tiramisukis, Alisha Henderson
54 Grapefruit creams, Emelia Jackson
59 Macadamia and wattleseed chocolate chip cookies, Michael James
61 Fluffy buttermilk scones, Belinda Jeffery
66 Crullers, Jesse Knierum and Aaron Morgan
71 London fog castagnole, cacao nib sugar and pots de crème, Giorgia McAllister Forte
73 Lemon, thyme and honey madeleines, Tilly Pamment
79 Ondeh ondeh, Raymond Tan
83 Mohn hamantaschen (poppyseed cookies), Maaryasha Werdiger

MORNING & AFTERNOON TEAS

90   Glazed fruit buns, Orlando Artavilla
92   Baker Bleu babka, Gad Assayag
99   Beetroot and apple cake with wattleseed icing, Jo Barrett
100 Ricotta cassateddi, Marianna Di Bartolo
102 Chu flans, Ryan and Seren Chu
107 Pear frangipane slab tart, Sophie Hansen
113 Bay gâteau d'émotion, Gillian Bell
115 Ginger and orange blossom cake, Gillian Bell
118 Peach and sour cream cake, Alisha Henderson
122 Chocolate, amaretto and sour cherry tart, Nadine Ingram
127 Lemon, polenta and raspberry tea cake, Michael James
128 Lemon curd shortbread tart, Belinda Jeffery
134 Plum, frangipane and cream cheese galettes, Dougal Muffet
139 Swedish semlor, Gregorio Montalbán Sánchez
142 Cinnamon braid, Gregorio Montalbán Sánchez
147 Buttermilk bundt with passionfruit icing, Tilly Pamment
148 Pandan drømmekage, Raymond Tan
150 Plum streusel cake, Maaryasha Werdiger

SPECIAL OCCASIONS

160 Inception cake, Rosemary Andrews

164 Hibiscus cake, Nornie Bero

167 Miss Trixie's classic chocolate cake, Alice Bennett

172 Hazelnut and apple cake with sour cream frosting and apple caramel, Natasha Brownfield

176 Preserved lemon layer cake with blackberry and olive oil buttercream, Patchanida Chimkire

182 Layered rhubarb meringue cake, Cherie Hausler

187 Chocolate cherry choux, Emelia Jackson

191 Strawberry, chocolate and balsamic lamington stack, Darren Purchese

SOMETHING SAVOURY

199 Spinach, leek and smoked cheddar cheese slab pie, Danielle Alvarez

203 Feta and dill biscuits with harissa honey butter, Danielle Alvarez

204 Little Picket potato bread with roasted garlic butter and parsley, Jo Barrett

206 Tomato, herb and quark tart, Natasha Brownfield

213 Fig-leaf sourdough tin loaf, Kimmy Gastmeier

215 Burnt fenugreek and sesame loaf, Dougal Muffet

218 Jerusalem artichoke, chilli greens and goat's cheese focaccias, Giorgia McAllister Forte

224 A1 pies, three ways (Za'atar manouche, Kafta manouche, Haloumi pies), Haikal Raji

230 Pea and feta tart, Gareth Whitton

TIME FOR DESSERT

239 Lemon tart, Audrey Allard

243 Negroni chocolate tart, Rosemary Andrews

246 Peaches and cream meringue tower, Anneliese Brancatisano

250 Chocolate and rye tart with olive oil mascarpone cream, Anneliese Brancatisano

255 Amaro crème caramel with salted, caramelised cacao, Charlie Duffy

257 Pandan, coconut and mango chiffon roll, Patchanida Chimkire

262 Cherry pie, Kimmy Gastmeier

267 Fig, chocolate and sweet dukkah sundaes, Sophie Hansen

268 Huon apple crumble, Jesse Knierum and Aaron Morgan

270 Basque cheesecake, Darren Purchese

273 Unbaked strawberry cheesecake, Akira Toyama

276 White chocolate and rhubarb pudding with lemon myrtle, Gareth Whitton

281 The baker's pantry

289 Find the bakers

292 The team

295 Thank you

297 Index

Contents by Baker

Audrey Allard 238
Lemon tart 239

Danielle Alvarez 198
Spinach, leek and smoked cheddar cheese slab pie 199
Feta and dill biscuits with harissa honey butter 203

Rosemary Andrews 158
Inception cake 160
Negroni chocolate tart 243

Orlando Artavilla 22
Marshmallow brownies 25
Glazed fruit buns 90

Gad Assayag 26
Chocolate rye tahini cookies 28
Baker Bleu babka 92

Jo Barrett 96
Beetroot and apple cake with wattleseed icing 99
Little Picket potato bread with roasted garlic butter and parsley 204

Gillian Bell 110
Bay gâteau d'émotion 113
Ginger and orange blossom cake 115

Alice Bennett 36
Miss Trixie's honey joy slice 39
Miss Trixie's classic chocolate cake 167

Nornie Bero 162
Hibiscus cake 164

Anneliese Brancatisano 244
Peaches and cream meringue tower 246
Chocolate and rye tart with olive oil mascarpone cream 250

Natasha Brownfield 170
Hazelnut and apple cake with sour cream frosting and apple caramel 172
Tomato, herb and quark tart 206

Patchanida Chimkire 174
Preserved lemon layer cake with blackberry and olive oil buttercream 176
Pandan, coconut and mango chiffon roll 257

Ryan and Seren Chu 30
Strawberry and matcha maritozzi 32
Chu flans 102

Marianna Di Bartolo 40
Pistachio amaretti 42
Ricotta cassateddi 100

Charlie Duffy 44
Burnt butter and pecan cakes 47
Amaro crème caramel with salted, caramelised cacao 255

Kimmy Gastmeier 210
Fig-leaf sourdough tin loaf 213
Cherry pie 262

Sophie Hansen 106
Pear frangipane slab tart 107
Fig, chocolate and sweet dukkah sundaes 267

Cherie Hausler 180
Layered rhubarb meringue cake 182

Alisha Henderson 48
Tiramisukis 51
Peach and sour cream cake 118

Nadine Ingram 120
Chocolate, amaretto and sour cherry tart 122

Emelia Jackson 52
Grapefruit creams 54
Chocolate cherry choux 187

Michael James 56
Macadamia and wattleseed chocolate chip cookies 59
Lemon, polenta and raspberry tea cake 127

Belinda Jeffery 60
Fluffy buttermilk scones 61
Lemon curd shortbread tart 128

Jesse Knierum and Aaron Morgan 64
Crullers 66
Huon apple crumble 268

Giorgia McAllister Forte 68
London fog castagnole, cacao nib sugar and pots de crème 71
Jerusalem artichoke, chilli greens and goat's cheese focaccias 218

Gregorio Montalbán Sánchez 138
Swedish semlor 139
Cinnamon braid 142

Dougal Muffet 132
Plum, frangipane and cream cheese galettes 134
Burnt fenugreek and sesame loaf 215

Tilly Pamment 72
Lemon, thyme and honey madeleines 73
Buttermilk bundt with passionfruit icing 147

Darren Purchese 190
Strawberry, chocolate and balsamic lamington stack 191
Basque cheesecake 270

Haikal Raji 222
A1 pies, three ways
(Za'atar manouche, Kafta manouche, Haloumi pies) 224

Raymond Tan 76
Ondeh ondeh 79
Pandan drømmekage 148

Akira Toyama 272
Unbaked strawberry cheesecake 273

Maaryasha Werdiger 80
Mohn hamantaschen (poppyseed cookies) 83
Plum streusel cake 150

Gareth Whitton 228
Pea and feta tart 230
White chocolate and rhubarb pudding with lemon myrtle 276

Introduction

Growing up in the suburban fringe of Melbourne, most of my childhood baking came from Mum's weathered copy of *Cookery the Australian Way*. Specifically, from a family friend's handwritten recipe, wedged permanently into the fold on the page for chocolate self-saucing pudding. Hers was for butterscotch and pecan, and it was craving incarnate.

We never had lavish pecans, but there was always a jar of golden syrup in the cupboard; I could climb up to the flour tin, and the butter would be in its dish if the cat (or I) hadn't got to it first.

It was a recipe, but it was also a magic trick. You mixed up a basic batter and poured it into a pudding basin – and then it got interesting. On top came a sprinkle of brown sugar and cornflour, and then – a moment of bravery – a careful pour of golden syrup and boiling water followed by a cartoonish shuffle to the oven. It went in looking suspiciously like mud-pie mix, but it would emerge a pudding, puffed up and triumphantly golden. The soupy top had become a caramel sauce that bubbled up the sides from underneath. Something transformative had occurred in the oven. At that age, I didn't question the process. I was happy enough to just dig my spoon in and enjoy.

Nowadays, I understand the reactions that happen: how the top liquid layer descends, thickens and caramelises while the soft batter turns fluffy as it cooks. But the thing is, understanding how baking works doesn't break its spell. If anything, it makes what you've baked feel that much more magic – especially when it comes out of the oven as you'd imagined it. Or better.

We set out to make a book that could capture this feeling. It started with the much-loved pastry chef Rosemary Andrews, who planted the seed of an idea to bring the most inspiring bakers in Australia together. And so we started dreaming up a book that would not only share recipes (and great ones, too), but the stories of the people who dedicate themselves to the craft day in, day out. Sprinkled with wisdom and advice, it's a book we imagined could be as inspiring as it was instructive. One that could give you insight into the graft, generosity and diversity of the baking community – and invite you in.

> Along the way, I asked every baker for a piece of advice – a lesson learned that changed everything

In these pages, you'll learn from pastry chefs, home bakers and community bakeries, from those starting out and our most respected baking voices alike. We asked for recipes that excited them, that they wanted to share, in the hope that this book might become something you treasure, like a passed-down community cookbook. Most importantly, we asked for recipes our bakers enjoyed making. This book has everything from everyday recipes for loaf cakes, slices and biscuits (useful for anyone who's ever said 'I can cook but I can't bake') to projects for tarts and pies to lose yourself in, all the way to decadent layer cakes, roulades and choux ready to mark occasions – or make them. We drew a vague line at laminated dough but were convinced otherwise by Perth baker Ryan Chu, who himself mastered the process at home. Maybe you will, too.

Along the way, I asked every baker for a piece of advice – a lesson learned that changed everything, a handy tip that's always in their back pocket. I became more confident in my own baking at home. After a lifetime of wilful ignorance, I followed the words of the thirty-five bakers in these pages and stopped ignoring the 'room temperature' note in ingredient lists – and let me tell you, it really did change everything. And the more conversations I had, the less I could ignore another trail of crumbs forming in my mind – that these were not just lessons that were useful for baking alone, but for life.

Baking is often mixed up with achieving perfection – but these conversations taught me that we would be misguided, and in fact we'd be miserable, to reach only and always for this. Baking, like life, is full of surprises. There are the whims of your ingredients, the temperature of your room, the reliability of your oven. You learn, over time, to work with them, not against them, and to find accomplishment in understanding a little more each day. You learn that getting anywhere is to put your trust in small but remarkable steps.

To bake, again and again and again, is to let this time-earned intuition guide you as much as intellect – to relish the moments when things do turn out as you'd hoped they would as much as learning to let go when they don't. It's to be kind to yourself, and to others, through this – and to let curiosity be the thing that keeps bringing you back.

And then there was the joy. That thing that started it all. I think I can speak for every baker in this book when I say that the pinnacle of baking's many joys is the very simple act of sharing something you love – and seeing, just for a moment, someone's face light up as a result.

Baking offers us kindness in many forms – from a woozy moment of sugary celebration or a slice of sourdough made from local wheat, to the honeycombed cross-section of a perfect croissant in the hand on an ordinary Wednesday morning.

What if I'm not being overly sentimental by relating baking to life? Something baked is, after all, a slice of life – it captures a moment, makes a memory to take along with you into the future, or offers that rarest of opportunities to taste the past and feel instantly borne back there. It's also a process – a destination that can only be reached by paying close attention to the journey. Which, the wise will tell you, is the only way to live.

It might not solve the bigger questions, but in those minutes it takes to eat a baked delight, there's discovery, nostalgia, a sliver of completeness. And so we bake again.

Stain these pages with melted butter and lodge flour in the folds. Find things to learn and to share. But mostly, I hope you find joy, mixing bowls full of it.

The legendary butterscotch pecan self-saucing pudding

Preheat the oven to 170°C. Grease a 4-cup ovenproof dish.

Sift 1 ¼ cups S.R. flour over ⅓ cup firmly packed brown sugar and combine.

Whisk ½ cup milk, 1 egg, 80 g melted and cooled butter and 2 tablespoons golden syrup together until combined.

Add the dry ingredients and beat until a smooth batter forms. Stir in 75 g chopped pecans. Pour into a dish and smooth the surface.

Sauce: Combine ½ cup firmly packed brown sugar and 1 tablespoon cornflour, then sprinkle it over the batter in the dish. Combine ¼ cup golden syrup and 1 ¼ cups boiling water, then pour it evenly over the sugar and cornflour mixture.

Bake for 50–55 minutes.

Before You Begin

Bakers love the accuracy of scales – so you'll find most measures here given in weight. This includes whole eggs, yolks and whites (but you'll find helpful approximations for whole eggs along the way). For rougher measures, you might find a cup here or there. And all milk is full cream.

Each recipe is stamped with an icon that indicates its complexity (see below). This takes into account preparation, resting and baking, but we leave the time it takes to measure ingredients to you, so come prepared.

Each recipe also includes a 'special equipment' list, which covers particular tins, stand mixers and other whizzing gadgets (though we're not stopping you from using your favourite hand-held electric beaters or your hands – often the latter are recommended), piping bags and nozzles, and so on. Regular items such as mixing bowls, standard baking trays, spatulas and sieves aren't listed – we imagine these are part and parcel of the baker's life. And where tea towels (dish towels) don't suffice, look out for biodegradable plastic wrap, which is thankfully now a thing.

On page 281, you'll find a list of producers recommended by the bakers in this book – if you live in Australia, we encourage seeking them out for top-notch ingredients and to support local traders and sustainable small businesses.

RECIPE KEY

Look out for these symbols – they'll help you assess you how complex a recipe is at a glance:

EVERYDAY BAKE: There's something for everyone here. These recipes use straightforward processes with techniques in the baker's everyday skill set.

EVERYDAY PLUS: These are everyday bakes that require some planning because of resting or proving times.

PROJECT BAKE: A level up from everyday bakes, these tend to be for yeasted doughs or tarts that have steps spanning a matter of days (or can be organised as such to ease the load). It's best to plan ahead for these.

SKILLED BAKE: These recipes contain multiple techniques, often including decoration. Don't be deterred – our bakers will walk you through every step so you can achieve them with confidence.

A NOTE ON FLOURS

The percentage of protein in your flour indicates how much gluten will develop. You want less gluten for cakey, short and finely crumbed creations, and more for a slice of bubbly focaccia or chewy sourdough.

BAKER'S FLOUR (STRONG FLOUR): Also called bread flour, this is a high-protein flour (and hence high in gluten-developing potential) and the choice for heftier bakes that require generous elasticity – think breads and highly enriched doughs (i.e. doughs that include a high-fat ingredient, such as milk, eggs, butter or oils). Baker's flour usually contains at least 13 per cent protein.

00 FLOUR: A relatively high-protein flour made of durum wheat. It's commonly used in pizza dough, as it forms just enough gluten to build strength but remain tender, and it's milled very finely to allow for thin, crisp bases. You'll also see it used in wider Italian-style baking. It usually contains 12–13 per cent protein.

PLAIN (ALL-PURPOSE) FLOUR: Does what it says on the flour tin. It's your everyday choice for soft yet chewy bakes, such as tea cakes, biscuits, scones and pancakes – and most likely the one you can get away with in a pinch. Plain flour usually contains 10–12 per cent protein.

CAKE FLOUR: The lowest of protein percentages for the lightest of bakes (think sponges and chiffons). Cake flour will help develop just enough gluten to give form and keep the final result fluffy (which is why we don't want to overbeat a cake batter – we want to keep the gluten lazy). Cake flour usually contains 7–9 per cent protein.

Small *Pleasures*

25 Marshmallow brownies

28 Chocolate rye tahini cookies

32 Strawberry and matcha maritozzi

39 Miss Trixie's honey joy slice

42 Pistachio amaretti

47 Burnt butter and pecan cakes

51 Tiramisukis

54 Grapefruit creams

59 Macadamia and wattleseed chocolate chip cookies

61 Fluffy buttermilk scones

66 Crullers

71 London fog castagnole, cacao nib sugar and pots de crème

73 Lemon, thyme and honey madeleines

79 Ondeh ondeh

83 Mohn hamantaschen (poppyseed cookies)

Orlando Artavilla

Marshmallow brownies (25)

Glazed fruit buns (90)

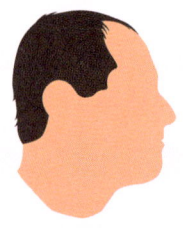

Co-owner and founder,
Candied Bakery

Melbourne, Vic
Boonwurrung/Bunurong
Country

The way Orlando Artavilla describes it, baking was the obvious choice. 'I was brought up in a Calabrian family and I'm just that classic kid that grew up around food.' He describes watching his grandmother make kilos of bread, mixing it by hand in a big wooden trough: 'Those memories are the most visual thing I have of her. And then she'd have leftover dough and she'd make the most beautiful pizzas, and then we'd eat that while the bread was baking.' Every night, there would be three or four dishes on the dinner table, prepared by his mother. 'It was something tasty, always,' he says.

With these beginnings in mind, the array on offer at Candied, the bakery he runs with his wife, Toula Ploumidis, in Spotswood in Melbourne's inner west, is not surprising. It's a real neighbourhood bakery, with crowd-pleasing cookies and brownies (see page 25), Toula's famous spanakopita, Orlando's potato focaccia and all manner of buns (see page 90) and bread. Orlando's baking goes back to Year 11, when he left school to begin as an apprentice. 'I was more excited about leaving school than baking – I don't think it really hit me until I realised it was a 3 am start!' he admits.

'It's not like I had thought about baking, but I was always interested in what Mum was doing or what my grandmother was doing,' says Orlando. 'I grew up in Cobram, up in country Victoria, so we didn't have access to anything great. And I suppose back then baking wasn't seen as something special. It was just a staple food. Bread was just sliced bread, there was no sourdough. Since then, the industry has changed so much for the better.'

But the craft gained dimension in his life – not only through the skills he learned but through the relationships he built with his bosses and mentors (see opposite). For many years, Orlando and Toula were behind the Brunswick East institution that was Sugardough Panificio and Patisserie. 'We never wanted to bake again,' he says. 'I don't think I was sick of baking. I think I was sick of the whole idea of having a business – where you don't really get to enjoy it as much as you would like.' A getaway unexpectedly changed their minds. It was the time of Milk Bar and Christina Tosi. 'Everything was back to nostalgia and just having things you grew up with. It wasn't over the top. They weren't trying to add a twist to everything,' says Orlando.

They came back, opened up Candied Bakery with a focus on straightforwardly delicious bakes – and something clicked. 'We've been here for over a decade, but it feels like five years,' he says. 'And it feels like we're nowhere near finished.' They still follow the pearls of

> 'You always go back to what's the most simple thing, I think. In the end, that's what people want and what they appreciate more, as long as it's done properly.'

wisdom they picked up overseas. 'You always go back to what's the most simple thing, I think. In the end, that's what people want and what they appreciate more, as long as it's done properly,' he says.

WORDS TO BAKE BY
'When I was starting out, I met a couple of people in the industry who really inspired me. The first bakery owner who took me under his wing, who gave me the apprenticeship initially, was key to me. Obviously for the baking aspect, but for life too. One of the things that sticks in my mind is something he said when saw I him many years later: "I wish I'd let go of it and let you do a lot more." And I really took that on board. I like to not get too involved. We've got some really great pastry chefs and bakers – this young generation shows so much passion. It's nice to be able to step back and just let them do what they want to do.'

Marshmallow brownies

Orlando Artavilla
Profiled on page 22

MAKES 15
SPECIAL EQUIPMENT 23 cm (9 inch) square or round baking tin

220 g (7¾ oz) unsalted butter
400 g (14 oz) dark chocolate, 70%
50 g (1¾ oz) ground espresso coffee beans
550 g (1 lb 4 oz) caster (superfine) sugar
6 eggs
1 teaspoon salt
2 teaspoons vanilla extract
270 g (9½ oz) plain (all-purpose) flour, sifted
about 20 marshmallows, or to taste

These brownies were the first bake we developed for Candied Bakery, along with our chocolate marshmallow cookies. We revised a recipe we got from a New York friend of ours who was visiting and changed it to what we like ... to great result.

Preheat the oven to 150°C/300°F fan-forced (170°C/350°F conventional). Line a 23 cm (9 inch) square or round baking tin with baking paper.
 Combine the butter, chocolate and espresso in a small heavy-based saucepan and warm over low heat until the butter and chocolate are melted and stir to combine. Remove immediately from the heat and set aside.
 Whisk the caster sugar and eggs in a large mixing bowl until combined but not fluffy. Whisk in the salt and vanilla. Fold the chocolate mixture into the egg mixture using a wooden spoon. Gently fold in the flour. Press the mixture into the prepared tin.
 Bake for about 40 minutes, then quickly open the oven door and place the marshmallows on top. Bake for another 40 minutes or until slightly set. Cool in the tin before cutting into 15 squares.

Gad Assayag

Chocolate rye tahini cookies (28)

Baker Bleu babka (92)

Executive pastry chef, Baker Bleu

Melbourne, Vic
Wurundjeri Country

For Gad Assayag, it begins – and continues – with babka. 'I'm from Jerusalem, so babka is what I grew up on,' he explains. 'It was always on the table on the weekend.' It was the thing he missed most after moving to Australia about twenty years ago. 'I never really found the same thing. So I tried to replicate it as much as I could – and then I started to make it more my own.' It's a weekend tradition he's carried on at home with his two daughters – and now with you (see page 92). 'I think the beautiful thing about babka is that the filling soaks into the dough just slightly without being fully absorbed by it, so you still feel the different textures of the dough and the filling.'

Gad moved into pastry production in bakeries several years ago, after life as a fine-dining chef. For him, baking is all about the excitement of beginning again. 'You can't beat a fresh product. There's something very special about it,' he says. You can hear the enthusiasm when he talks about his craft. 'It's incredible really. In bakeries we're making similar products over and over again, but you always continue to learn and develop. When you work with a live product, you sort of build a bit of a relationship with it – and a relationship with the process as well, particularly with sourdough.'

Gad continues to find inspiration in an early love – books. 'I read a lot of recipe books. All the time. That's where you get all the little tips and tricks and an understanding of the process. In every recipe, there are a few things that you really have to focus on, the critical points.'

You can see this in the recipes Gad shares in this book. Despite working in a commercial kitchen at Baker Bleu (beloved bakeries in Melbourne and Sydney), he has an intuitive understanding of baking at home, and how to tweak the experience to get better results.

He and Baker Bleu's founder, Mike Russell, bounce ideas off each other in the way only a baker and a pastry chef can, he explains (see opposite). 'The philosophy here is what really inspired me to work with Mike, even though I've been so long in the industry. It's his respect for ingredients, using the best ingredients, the best processes.'

Then there's also going back to the roots of what it means to bake: 'I think of everybody sitting around the table and having the pastries, and it's the whole thing of bringing people together,' says Gad. 'I love the small joy of having a croissant in the morning. It's just two minutes of your day to enjoy this crunchy buttery thing, and then life keeps going. To create this moment for people is something quite special. It's very rewarding.'

'I love the small joy of having a croissant in the morning. It's just a few minutes of your day to enjoy this crunchy buttery thing, then life keeps going. To create this moment for people is something quite special.'

NOTES ON BAKERS AND PASTRY CHEFS

'Morning pastries are where the skills of pastry chefs and bakers meet. Bakers and pastry chefs often come from very different perspectives. There's a little bit of teasing each other, but at the same time they complete each other. That's something I really enjoy about working with Mike: we're able to bring our different skills and perspectives together and bounce ideas off each other. It really helps with creativity.'

WORDS TO BAKE BY

'Baking is all about organisation. It's probably 70 per cent of the process. The more you organise, the better your result. Look at your recipe, read it very well. And start weighing up your ingredients and then tick whatever you did, so you know that everything is organised. And only then, once everything is organised, your tools are there, then you start working. Then you'll get much more of a chance of better results. You have to understand the process and understand where you're going before you actually start.'

Chocolate rye tahini cookies

Gad Assayag
Profiled on page 26

MAKES 16
SPECIAL EQUIPMENT stand mixer with paddle attachment

195 g (6¾ oz) plain (all-purpose) flour
80 g (2¾ oz) rye flour
25 g (1 oz) unsweetened cocoa powder
3 g (⅛ oz) baking powder
6 g (¼ oz) bicarbonate of soda (baking soda)
6 g (¼ oz) salt
135 g (4¾ oz) unsalted butter, at room temperature
105 g (3¾ oz) hulled tahini
265 g (9¼ oz) brown sugar
65 g (2¼ oz) caster (superfine) sugar
65 g (2¼ oz) egg (from about 2 eggs)
40 g (1½ oz) egg yolk (from about 2 eggs)
300 g (10½ oz) dark chocolate, 70%, roughly chopped
50 g (1¾ oz) sesame seeds or Tasman Sea salt, for sprinkling (optional)

At Baker Bleu, cookies are always on offer and we are constantly looking for new and exciting flavours. While Mike was on his last bakery tour of France, he sent me a photo of a cookie with the message: 'Best cookie I've ever had.' It was a chocolate and tahini cookie, and I instantly knew this would be my next project. To make it more exciting and unique, I used dark chocolate and added rye flour, which creates a very fudgy texture – like a brownie in a cookie. I recommend buying tahini produced in a Middle Eastern country, as it is creamier and tends to have more flavour.

Combine the flours, cocoa powder, baking powder, bicarbonate of soda and salt in a large bowl and mix with a whisk. Set aside.

Combine the butter, tahini, brown sugar and caster sugar in the bowl of a stand mixer with the paddle attachment. Cream on medium speed until light and fluffy, about 5 minutes.

Switch to low speed and add half the egg and half the yolk, mixing well and scraping down the side of the bowl before repeating with the remaining egg and yolk. Mix until incorporated. Add the dry ingredients and mix on low speed until just combined. Add the dark chocolate and mix until just combined.

Line two baking trays with baking paper.

Use a large spoon or a ¼ cup measuring cup to scoop out pieces of cookie dough of about 80 g (2¾ oz). Roll each into a ball, arrange on the prepared baking trays and press to flatten into discs. Make sure they are about 5 cm (2 inches) apart. You should have about 16 cookies. Cover and refrigerate for 4 hours or overnight.

Preheat the oven to 175°C/350°F fan-forced (195°C/375°F conventional).

Remove the cookies from the fridge at least 10 minutes before baking to bring them to room temperature. If you're using sesame seeds, put the seeds on a small plate and press the top of each cookie into the seeds to coat. Put the cookies back on the baking trays. Alternatively, you could sprinkle the cookies lightly with sea salt.

Bake for 7 minutes, then remove the trays from the oven and gently tap them on a bench before returning them to the oven for 3–4 minutes, until the cookies are browned around the edges. (The tapping will give you nice flat cookies with a chewy texture.)

Cool the cookies on the trays for 10 minutes before transferring to a wire rack to cool completely.

The cookies will keep in an airtight container for 3 days.

Ryan and Seren Chu

Strawberry and matcha maritozzi (32)

Chu flans (102)

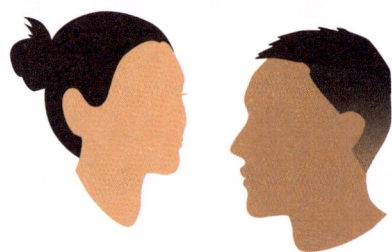

Ryan and Seren Chu, of Perth's go-to Chu Bakery, do classic French bakes their way. 'Light and uplifting' is the desired effect of a Chu bake, says Ryan. Something 'indulgent that doesn't leave you feeling burdened,' adds Seren. Then there's the focus on texture. Contrast and variety as you bite through is key. 'It's a very Chinese thing, I think,' Ryan says. 'Chinese people love texture – crunchy, chewy, gelatinous. I think about that with our baguettes, which are super crispy on the outside and really soft in the middle. It just makes it more exciting when you bite into it.'

But when they met, their views on baking were not in sync. Ryan was a town planner in Perth, prone to daydreams of making a living selling egg tarts like the kind he'd eat when visiting Hong Kong (China). Seren was managing her parents' bakery a few hours away in the coastal town of Busselton, but had no romantic dreams of staying in the trade. 'It was a standard Australian-style bakery, with lamingtons, hedgehog slices, vanilla slices,' she says. 'I wasn't proud of it and I wasn't loving it. That era in baking in Australia, in the early nineties to two-thousands was all about commercial pre-mixes,' says Seren.

When Ryan moved to Busselton and couldn't find work, he took up Seren's suggestion that he could work in the bakery. 'It was really tough,' he says. 'Everything was sharp and hot and heavy. I wasn't super in love with the actual product, but it was enjoyable because I was

Baker and pastry chef, and founders of Chu Bakery

Perth, WA
Whadjuk Nyoongar Country

making things with my hands.' Then came the global sourdough craze, upending Ryan's feelings about 'vinegar bread' – his nickname for the loaves his mum brought home from Coles supermarket when he was a kid. He got a textbook, read it from cover to cover and taught himself how to make classic French bakes: éclairs, brioche, croissants and sourdough baguettes.

After disasters and trial and error alike, Ryan's 'romantic idea' to have his own bakery only grew. For years, Seren was resistant: 'I never thought I would follow in my parents' footsteps because they worked seven days a week. It was hard and laborious. I kept saying no. I had all the trauma.' But she was finally swayed by the size of the dream – a residential bakery, small in scale, high in quality and across from a park – and by the opportunity to make a living from something she was proud of.

Eventually, they found an old deli space listed on Gumtree that, yes, overlooked a park – and in 2015 they opened Chu Bakery. Ryan focused on bread and Seren, also self-taught, took care of pastry, working from her love of cold French desserts. Soon there were queues around the block. 'It was just the two of us in the back, one person making coffee and one person serving, and a dishy,' Seren recalls. These days, Chu is a local institution that employs a team of thirty-five. The story of Chu is a little like their bakes – uplifting. It's about letting yourself indulge your dreams, and what you make of the work it takes to get there.

NOTES ON CONFIDENCE

Seren: 'My parents were very confident people. I feel like I've always had that natural confidence in what I do. They've always had a very strong work ethic, being boat people and coming to Australia with no money and then working and opening a business. My dad captained the ship and brought his whole family and some other passengers, and they ended up in the Philippines. They were out at sea for fourteen days and nights – a really long time. When you were in the refugee camp and you were about to come to Australia, they taught you skill sets, so that's how they started their baking journey. So even when we failed, I always felt, "We'll just keep trying," and we never stopped, even after so many attempts. I feel like all the mistakes that you make in the kitchen really shape you.'

WORDS TO BAKE BY

Ryan: 'I want to create something really beautiful to eat, like a potter wants to create a really nice cup to drink from – a really beautiful loaf of bread or a really beautiful croissant. I always have this image, like you see in paintings, of people gathering around a giant loaf of bread on the dinner table. You want to create this beautiful thing that you can imagine people will take home and share around with their family.'

'You want to create this beautiful thing that you can imagine people will take home and share around with their family.'

Strawberry and matcha maritozzi

Ryan and Seren Chu
Profiled on page 30

MAKES 8
SPECIAL EQUIPMENT stand mixer with dough hook and whisk attachments, stick blender, rolling pin, dough scraper, sugar thermometer, palette knife, two disposable piping bags

Brioche dough
103 g (3½ oz) water
5 g (⅛ oz) dried yeast
250 g (9 oz) baker's flour, plus extra for dusting
75 g (2¾ oz) egg (from about 2 eggs)
30 g (1 oz) caster (superfine) sugar
5 g (⅛ oz) salt
50 g (1¾ oz) unsalted butter, at room temperature

Egg wash
1 egg
1 teaspoon milk

When we were growing up in the nineties, every bakery and supermarket sold cream buns – giant dough pillows with a decadent amount of cream. We wanted to create a version of this classic but with our sensibility and contrasts in flavours and texture. This is our take on the Roman maritozzi, with a light brioche bun and the slightly earthy flavour of matcha paired with a sweet and bright burst of strawberries.

To make the brioche dough, pour the water into the bowl of your stand mixer. Add the yeast and let it hydrate for 5 minutes, then stir vigorously with a hand whisk until the yeast is well dissolved in the water.

Add all the ingredients except the butter. Fit the bowl to your stand mixer with the dough hook attachment and mix on low speed until all the ingredients are combined. Stop the mixer and scrape the bowl to make sure nothing is stuck to the side. Continue to mix on slow speed, then gradually increase to high speed until a cohesive and tacky dough forms. Give it a stretch to see if the gluten network has developed. If it breaks apart very quickly, mix the dough for another minute on high speed.

Add the butter and mix on low speed until it coats the dough. Gradually increase the speed until the dough starts to pull away from the side and makes a slapping noise.

Transfer the dough to a large greased bowl, cover tightly with biodegradable plastic wrap and leave to rest at room temperature (the ideal range is 20–24°C/68–75°F) for 1 hour or until doubled in volume.

Gently peel off the plastic wrap and knock the gas out of the dough by punching it. Fold the left side of the dough into the centre, then the right side, and turn the dough over. Cover with biodegradable plastic wrap and refrigerate overnight.

The next day, generously dust a work surface with flour. Unwrap the dough and place on the floured work surface. Use a rolling to pin to squash it into a rectangle, then roll out to about 1 cm (½ inch) thick. Gently turn the dough over to prevent it sticking to the work surface.

Let the dough relax for 15 minutes.

Using a dough scraper or knife, divide the dough into eight 65 g (2¼ oz) portions. Shape each portion into a ball and place on a baking tray lined with baking paper. Cover loosely with biodegradable plastic wrap and leave at room temperature for 1–2 hours, until doubled in volume.

Preheat your oven to 180°C/350°F fan-forced (200°C/400°F conventional).

Make an egg wash by beating the egg with the milk. Glaze the buns with the egg wash and bake for about 20 minutes, until deep golden brown.

Matcha chantilly

5 g (⅛ oz) gold-strength leaf gelatine

202 g (7 oz) whipping cream

30 g (1 oz) icing (confectioners') sugar

7 g (¼ oz) best-quality matcha powder

120 g (4¼ oz) milk

103 g (3½ oz) white chocolate, roughly chopped

Strawberry gel

69 g (2½ oz) caster (superfine) sugar

3 g (⅛ oz) agar-agar

290 g (10¼ oz) strawberries, hulled and puréed

To serve

hulled and sliced strawberries or crumbled freeze-dried strawberries

To make the matcha chantilly, first soak your gelatine in a bowl of cold water. Whisk the cream and icing sugar in a stand mixer with the whisk attachment at low speed, then gradually increase to medium speed until soft peaks form.

Put the matcha in a small bowl. Heat the milk until just boiling, then slowly pour it over the matcha powder while whisking away any lumps.

Put the white chocolate in a medium bowl and pour the matcha milk over it. Squeeze out the gelatine leaf, add to the bowl and blitz the mixture with a stick blender until smooth. Pour the matcha mixture into the whipped cream and slowly incorporate using a hand whisk.

For the strawberry gel, whisk together the sugar and agar-agar in a small bowl.

Bring the strawberry purée to the boil in small saucepan, then add the sugar and agar mixture and whisk until dissolved. When the strawberry purée reaches 85°C/185°F, turn the heat to the lowest setting and continue cooking for 5 minutes. Remove from the heat, cover with biodegradable plastic wrap, cool to room temperature, then refrigerate until set. Remove from the fridge and blitz with a stick blender or in a food processor

To assemble, using a serrated knife, cut each cooled brioche bun vertically down the middle, making sure not to cut all the way through so the bun can be opened up like a taco.

Prepare two disposable piping bags by measuring 5 cm (2 inches) from the tips and slicing off the ends – no piping nozzle needed. Pipe a generous amount of strawberry gel into the centre of each bun, then fill the entire bun by piping in the matcha chantilly. Use a palette knife to smooth out the filling and remove any excess. Scatter the fresh or freeze-dried strawberries over the matcha filling to serve.

Alice Bennett

Miss Trixie's honey joy slice (39)

Miss Trixie's classic chocolate cake (167)

Founder and head pastry chef, Miss Trixie Drinks Tea

Melbourne, Vic
Wurundjeri Country

Alice Bennett is a dessert person. 'I just love sugar,' she says. 'Growing up, I had an incredibly sweet tooth. I would open a menu and look straight to the desserts to methodically plan what I'd eat to ensure that I'd have room for dessert. And I still do that now.' Alice was the kind of kid who recruited friends and family into pretend cooking-show extravaganzas inspired by recipes in her mum's copies of *Women's Weekly*, *Feast* and *delicious* magazines, and who clicked instantly with an early stint living in America ('You open a bag of bread there and sugar pours out,' she jokes).

Today, her cake alter ego, Miss Trixie Drinks Tea, is all about turning back the clock to those first sugary moments. 'I just want those simple pleasures in life. And typically, if I were to trace them back, it goes back to a moment in my childhood when I loved that and felt joy,' says Alice. For the big celebrations, sometimes it's the simplest flavours that bring the greatest emotional return – her malted vanilla cake is a crowd-pleaser. 'As an adult, you're probably not making yourself a malted milk,' she says, 'but you might treat yourself to that in a cake form.' Likewise, her honey joy slice (page 39) is an instant sell-out at pop-ups; the inspiration for her buttercream (see page 167) is the particular taste of melted vanilla ice cream; and her birthday cakes, bejewelled with lolly-bag sweets, reduce adults to childish squeals. 'Visually, it's always just been colour, bright, fun, nothing too serious,' says Alice.

Though she left media and production to grow her baking side hustle into a business, Alice is still all about spreading a message – today, it's to champion emerging bakers. A big slice of the baking community is now made up of self-starters running their own businesses, many of them online. As delicious as the end results might be, working solo can be isolating. 'Knowledge is power, so being able to share my experience, especially with people who are starting out and operating on their own, is a really nice thing,' says Alice. 'I've always felt very proud of the work I do, but I've had imposter syndrome for most of my life, particularly coming out of production and then into this. It's easy to think: "I'm not trained in this, so why would anyone buy my product?"' But they do, and they line up around the block when Alice hosts a Bake Sale at Co.Bake – the shared kitchen and pop-up space she founded with Alisha Henderson (page 48). The pop-ups at Co.Bake give independent bakers a chance to connect with customers and be enthusiastically pepped up by fellow bakers.

There's room for everyone. 'If you're a starting baker and you're looking to build a business, I think it's really important to try to create something that's evidently yours. It doesn't have to be original, but people come up with new ideas and different looks every day,' she says. 'Take inspiration from something and work on making it yours. That's how everyone begins.'

'Take inspiration from something and work on making it yours. That's how everyone begins.'

NOTES ON INGREDIENTS

'Baking is precision, but at the same time, there's a little bit of wiggle room – especially when it comes to ingredients. We always make our own buttermilk because it's just soured milk – add vinegar to milk and you've got it. If you're making a sour cream cake, you could use Greek yoghurt and it'll be fine. Or if you don't have a neutral-flavoured oil, you could definitely use olive oil. It's just going to give you a nuttiness, but if you're happy and prepared for that, it will be fine. It might be just what your banana bread needs.'

WORDS TO BAKE BY

'Go low and slow. We have our ovens on at about 145°C/300°F on low fan. Typically, a lot of cookbooks will tell you something like 160°C/325°F. I've always gone a little bit lower and slower with temperatures – and you can apply this before you even put your cake in the oven. If you slow down the whole process, mistakes will be eliminated. You've monitored every single aspect along the way. You haven't been overbeating something, because you've just taken your time getting there.'

Miss Trixie's honey joy slice

Alice Bennett
Profiled on page 36

MAKES 16
SPECIAL EQUIPMENT 22 cm (8½ inch) square brownie tin, stand mixer with paddle attachment

Cookie dough base
250 g (9 oz) unsalted butter, softened
225 g (8 oz) brown sugar
150 g (5½ oz) caster (superfine) sugar
generous pinch of sea salt flakes
2 eggs, at room temperature
450 g (1 lb) plain (all-purpose) flour
5 g (⅛ oz) bicarbonate of soda (baking soda)

Honey joy top
215 g (7½ oz) unsalted butter
250 g (9 oz) caster (superfine) sugar
75 g (2¾ oz) honey
145 g (5 oz) cornflakes
10 g (¼ oz) sea salt flakes

I feel like the ultimate debate in Australia is whether you were a chocolate crackle kid or a honey joy kid – rice puffs, cocoa, coconut and sugar held together with coconut shortening, or cornflakes and sugar held together with butter and honey, both served in cupcake papers. I was positively the former. And I think it was because I just didn't get enough from the honey joy. I wanted more! This recipe was developed alongside my second-in-charge and right-hand woman, Katie, who I tasked with making a honey joy slice for a bake sale. We married our classic cookie dough with the honey joy mixture, inspired by the original Kellogg's recipe, and added a good whack of salt. The result is arguably better that the original, and it's a slice I want to see at every kids' party from now on.

Line your 22 cm (8½ inch) square brownie tin with baking paper. Be sure to bring the paper up the sides of the tin with a slight overhang. This will make getting your slice out of the tin a breeze.

For the cookie dough base, using a stand mixer with the paddle attachment, beat your butter, sugars and salt on medium speed until pale and creamy, about 4 minutes. Add the eggs and beat until well combined. Using a wooden spoon, mix your flour and bicarbonate of soda through until combined. Press your dough into the prepared tin and freeze for a minimum of 3 hours (I like to freeze mine overnight).

Preheat your oven to 140°C/275°F fan-forced (160°C/325°F conventional).

Bake the base for 25 minutes or until the edges are starting to turn slightly golden.

Leave the dough in the tin to cool slightly. You'll notice that your base will rise and then collapse again – this is completely normal.

Make the honey joy top while the base is baking. Melt your butter with your sugar and honey in a medium saucepan over medium heat until the mixture starts to bubble and turn golden. Take the pan off the heat, add your cornflakes and sea salt, then gently fold through (taking care not to break your cornflakes).

Pop the cornflake mixture on top of your cooked dough base and return to the oven for a further 15 minutes. You want your cornflakes to have turned a luscious golden colour.

Cool in the tin for 30 minutes before taking out and slicing into squares or bars.

Marianna Di Bartolo

Pistachio amaretti (42)

Ricotta cassateddi (100)

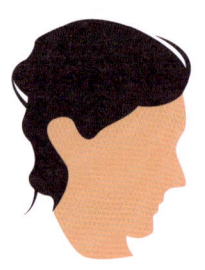

Pastry chef

Melbourne, Vic
Wurundjeri Country

For Marianna Di Bartolo, it always goes back to amaretti. 'I'll never forget discovering amaretti that have citrus in them. And it's a citrus that has been preserved – it's been there for the whole year, waiting to be turned into something really beautiful,' she says. This is the style of baking from her parents' homeland of south-eastern Sicily, a place that heaves with orchards of oranges, lemons and almonds. 'The palate is more simple because it's really about the ingredient, that sense of "You know how good this almond is? Have a taste."' When Marianna was growing up in Melbourne, her mother would give her some of the cake batter to use in her very own stand mixer. They made the famous amaretti, crostata with home-made jam, and Italian custard that would coax old cake into dessert. Marianna counts herself lucky. Her friends often swapped stories of never being allowed into their home kitchens. 'I had an Italian mother who let me make a mess in the kitchen as long as I cleaned it,' she says.

After finishing school, Marianna began an apprenticeship that would open up the world of pastry to her, but she knew the traditions of Italy would continue to guide her. 'It was what I had been baking since I was a kid, it was my palette, it was all I knew – but I think what drew me to Italian baking was the seasonal aspect, the preserving aspect. The sense that it came from somewhere. The recipe had a history, a connection to the earth,' she says. 'And I thought, "I really want to hold on to that part of me."' This wasn't the case for everyone, she reflects. 'Growing up in the seventies, I felt a little bit of racism, but not so much that I disowned my Italian heritage. It allowed me to discover and appreciate the traditions of my parents. I've spoken to a few people who are a little bit older than me who struggled with that and completely disowned that side,' she says.

Food has always loomed large in Marianna's family and their Sicilian community – celebrations were always around food, and food was always celebrated. Sweets, for instance, were not just sweets. 'The pleasure of dessert, or anything sweet, is very special because of poverty they experienced. When they had an amaretti biscuit, it was for a special occasion, because when they were children, they couldn't afford the almonds or the sugar. It was only as they got older,' she says. 'A lot of these recipes are also really special for them because it's about luxury. And now it's a luxury that they can afford.'

Marianna has brought this joy to so many lives. She's worked at Laurent and Baker Di Chirico and now teaches baking. For more than a decade, she ran her own pasticceria in West Melbourne where she could share her knowledge and recipes with the public. After she closed Dolcetti in 2020, she decided to walk away from baking but found she couldn't stay away – and now is devoted to teaching the craft. 'You get me back in the kitchen and I'm happy baking. I've understood that. I can't stop the baking.'

'What drew me to Italian baking was the seasonal aspect, the preserving aspect. The sense that it came from somewhere. The recipe had a history, a connection to the earth.'

ON THE THINGS THAT STAY WITH US

'Every Christmas and Easter, just before those big celebrations, the women that I grew up with would get together and we'd bake some favourite biscuits for that season. I had such beautiful memories of that tradition, so when I had my shop, I wanted to continue it. These women were now in their sixties, seventies, some in their eighties. But they'd come in on my day off and we would bake whatever they wanted to bake, something that meant something special to them. Usually it was a rustic Sicilian biscuit. One year, just before Easter, we made a bread dough and they created these amazing baskets, porcupines, horses, handbags, all made of dough. I was blown away by the skill that they had, the plaiting. It was just so pleasurable to watch these women, because it was like they had stepped back into another world. There was one woman there, she was the matriarch. She was ninety, she had dementia, but we got her there and she made a horse. She made a horse out of this bread dough that she would have made when she was ten years old. That was a really special day for me because I never expected that, but it's the power of baking.'

Pistachio amaretti

Marianna Di Bartolo
Profiled on page 40

MAKES 20
SPECIAL EQUIPMENT spice or coffee grinder

100 g (3½ oz) raw pistachio nut kernels
180 g (6¼ oz) caster (superfine) sugar
150 g (5½ oz) almond meal
50 g (1¾ oz) egg white (from about 2 eggs)
20 g (¾ oz) icing (confectioners') sugar

Coating
150 g (5½ oz) raw pistachio nut kernels, chopped

To finish
20 maraschino amarena cherries, drained

Amaretti are one of my favourite biscuits and something I always looked forward to in Sicily, especially visiting my mother's family, who grew and harvested almonds. These biscuits are full of flavour, sweet, dense and nutty, with a mild hint of floral marzipan – which, combined with a bit of sugar and a preserve of lemon or mandarin (which grow there abundantly), is a perfect way to taste Sicily. I came up with this combination back in my wholesale business days. I am always at my most creative when I need to use up an excess of produce, and in this case it was pistachios. They became my most popular amaretti.

Preheat the oven to 160°C/325°F fan-forced (180°C/350°F conventional). Line a baking tray with baking paper.

Grind the pistachios with 2 tablespoons of the caster sugar in a spice or coffee grinder until fine, taking care not to overgrind into a paste.

Combine the remaining caster sugar, almond meal and ground pistachios and sugar in a large mixing bowl and stir until well mixed. Add the egg white and mix with large spoon or by hand until it comes together into a slightly sticky but firm ball. It should hold its shape when rolled into a ball, so if it feels dry add an extra 10 g (¼ oz) of egg white. Sift the icing sugar onto your work surface and roll your dough into a smooth ball (don't be tempted to add more icing sugar, or the pistachio coating won't stick).

Roll into a log and cut into 20 equal pieces. To coat, put the chopped pistachios on a small chopping board or tray. Roll each piece of dough into a ball then, making sure the dough is slightly sticky, roll it in the pistachios to coat. If the pistachios aren't sticking to the dough, dampen your palms with a drop or two of water, roll the ball between your hands to create a sticky surface, then roll in the chopped pistachios.

Arrange the coated balls on the prepared baking tray, about 5 cm (2 inches) apart. Place a cherry in the centre of each and push lightly so the cherry sticks as the biscuit cooks (it will fall off otherwise). Try not to flatten the biscuit too much, as you want to keep a round shape.

Bake for 15 minutes, or until the biscuits are slightly golden on the bottom. Cool on the tray for 15 minutes before serving.

Charlie Duffy

Burnt butter and pecan cakes (47)

Amaro crème caramel with salted, caramelised cacao (255)

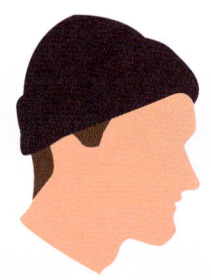

Head pastry chef, Small Batch Roasting Co.

Melbourne, Vic
Wurundjeri Country

'I wish I could tell you a romantic story about how I came to baking,' says Charlie Duffy. 'I didn't grow up baking with my grandma. It was more that I sort of flunked at school, looked at my grades and thought what could I do?' This might be his humble admission, but anyone encountering Charlie's work today would have a hard time taking the romance out of it. His pastries are beautifully composed things: you can spot the artist's hand in intricate viennoiserie with perfect plissé-like crinkles and fresh ingredients prepared and arranged just so.

And Charlie's artistry extends to – or rather begins with – the way he talks about ideas. 'Some things just sound dreamy together on the page. My phone is full of notes, full of ideas that'll come to me in the car,' he says. It's not hard to find the poetry in them. You might hear it as full-bodied verse ('blood plum, beeswax cream, hazelnut frangipane and thyme') or in the simplest phrasings ('rosella wheat croissants'). 'I just love finding new stuff,' says Charlie, describing his excitement at the increasingly available Australian native ingredients to work with, from tart lilly pillies to bell-shaped rainforest cherries. 'I just love that experience of having something unique and new for the first time,' he says.

And through Charlie's considered approach, even the most familiar of things can become surprising – and new again. 'I'm always trying to introduce something slightly different in terms of flavour combinations and couple them with a really interesting technique, even with the simplest pairing,' he says. It might be brown butter cakes finished with a microplaning of shaved pecans that fall like delicate leaves (see page 47) or pastries with melon-scoops of pearlescent poached pear.

Curiosity has persisted throughout Charlie's career. He caught the cooking bug as a teenager while working in a football stadium in Sheffield, UK, then trained as a chef before switching fully to pastry, including a stint at Melbourne's Tivoli Road Bakery with Michael James (see page 56), and trained his eye for composition further by dabbling in food styling. 'I remember one chef in particular, I just was in awe of the way he could plate stuff up. This flair, it was just beautiful. I knew I wanted to be like that. I used to go home and practise with tomato ketchup and random bits of food just to be better at those skills, to have that flair.'

Charlie is constantly tuning in and assembling ideas. 'I have so many cookbooks. Just to see beautiful food is quite inspiring – the way drops of oil fall on the plate or are interspersed with liquid and colours and shapes,' he says. 'Even if it's really simple baking: sometimes a cookie can look beautiful if the texture is lovely. It's cracked and slightly blistered and there are little pools of chocolate.' See? Plenty of romance there.

WORDS TO BAKE BY

'I went to the pastry section thinking: "I've been a chef for a good few years now and I've worked in good places, I've got a fair idea about cooking," but I killed so many recipes and it was a bit of a wake-up call. But I found the joys in the process of getting better at each recipe every time I made it and learning different ways to make it better. Every recipe can be tweaked slightly by so many different variables to try to get that extra two per cent improvement each time. When things don't go to plan it's a good time to take a lesson from it. When I do something wrong and I can't work out why, it's exciting, because I know I'm going to learn something new that I won't do again.'

NOTES ON INGREDIENTS

'Spend some time sourcing and connecting with producers of the best-tasting dairy, wheat, fruit, nuts and chocolate in your area. It's a simple way to improve the taste of your baking, and the connections you form make it all the more rewarding. Then pay attention to your produce – not every strawberry, for example, will have the same level of sweetness or acidity. Taste before making, adjust your sugar levels and experiment, even if it goes against the quantities given in the recipe.'

'Pay attention to your produce ... taste before making, adjust your sugar levels and experiment, even if it goes against the quantities given in the recipe.'

Burnt butter and pecan cakes

Charlie Duffy
Profiled on page 44

MAKES 20

SPECIAL EQUIPMENT twenty 7 × 2 cm (2¾ × ¾ inch) oval cake moulds, food processor, sugar thermometer, cheesecloth or coffee filter paper, disposable piping bag, mandoline

If you don't have oval cake moulds or a cupcake tin with oval holes, any muffin or mini-cupcake tin, or one with more traditional rectangular holes, will work. You may need to adjust your baking time slightly.

170 g (6 oz) unsalted butter
100 g (3½ oz) brown sugar
75 g (2¾ oz) caster (superfine) sugar
75 g (2¾ oz) panela sugar
45 g (1½ oz) almond meal
45 g (1½ oz) pecans
70 g (2½ oz) plain (all-purpose) flour
4 g (⅛ oz) salt
1 g (1/32 oz) ground cinnamon
½ vanilla bean, seeds scraped
160 g (5¾ oz) egg white
   (from about 6 eggs)

To finish
150 g (5½ oz) pecans

These moreish little cakes hit all the right notes. Salty, sweet, rich and nutty, with a crisp exterior that gives way to a soft centre (be sure to brown the butter well, as that's where all the nutty aromas will form). Inspired by a friend's pecan farm in northern New South Wales called Marlivale Farm, these cakes celebrate the humble pecan.

Lightly grease twenty 7 × 2 cm (2¾ × ¾ inch) oval cake moulds and arrange on a baking tray evenly spaced apart.

Melt the butter in a small saucepan over medium–high heat. When it starts to foam, stir frequently with a whisk. Continue cooking and stirring until the colour starts to turn deep brown and the smell is nutty and toasty. Strain the burnt butter through a sieve lined with cheesecloth or coffee filter paper into a heatproof bowl. Set aside to cool to about 65°C/150°F.

Meanwhile, combine all the dry ingredients in a food processor and blitz until the pecans have broken down to a fine texture (similar to the almond meal). Empty into a large mixing bowl and add the vanilla seeds.

Add the egg white to the dry ingredients and mix with a spatula until just combined, then follow with the still-warm burnt butter and mix with the spatula until just combined. Pour into a disposable piping bag and cut a small opening in the tip, then pipe the mixture into each mould until it is a couple of millimetres away from the top (I weighed mine to 35 g/1¼ oz each). Refrigerate overnight to rest (or for up to 5 days) – this will ensure an even rise. Skipping this step will risk the cakes popping out of the moulds unevenly during baking.

Preheat the oven to 185°C/375°F fan-forced (205°C/400°F conventional).

To finish the cakes, place one whole pecan in the centre of each cake. Working carefully with a mandoline, shave the remaining pecans into very thin, paper-like shavings. Loosely pile shavings onto each cake.

Bake for 14–15 minutes, or until the edges have browned slightly and the cake feels firm to touch. Cool in the moulds for 2 minutes, then use the tip of a small knife to remove each cake from its mould.

Panela sugar lends a lovely toasted caramel-like flavour to the mix, but if it's not available replace it with more brown sugar.

Alisha Henderson

Tiramisukis (51)

Peach and sour cream cake (118)

Pastry chef and founder,
Sweet Bakes

Melbourne, Vic
Wurundjeri Country

'Cake has always been my job, just in various formats,' says Alisha Henderson. It all took off when she started posting hand-painted creations on Instagram at nineteen – to viral effect – and launched her cake business, Sweet Bakes. Not long after, she ventured into the marzipan- and fondant-laced world of wedding cakes, but quickly strayed from the traditional. With nostalgic Australian flavours (think lamington–vanilla slice–Golden Gaytime dreams) and textural layers ('There has to be something crunchy or crispy in every single cake,' she says), Alisha's cakes were – and are – as fun to eat as they are to look at, painted in dreamy watercolours, penned with tongue-in-cheek messages and piped to perfection.

There have been many evolutions since then. Alisha has applied her illustrative talents to a children's book, taught cake-decorating workshops, and launched a 'Cake Mail' service during the pandemic that went, she says, 'bananas'. Then there's Co.Bake, a creative space for hire founded with fellow baker Alice Bennett (see page 36). They run their businesses separately from the commercial kitchen out the back, and rent the front studio space, decorated in frosted peach, out to other small businesses for pop-up events. Whether they're hosting their own bake sales, or a pop-up for the boom of independent bakers, queues squiggle around the block. It's part of Alisha's intention to support fellow bakers. 'I personally found it hardest to gain the respect of other people, particularly chefs, because I'm self-taught and it's cake. I grew an Instagram following really quickly. I think people just thought, "Pretty pictures, cake, Instagram, no skill whatsoever," she says. 'But my motivation for anything is being underestimated.' For any self-starters, her advice is: 'Be audacious in your approach.'

Alisha's way is to lean into joy. 'Everything always comes back to making it joyful for me. Sure, I want to be taken seriously in what I do, but I want to go about that in the most un-serious way possible. Cake is just this embodiment of fun and joy and celebration. Cake's not serious. And I love that.'

NOTES ON PIPING

'I learned how to pipe from YouTube and from making every kind of mistake. I would keep a cake in the freezer and reuse it as a practice cake. Instead of going through that process of baking a cake every single time, you can bring it out, decorate it, try out all your new techniques, wipe it off, and chuck it back in the freezer. Don't eat it, obviously, but use it again and again to keep practising all those bits and pieces on.'

'Cake is just this embodiment of fun and joy and celebration. Cake's not serious. And I love that.'

WORDS TO BAKE BY

'My creative process is led by the question, "How can cake be the reason that you enjoy yourself?" I'm drawn to the storytelling element. Hearing stories from other people about how I helped bring about a joyful moment in their life is why I keep coming back to it. It can honestly reignite my passion for it all sometimes. There are months where it's a real slog, but then I'll get feedback and it absolutely propels me forward. Even though I'm on a mission to change people's perceptions about decorated cakes, and the fact that they can look good *and* be utterly delicious, that isn't my primary motivator. What gets me going is knowing there is a core memory that's being created around one of my cakes. A couple may very well show that photo of something I made for them to their kids or their kids' kids. It's something that's just carried on beyond the moment itself.'

Tiramisukis

Alisha Henderson
Profiled on page 48

MAKES 12
SPECIAL EQUIPMENT stand mixer with paddle and whisk attachments

Cookie dough
1 tablespoon ground espresso coffee beans
225 g (8 oz) butter, at room temperature
80 g (2¾ oz) brown sugar
200 g (7 oz) caster (superfine) sugar
80 g (2¾ oz) mascarpone cheese
1 tablespoon Kahlua (optional)
250 g (9 oz) plain (all-purpose) flour
50 g (1¾ oz) cornflour (cornstarch)
1 teaspoon salt
2 teaspoons baking powder
120 g (4¼ oz) dark chocolate chips

Tiramisu frosting
1 tablespoon ground espresso coffee beans
150 g (5½ oz) mascarpone cheese
⅓ cup (40 g) icing (confectioners') sugar
1 teaspoon vanilla extract or vanilla bean paste
1 teaspoon Kahlua (optional)

To finish
unsweetened cocoa powder, for dusting

My criteria for the perfect cookie is one that's thin rather than chunky, and tender and gooey in the centre with buttery crackly edges. These cookies are precisely that and can stand on their own, but tiramisu on top takes them to another decadent level.

For the cookie dough, start by stirring the ground coffee with a little hot water to steep.

In a stand mixer with the paddle attachment, cream the butter and sugars for 4 minutes on medium–high speed. Scrape down the bowl, add the mascarpone and beat for a further 2 minutes. Add the steeped coffee and Kahlua, if using, and beat for 1 minute. Add the flour, cornflour, salt and baking powder and beat on low speed to combine. With the mixer still on low speed, stir the chocolate chips through the mixture.

Divide the dough (it's quite a sticky batter) into 24 pieces about 55 g (2 oz) each, roll them into balls and seal in an airtight container. Freeze for at least 12 hours (and up to 2 months). The long resting time ensures a tender cookie in the end.

Preheat the oven to 180°C/350°F fan-forced (200°F/400°F conventional) and line a baking tray with baking paper.

Arrange the cookie balls on the prepared tray about 3 cm (1¼ inches) apart. Bake for 12 minutes, or until the edges are golden brown. Leave the cookies on the tray to cool completely before frosting.

For the tiramisu frosting, again start by stirring the ground coffee with a little hot water to steep.

In a stand mixer with the whisk attachment, beat the mascarpone, icing sugar, steeped coffee, vanilla and Kahlua, if using, on high until stiff – don't overbeat or the mixture will split. Spread the tiramisu frosting across the tops of the cookies. Finish with a dusting of cocoa powder.

The cookies will keep for 2 days in the fridge.

The cookies will go softer/soggy in the fridge (sort of like a savoiardi would in a tiramisu). I prefer to eat these fresh with their crispy edges, gooey centre and creamy tiramisu on top.

Emelia Jackson

Grapefruit creams (54)

Chocolate cherry choux (187)

Cookbook author and pastry chef

Melbourne, Vic
Wurundjeri Country

For all her achievements, 2020 *MasterChef* winner and cookbook author Emelia Jackson is happy to call herself a 'lazyish' baker. Corners in her recipes are cut (she sifts flour only for sponges), and could-be complex recipes smoothed out like icing on a cake. She is an expert at speaking to home cooks, since it's where her own baking education began.

When Emelia was a child, her mother had her sitting up on the bench rolling out gingerbread and making an utter joyful mess. Then, there was her baba. 'She didn't actually let us touch anything. All of the wisdom she passed down to us was through watching only – and us trying to sneak little bites of it here and there. But I learned so much from her and I so admire how she could turn nothing into something.'

In the spirit of her baba, Emelia encourages us all to get back into the motions of what it means to bake at home. 'I think we've all become a little bit obsessed with thinking that baking needs to be perfect,' she says. 'Yes, it is very scientific, and a lot of it's based on chemical reactions. But then there's just so much instinct that goes into baking. When I think about how my baba used to bake, it was always a handful of that and a Turkish coffee cup full of this, and none of it was to the gram.'

The science, she says, is moot unless underpinned by experience and the desire to learn. Patience and curiosity are key. And it's exactly this lesson Emelia is passing down in her own family. 'I was raised being so openly allowed in the kitchen, so I was conscious of making it a happy place for my daughter, Addie, too. I don't ever want it to feel stressful for her. I've got to constantly remind myself that the mess is fine. It doesn't matter if it doesn't work out. It's all part of the process, but it's definitely in there for me to be a little control freak-ish like my baba.'

WHY KNEADING DOUGH IS LIKE READING A BOOK

'I love kneading. I get real joy out of punching a dough down, the first rise. I think that's directly linked to my baba, because she was always making her own bread. She made tsoureki for Easter, which is in my first book, so it's really intertwined with my memories. I also love it because anything yeasted is a long process. It's almost like my version of sitting down and reading a novel. There are chapters of activity to it and you don't know what the ending is really going to be yet. It feels like a quite indulgent me-time, which I love.'

TO MAKE YOUR OWN PRALINE PASTES

'Praline pastes add the most beautiful, truest flavour of whatever nut you're using. They can be quite hard to find in store and they're also quite expensive, but they're really just like peanut butter. You can easily make them at home with a blender and really elevate your bakes. You can put some pistachio praline paste through a pistachio cake to really enhance the flavour or you can mix a praline through icing, ganache or buttercream to flavour them that way. Or you could use one as a filling in a sandwich cookie. I'll do a hazelnut chocolate chip cookie and I'll lightly mix some hazelnut praline paste through the dough at the end. And then when I scoop the cookies with a cookie scoop, they're kind of swirled with praline paste, which then caramelises in the oven. It's just a little special add-on. You can just use Nutella to start, and then when you begin to venture into the wonderful world of pure praline pastes, you'll leave it for dead.'

Grapefruit creams

Emelia Jackson
Profiled on page 52

MAKES 18
SPECIAL EQUIPMENT stand mixer with paddle and whisk attachments, rolling pin, fluted 5 cm (2 inch) round cookie cutter, piping bag and 1 cm (½ inch) star nozzle

Cookies
300 g (10½ oz) plain (all-purpose) flour, plus extra for dusting
½ teaspoon baking powder
½ teaspoon salt
½ cup (110 g) caster (superfine) sugar
finely grated zest of 1 grapefruit
165 g (5¾ oz) unsalted butter, softened
1 egg yolk
½ teaspoon vanilla bean paste

Level up your cookies by sandwiching them together with a bright and fragrant grapefruit buttercream. These melt-in-your-mouth buttery sable cookies are amped up with a pop of bright grapefruit zest and are perfect if you want to impress at tea time. If you can't get your hands on grapefruit, you can use any of the usual citrusy suspects: lemon, lime, orange, mandarin or even fresh yuzu (if you're lucky enough to find some).

For the cookies, combine the flour, baking powder and salt in a medium bowl. Give these dry ingredients a good whisk and set aside.

Using a stand mixer with the paddle attachment, mix the caster sugar and zest on medium speed – this will help release the grapefruit oils into the sugar, giving an even more vibrant flavour. Add the butter, egg yolk and vanilla and mix until thoroughly combined but not aerated (we don't want the cookies to spread too much in the oven). Finally, add the dry ingredients and mix until a soft dough forms.

Wrap the dough in biodegradable plastic wrap and refrigerate for 1–2 hours. This will also ensure that the biscuits don't spread too much while baking.

Preheat the oven to 180°C/350°F fan-forced (200°C/400°F conventional) and line two baking trays with baking paper or silicone baking mats.

Lightly dust a work surface with flour. Using a rolling pin, roll out the chilled dough to 3–4 mm (⅛–³⁄₁₆ inches) thick. Using a fluted 5 cm (2 inch) round cookie cutter, cut out 36 rounds and arrange them on the baking trays, with 2–3 cm (¾–1¼ inches) between them.

Bake for 12–15 minutes, or until the cookies look dry all the way to the centre but are still blond. Transfer to a wire rack to cool completely while you make the filling.

Grapefruit cream

150 g (5½ oz) unsalted butter, softened

210 g (7½ oz) icing (confectioners') sugar, plus extra for dusting

juice of ¾ ruby grapefruit

½ teaspoon citric acid (optional)

For the grapefruit cream, combine all the ingredients in a stand mixer with the whisk attachment. Whisk on medium speed until cohesive and aerated – it will appear to split because of the grapefruit juice, but keep mixing until it comes together.

Spoon the cream into a piping bag fitted with a 1 cm (½ inch) star nozzle. Pipe 1–2 teaspoons of the cream in the centre of half the cookies and sandwich with the remaining cookies. Lightly dust the filled grapefruit creams with icing sugar.

To create the half-dusted effect, mask half of the top cookie with paper.

Michael James

Macadamia and wattleseed chocolate chip cookies (59)

Lemon, polenta and raspberry tea cake (127)

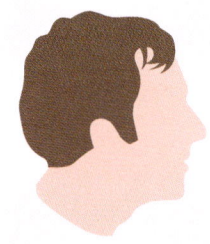

Baker, cookbook author and founder/co-owner of Urbanstead

Melbourne, Vic
Wurundjeri Country

'Bread keeps you honest; it keeps you on your toes,' says Michael James. 'It's a bit like life: you've got to let it take you on its journey. There are a lot of variables, so it's about guiding it.' Guiding is something he's become rather good at. For Michael, baking goes hand in hand with community. Growing up in Cornwall, UK, he'd help his nan crimp pasties on an ironing board and join her making heavy cake, a local specialty originally made to celebrate the fisherman's catch. 'In those days we didn't lock the front door; ours was kind of an open house, with family, cousins and all sorts. People would come in from the country, mainly farmers and workers,' he says. 'There was always cake on the table, and all of a sudden someone would drop in for a brandy or a tea in the afternoon. That's probably where the community bit comes from, for me.'

He found his way into baking professionally after leaving Cornwall for London, where he worked his way up in Michelin-starred restaurants, but, most importantly, discovered the bread and pastry section. Until 2018, Michael and his wife, Pippa, owned the Tivoli Road Bakery in Melbourne, which in their debut cookbook he tellingly called 'a network of relationships'. It was a place that nurtured many people's talent, from bakers in these pages (Jo Barrett, page 96, and Charlie Duffy, page 44) to those in search of a career change (a lawyer and a biochemist among them). 'We tried to get everybody to do all sections and have them work side by side with another baker and learn business skills, to encourage them and support them and their passion and enthusiasm. Once you've got that and a bit of common sense, everybody can have a go at it.'

The Tivoli Road Bakery was also a place to nurture what it meant to bake in Australia. It was a no-brainer, says Michael, to use local grains and native ingredients: 'Adding the Indigenous ingredients, you're adding more story, supporting local people – and it's also a whole other palette. A lot of that information has been lost, stolen or destroyed, so it was important to go out and learn about these ingredients, take them back to the bakery and share them with staff and customers.'

In the years since, in his own work and as a co-founder of Grainz, a local grain-sharing initiative that Michael says is quite simply 'trying to make the world a better place', he's continued to champion local baking networks. 'Bakeries are community-focused anyway, so we just tried to do that in our baking community as well,' he says. 'We want to try to give back and make other people feel supported.' He connects bakeries with local producers, encouraging them to use local ingredients, from whole grains all the way down to regionally made butter (instead of importing it from Europe). He's also been active helping the boom of new bakers open up bricks-and-mortar businesses and in 2024, alongside Pippa, founded Urbanstead, which offers baking classes and consulting. It sounds like a lot – or maybe it's just right. 'When you're there working at a communal bench with the team, it's kind of not really a job, it's more something to do. You just love it, you're grateful to have these skills and do it with these particular people.'

'Bread keeps you honest; it keeps you on your toes. It's a bit like life: you've got to let it take you on its journey.'

WORDS TO BAKE BY

'When you're dealing with fresh local ingredients, whether it's butter or flour or even sugars, just be mindful that they're a bit more alive. It makes you a better baker, too. You'll get better flavour, but they also push the boundaries of the baker as well, which is important – you have to get comfortable with being uncomfortable. Grain is kind of like coffee. We have fresh coffee, so why shouldn't we have fresh grain? The fresher it is, the more oils you get, and it's more enzyme active – it ferments much nicer and faster. And the bran is also good for you to start, the fibre in it. It's also better for, again, the food miles and the environment. It's a hard graft, so I get why people use ultra-processed, high-protein flour for their breads or pastries. But using local alternatives, down to your sugars, you gain different flavours, and with whole grains even more flavour, and more nutrition as well.'

Macadamia and wattleseed chocolate chip cookies

Michael James
Profiled on page 56

MAKES 18
SPECIAL EQUIPMENT stand mixer with paddle attachment, food processor (or spice grinder or mortar and pestle)

40 g (1½ oz) freshly ground wattleseed (available online and in specialty spice stores)
220 g (7¾ oz) unsalted butter, softened
170 g (6 oz) brown sugar
130 g (4½ oz) raw caster (superfine) sugar
8 g (¼ oz) salt
1 vanilla bean, split lengthways and seeds scraped, or 1 teaspoon vanilla extract
280 g (10 oz) plain (all-purpose) flour
5 g (⅛ oz) baking powder
3 g (⅛ oz) bicarbonate of soda (baking soda)
1 egg (60 g), lightly beaten
350 g (12 oz) dark chocolate, 60%, roughly chopped
150 g (5½ oz) macadamia nuts, roughly chopped

With food and baking, it's always a good idea to use what's around you, in season or abundant. Often they taste good together, and they're probably cheaper. Since moving to Australia, I have discovered a whole new palette of flavours and combinations. Macadamia and wattleseed in a cookie is one such combination to be tried and enjoyed. The freshly ground wattleseed complements the nuts and adds depth of flavour, resulting in a cookie that's the perfect balance of sweet, salty and nutty. And with the bitterness of the chocolate and wattleseed, it makes for one of the tastiest cookies.

If the wattleseeds are still a little coarse, blitz them in a food processor or spice grinder, or grind them with a mortar and pestle.

In a stand mixer with the paddle attachment, cream together the butter, sugars, salt and vanilla seeds or extract. Start on a low speed and gradually increase the speed to high, until the mixture is pale and fluffy. Scrape down the side of the bowl.

Sift the flour, baking powder and bicarbonate of soda onto a large sheet of baking paper or into a medium bowl.

With the mixer speed on low, add the egg in two or three batches. Run the mixer on high speed between each addition to fully incorporate before adding the next. Scrape down the side of the bowl as necessary.

With the mixer turned off, add the flour mixture. Mix on low speed until just incorporated.

Add the chocolate, macadamias and wattleseed. Mix on low speed until just incorporated.

Transfer your cookie dough to an airtight container and refrigerate overnight. This will help the flavours to mature and your cookies to taste even better.

The next day, preheat the oven to 170°C/350°F fan-forced (190°C/375°F conventional) and line a baking tray with baking paper.

Divide the dough into 18 equal portions, roughly 75 g (2¾ oz) each (halve the dough, then divide into three, then three again). With clean hands, roll each portion into a ball, then slightly squash each one into a puck. (At this stage, you can freeze some or all of your cookies for future use.)

Arrange the cookie pucks on the prepared baking tray with space between them – they will spread quite a lot during baking.

Bake for 16–18 minutes, until golden and crisp. If you like them really crunchy, bake for a little longer. Cool on the tray for a few minutes and enjoy a warm cookie, then transfer the remainder to a wire rack to cool completely. Store in an airtight container for up to 3 days.

Having cookies in the freezer is like having a secret stash of loot. They keep for up to 3 months and can be baked from frozen – just add a couple of minutes to the baking time.

Belinda Jeffery

Fluffy buttermilk scones (opposite)
Lemon curd shortbread tart (128)

Cookbook author,
TV presenter and
food writer

Yamba, NSW
Yaegl/Bundjalung Country

When Belinda Jeffery writes a recipe, she wants you to feel like she's standing beside you in the kitchen. That's how she learned. Belinda has a distinct memory of her early baking – she insisted that her mother give her some of her 'own' mixture in her 'own' enamel mixing bowl – and that her cake should bake it in it, too. She got her way – and vividly remembers the flush of pride that came with creating something.

In her recipes, and in her classes, she aims for the same reaction. There's a familiarity in Belinda's tone and a generosity of instruction. 'It's never about just following the recipe,' she says. 'It's about learning how to get things to the point that you go, "That's it, that's how it should be." I think if people start to trust their instincts more, that's when you really start to enjoy cooking, because you've got all of that knowledge in you to be able to then experiment.' And according to Belinda, learning to bake is really learning how to feel your way through things. 'Hands are the greatest tools of all. I'm always trying to get people to be confident using their hands. There is so much knowledge in them.'

Belinda tells a story of working for Millie Sherman at her bakery, Otello, in Sydney's Cremorne. 'We'd mix sponges in huge bowls because we'd be making six at a time. And you know, what you'd do is just roll your jacket back, wash your arms really well, and then you'd fold the flour in by hand, because otherwise you'd lose too much volume.' It's one of many tips she quite literally keeps up her sleeve. 'If you're making something where you want to fold one ingredient into another and keep it light, the best thing you can use is your hand, because you know exactly how it feels and you get right round the bowl.'

Skills aside, she thinks a recipe should leave you with something more. 'I've got to this stage in my life where I prefer cookbooks for the stories,' she laughs. 'What I love are the stories of the people and how they've ended up where they are, or why a recipe has meaning for them.' Fans of Belinda's cookbooks know this is what she does herself – and perhaps best in her baking recipes, particularly those quick, resourceful comforts. 'I suppose that's the baking that's closest to my heart,' she says. 'It's simpler cakes that have the most appeal for me. And I think that there's also the link to the past too, as those were the cakes I grew up with. And that stayed with me, that little bit of joy you could get from making something for someone.'

ON CREAMING BUTTER AND SUGAR

'I started like everybody else, I suppose. I put the butter and sugar in the bowl of my mum's old Kenwood beater and beat the hell out of them. In more recent years, I don't do that. I cream them on medium speed for three to four minutes, until they're well mixed but not all white, light and fluffy. Because if you beat them too rapidly for too long, it's possible to overbeat the mixture and incorporate too much air, which makes the cake rise ... and then collapse.'

ON BEATING EGG WHITES

'It's easy to overbeat egg whites when they need to be folded into a mixture. They should be just beyond sloppy, because otherwise, if you beat them until they're firm, it's so much harder to incorporate them into the batter. You want to be able to gently fold the two together, otherwise you end up with a wet batter and fairly firm egg white mixture that doesn't want to fold in. I tend to start off whisking in a stand mixer, but I always stop before I get to when I know they're ready. And I do the rest by hand, just with a balloon whisk, so I don't overbeat them.'

Fluffy buttermilk scones

MAKES 18–20
SPECIAL EQUIPMENT heavy baking tray (optional), food processor (optional), scone cutter (about 5.5 cm/2¼ inches in diameter)

3 cups (450 g) self-raising flour
1 cup (150 g) whole-wheat self-raising flour
¼ cup (55 g) caster (superfine) sugar
1 teaspoon salt
180 g (6¼ oz) chilled, unsalted cultured butter, finely diced
200 g (7 oz) sultanas (golden raisins) or roughly chopped, pitted dates (optional)
2 cups (500 ml) buttermilk or milk kefir
plain (all-purpose) flour, for dusting

To serve
butter, or jam and softly whipped cream

My mum, Cooee, was a wonderful scone maker. If anyone arrived unexpectedly for afternoon tea, she would duck into the kitchen, and it seemed within minutes a basket of warm scones wrapped in a starched tea towel was being popped on the table, along with a bowl of home-made strawberry jam, softly whipped cream and a dish of butter triangles.

I used to love helping her make them. She'd stand me on a stool beside her and show me how to rub the cold butter (yes, it always had to be cold) into the flour. Then she would add a big handful of chopped dates or sultanas, and finally the milk. I remember watching in fascination as she added a splash of vinegar to the milk to curdle it. 'Why?' I would ask. 'Because it helps make them light and tender,' she would reply. It was only when I started my career as a cook many years later that I learned buttermilk would do the same thing ... only better. Its gentle tang adds a more subtle flavour to the scones, and its mild acidity reacts with the baking powder to make them really light. I would delight in watching them puff up in the oven, their tops turning golden as they did.

Mum always left her scones to sit, wrapped in a tea towel, for a few minutes before we ate them. Much as I protested about this waiting time, she insisted on it so the steam from the scones would be trapped inside and help keep them moist.

There was no jam and cream when it was just family. They were split open and a big dollop of butter was tucked into each one. How I loved them: the warm buttery crumb dotted with succulent dried fruit. To this day, I can't think of anything more delicious for afternoon tea.

This recipe is a version of Mum's scones. I like to use a mixture of whole-wheat and self-raising flour to give the scones a gentle 'wheaty' flavour and, of course, I always add buttermilk for lightness and dried fruit for sweetness. I'd have to say, though, that they're just as delicious without the fruit, especially once the jam and cream are dolloped on top. I hope you enjoy them.

Preheat your oven to 180°C/350°F fan-forced (200°C/400°F conventional). Dust a heavy baking tray with flour and set it aside. (If you don't have a heavy baking tray, you can use a lightweight one, but line it with a double thickness of baking paper so the bottoms of the scones don't burn.)

Combine the flours, sugar and salt in a large bowl. Mix them together with a hand whisk for 1 minute so they're thoroughly combined and aerated. Scatter the little chunks of butter over the top, and use clean fingers to rub the butter into the flour mixture until it resembles coarse breadcrumbs. (If you like, you can mix the dry ingredients and cut in the butter using a food processor, then transfer the mixture to a large bowl.)

Add the sultanas or dates and toss them about so they're well coated. Now make a well in the centre. Pour in the buttermilk and stir it in very lightly until the mixture starts to come together into a somewhat sticky dough. >

Dust a work surface with flour and turn the mixture out onto it. Knead gently until just combined – don't overdo this or the scones will toughen. Pat the dough out into a round about 4 cm (1½ inches) thick. Dip a scone cutter (the one I use is 5.5 cm/2¼ inches in diameter) or a small tumbler into some flour to prevent the dough sticking to it, then stamp out the scones, dunking the cutter back into the flour before each one. Gently knead together any scraps and cut them again.

Snuggle the scones close together on the prepared baking tray and dust them very lightly with flour. Bake for about 20 minutes, until golden. Remove them from the oven and wrap immediately in a clean tea towel (dish towel). Leave for 5 minutes, then serve with butter or lashings of jam and cream.

Belinda Jeffery

Jesse Knierum and Aaron Morgan

Crullers (66)

Huon apple crumble (268)

Co-founders: head baker and head pastry chef, Poolish & Co.

Cygnet, Tas
Palawa Country

Cygnet, Tasmania, is a town of 4000 people and one bakery – Poolish & Co. In the few short years since Aaron Morgan, Jesse Knierum and Chelsea Martin fired up the wood oven, they've put themselves at the heart of the community. Aaron is the viennoiserie master, Jesse is the bread maker, and Chelsea (Jesse's partner) runs the business and front of house. Their starting point was clear, says Aaron: 'Bread and pastry and everything else will work out. We'll keep it simple.'

Both Aaron and Jesse come from hospitality families and have carried on the torch with years of work in cafes, bakeries and fine-dining establishments between them. Their own bakery embodies what service truly means to them. Jesse, who moved with Chelsea from Perth, Western Australia, for a 'tree change', came to breadmaking after becoming disillusioned with high-end cooking. 'I was getting frustrated with the fact that the really high-quality food and ingredients weren't accessible to everybody. I came from a hospitality family, so we didn't have any money for anything like that, and it frustrated me that I wouldn't be able to afford that, my friends couldn't afford that,' he says. 'It was one of the reasons I started cooking in those kinds of restaurants – I wanted to try the food, but it was the only way I could get in there. With bread, I just completely fell in love with that thought: "This is the way that I can feed people good food without it being something just for a certain demographic of people." Food should be for everyone, that's what I've always felt.' And at Poolish, they've made it so.

They have a donations-based community fund that means nobody in need is priced out. 'It makes sure everyone has access to what we have,' says Jesse. 'It's not a question of "Do I deserve this?" Everyone deserves it. No one has to walk in and feel embarrassed when they ask to have a loaf of bread from the community fund – and that's important to us.' Then there's the local food swap – in which locals can drop off their overflow of homegrown produce and see what magic Poolish can make out of it. This complements the natural abundance of produce around them in the Huon Valley – apples and pears, mushrooms, berries and Franklin stone fruit, for instance.

And then it's back into the kitchen. 'I think working together helps us,' says Aaron. 'We work on a bench facing each other for most of the day. We throw some ideas around. We talk a lot of smack. Lifestyle is important to us.' Aaron describes the rhythm of their 'reasonable' working hours that, unlike those in other avenues of hospitality, give them more time with the people in their lives. The measure of success at Poolish lies in building a bakery that both sustains and is sustainable. 'We're comfortable because we're very hands-on in what we do. It goes back to the bread and pastries. That's what our passion is,' says Aaron. 'It was important right from the start that we could maintain this for as long as we wanted to without being burnt out. The window's open for us to be here for twenty years.'

'Remember that things are going to change and you'll need to readjust every few months. Because you might think you're hot shit – and then the weather changes.'

NOTES ON BAKING IN DIFFERENT PLACES

Jesse: 'Be mindful of the conditions you're working in. One of those things is room temperature. Moving from WA to Tasmania, I had to re-attune to what I was doing. Over there, it's about keeping everything as cold as you can and slowing it down. But here it's more about giving it a bit of a push and getting a bit more life back into it. The idea of putting 30°C/85°F water into my bread was mind-blowing, whereas I was using iced water back in Perth. Every time the season changes, I still get a little shock and think, "Why isn't this working for me?" I can't be on autopilot. Remember that things are going to change and you'll need to readjust every few months. Because you might think you're hot shit – and then the weather changes.'

WORDS TO BAKE BY

Aaron: 'Stop working when you're getting overwhelmed, when you're getting lost in your thoughts and overthinking a process. Sometimes you just need to stop, take a breather, pull back and think, "What am I actually doing here?" Just slow your brain down to go down the path of one step at a time instead of thinking of six or seven things to do. Just worry about the next step in front of you.'

Crullers

Jesse Knierum and Aaron Morgan
Profiled on page 64

MAKES 12
SPECIAL EQUIPMENT stand mixer with paddle attachment, sugar thermometer, piping bag and 827 star nozzle

Crullers
160 g (5¾ oz) milk
160 g (5¾ oz) water
8 g (¼ oz) sugar
6 g (¼ oz) salt
148 g (5¼ oz) unsalted butter
180 g (6¼ oz) baker's flour
20 g (¾ oz) rice flour
280 g (10 oz) egg (from about 6 eggs)
vegetable oil, for deep-frying

In keeping with everything else we tend to offer at Poolish & Co., we leaned into making crullers because they're deceptively light but somehow also incredibly buttery and rich. Also, who doesn't love choux dough? Crullers are perfect to pair with seasonal fruit or with chocolates and spices in the winter. Or simply to fry and toss in cinnamon sugar. Yum!

Cut twelve 12 cm (4½ inch) square pieces of baking paper.

For the crullers, combine the milk, water, sugar, salt and butter in a large saucepan and bring to a very gentle simmer over medium heat. Once simmering, add the flours, stirring quickly to make sure there is no dry flour or lumps.

With a silicone spatula or a flat-ended wooden spoon, keep stirring the mixture, making sure to scrape the bottom of the pot as you stir. Continue for about 5 minutes, until the mix thickens and turns a little glossy. It will stick to the bottom of the pan, but do your best to keep it from sticking as long as you can. Once there is a layer stuck across the bottom of the pan, remove from the heat and transfer the dough to the bowl of a stand mixer.

With the paddle attachment, beat the mix on medium–high speed until it doesn't hurt to hold your hand against the bowl but it's still quite warm. While still mixing, add the egg one-third at a time, mixing until fully incorporated each time. Run the mixer for a couple more minutes, taking a moment to scrape down the side. Transfer the cruller mixture to a bowl and cover with biodegradable plastic wrap; make sure it touches the surface of the mixture to stop a skin forming. Refrigerate overnight or for up to 3 days.

Put some of your cruller mix in a piping bag fitted with an 827 star nozzle and pipe an 8 cm (3¼ inch) diameter ring onto each of the prepared pieces of baking paper, keeping the nozzle about 2 cm (¾ inch) above the paper at all times. (Tip: Draw an 8 cm circle on a sheet of paper, place it under each of your baking paper sheets in turn and trace over the top to keep the size consistent.) At this point the crullers are ready to fry, but if you refrigerate the piped mix uncovered overnight, they'll have crisper definition.

Bring a 7 cm (2¾ inch) depth of oil to 190°C/374°F in a heavy-based, high-sided pot or saucepan. Deep-fry the crullers in batches by carefully placing them in the hot oil, face down, leaving the baking paper attached – after 10 seconds you should be able to peel off the baking paper easily using tongs.

Continue to fry the crullers face down until the mixture bubbles and sets (very similar to making a pancake), about 2 minutes, then turn them over and fry for another 2 minutes. (If your crullers burst out at the seams a little, this means they need to fry for longer face down, so try this for the next batch.)

Finally, flip them back to fry face down for 20 seconds, then pull them out with the tongs and drain face up on a wire rack. (If your crullers deflate a little at this point, flip them again and fry for a little longer.) Leave to cool completely.

Sour cream glaze
100 g (3½ oz) icing (confectioners') sugar, plus extra as needed
20 g (¾ oz) pouring cream
80 g (2¾ oz) sour cream
pinch of citric acid, or a squeeze of lemon juice
pinch of salt

To finish
1 orange, for zesting

Use whatever you like to flavour the glaze: lemon juice, sour cream, puréed plums – highly flavourful liquid mixes are what you want.

For the sour cream glaze, sift the icing sugar into a medium bowl, then mix in the cream, sour cream and citric acid or lemon juice (to boost the acidity), and whisk until incorporated. It takes a lot of icing sugar and we're looking for the texture of a thick soup or thin purée. So just keep mixing in extra icing sugar until the texture is good, then taste. If it's too sweet, add a bit more citric acid or lemon juice. (And a pinch of salt never goes astray.)

Dip each cruller in the glaze, put it on the wire rack and allow excess glaze to drip off and the glaze to firm up a bit. Finely grate the orange zest over the dipped crullers, allowing the oils from the orange to drop onto them.

Giorgia McAllister Forte

London fog castagnole, cacao nib sugar and pots de crème (71)
Jerusalem artichoke, chilli greens and goat's cheese focaccias (218)

Pastry chef and founder, Monforte Viennoiserie

Melbourne, Vic
Wurundjeri Country

Giorgia McAllister Forte was twelve when she decided she'd be a pastry chef. She hadn't, admittedly, baked a great deal yet, but it was half-term in London, she was helping out in the kitchen of a family friend's restaurant – and the dream stuck. When she looks back on this early decision to become a pastry chef, it strikes her that it didn't feel like a choice at all, more: 'This is what I'm going to do, why would I do anything else? It just made sense.' It's been that way ever since.

Today she is the owner of Monforte Viennoiserie, a small-batch neighbourhood pasticceria in Melbourne's North Carlton. At any one time, there are eight, always eight, perfectly baked goods on the menu, all lined up in the single window cabinet – it's the maximum squeeze-out of a ten-square-metre (hundred-square-foot) kitchen, and it wants for nothing. Viennoiserie, every which way, is the ticket: croissants are dark and glossy on the outside and silkily honeycombed on the inside; one, drizzled with fragrant leatherwood honey and flecked with flaky sea salt, has become a non-negotiable staple (there would be neighbourhood uproar if it disappeared). The rest of the menu changes every three to four weeks. In the variety, Giorgia's always looking for one thing: 'I just try to find balance with everything. I don't really have a super-sweet palate, so a lot of the time we get the questions: "Is it sweet?" "Is it savoury?" But it's somewhere in the middle.'

Giorgia and her team test out their creations on squares of laminated dough squirrelled from their rolling production, making the most of what's in season, what their producers have been growing, and what they've been seeing on plates in local haunts. 'I like the saying that if it grows together, it goes together. So I use that,' she says. 'Or if there are things that I know would be good to introduce to bring a bit of brightness when it's miserable outside.' In the summer months, there's soft-serve flavoured peach one week, coffee and wattleseed the next, and it is so smooth and balanced that you can feasibly find yourself seeing one off at nine in the morning.

Early on in her career, Giorgia worked for Claire Ptak at Violet Cakes in London, which is where she first learned to stretch the limits of a single format – at that time, cake. 'She taught me all about cakes, and it was all less sugar, more of the actual fruits, and also vegetables. It was a lot more balance, and learning about that changed how I viewed baking, because you can do so much with lots of different things. It doesn't need to be so prescriptive.'

'The best things are usually the most simple and considered. You can get so much more out of simple flavours by treating them in different ways.'

A NOTE ON FLAVOUR

'I think often people get a bit hung up on what's going to be the most extravagant and impressive bake to make, and while those things are often delicious, the best things are usually the most simple and considered. You can get so much more out of simple flavours by treating them in different ways. If we pull right back to vanilla – what most people would consider a "basic" flavour, then depending on how it's used and the quality of the beans, it can taste a number of different ways. This could be anything from dry-roasting the beans to get a deeper, richer and more caramelly flavour, to simply using the seeds inside for a quintessential nostalgic nod, or infusing the empty beans in vodka for your own essence to get a brighter and more floral note. This can be applied to so many of the most accessible ingredients, and you'll always get a lovely result.'

WORDS TO BAKE BY

'Always, always listen to your gut when you're baking. Sometimes it's easy to get a little bit lazy or just think, "I don't need to do this, it'll be fine." But in your gut you know you should be doing something differently. Instead you keep going and it comes out terribly, and you know you could have fixed it. It takes much less time to fix something earlier on in the process than going all the way through to the end. Try to fix as you go. Ask yourself questions: "Does this feel right?" "Does it look right?" "Is there something I can do now that will save me some time later?"'

London fog castagnole, cacao nib sugar and pots de crème

Giorgia McAllister Forte
Profiled on page 68

MAKES 12
SPECIAL EQUIPMENT four 5–6 cm (2–2½ inch) ramekins, high-speed blender or mortar and pestle, pastry brush, sugar thermometer

Cacao nib sugar
200 g (7 oz) caster (superfine) sugar
25 g (1 oz) salted butter
150 g (5½ oz) cacao nibs

Pots de crème
300 g (10½ oz) dark chocolate, 55%, chopped
140 g (5 oz) milk
150 g (5½ oz) pouring cream
4 g (⅛ oz) loose-leaf earl grey tea
2 g (1/16 oz) sea salt
2 g (1/16 oz) dried lavender or liquid natural lavender flavour (optional)

Castagnole
1 g (1/32 oz) loose-leaf earl grey
255 g (9 oz) fresh ricotta cheese
50 g (1¾ oz) egg (from about 1 egg)
25 g (1 oz) caster (superfine) sugar
1 g (1/32 oz) lemon zest
12 g (½ oz) Marsala
70 g (2½ oz) plain (all-purpose) flour
4 g (⅛ oz) baking powder
50 g (1¾ oz) dark chocolate, 50–70%, chopped
sunflower oil, for deep-frying

Castagnole are a traditional fritter, named for their chestnut shape and eaten during carnival season throughout Italy. Here I've combined them with chocolate and Earl Grey – one of my favourite flavours. The interior offers chipped chocolate throughout, reminiscent of stracciatella ice cream. Eaten alongside lashings of chocolate crème, they make an excellent after-supper snack.

Line a baking tray with baking paper.
For the cacao nib sugar, in a heavy-based saucepan, combine half the caster sugar with just enough water to give it the texture of wet sand. Stir the sugar and water together off the heat then, using a bowl of water and a pastry brush, brush away any granules of sugar left on the side of the saucepan.

Once no granules remain, place over medium–high heat. Allow it to come to the boil without stirring (or the sugar will crystallise), then cook, still without stirring, until the sugar begins to caramelise, turning golden brown.

Add the butter and swirl the pan to melt it, taking care as it will bubble up and can spit. Once the butter is melted, stir through the cacao nibs to coat thoroughly with the caramel. Remove from the heat, pour onto the prepared baking tray and leave to cool. Once completely cool, break into chunks and blitz to a fine powder in a high-speed blender.

Transfer the mixture to a bowl and add the remaining caster sugar, tossing to combine.

For the pots de crème, put the chocolate in a large bowl and set aside. Combine the milk, cream, tea, salt and lavender, if using, in a heavy-based saucepan over medium heat. Bring to the boil, then remove from the heat and leave for 1 hour to infuse.

Re-boil the milk and cream, then strain over the chocolate. Leave to sit for 2 minutes for the chocolate to temper, then whisk to combine. Pour about 140 g (5 oz) into each of four 5–6 cm (2–2½ inch) ramekins and refrigerate until set, 2–3 hours.

For the castagnole, blitz the earl grey in a high-speed blender or crush to a fine powder using a mortar and pestle. In a large bowl, whisk together the ricotta, egg, sugar, earl grey, lemon zest and Marsala. Sift the flour and baking powder into the ricotta mixture. Whisk gently to combine, taking care not to overwork the batter. Using a spatula, fold through the chocolate until evenly combined.

Half-fill a large, heavy-based saucepan with sunflower oil and heat over medium heat to 165°C/325°F. Working in batches and using two teaspoons to make fritters, carefully drop small mounds of batter into the oil. Fry for 3–4 minutes, using a slotted spoon to flip them occasionally, until they are a deep golden brown.

Drain in a bowl lined with paper towel, then toss them in the cacao nib sugar. They are best eaten immediately, dipped in the pots de crème.

Tilly Pamment

Lemon, thyme and honey madeleines (opposite)
Buttermilk bundt with passionfruit icing (147)

Baker and cookbook author

Blue Mountains, NSW
Dharug & Gundungurra Country

'For generations, people baked every day. If you wanted cake, you had to bake it,' says Blue Mountains–based baker Tilly Pamment. Her work is inspired by community-style baking, the kind she grew up with in the regional city of Armidale, New South Wales, and the kind made famous by the Country Women's Association. Generous and unfussy are Tilly's adjectives of choice.

Her Plain Cake Appreciation Society, and now her book of the same name, took off during the pandemic, offering comfort-giving cakes you could knock together with ease. The message: 'You don't have to wait for a special occasion to bake. Baking can be a simple, everyday thing.' This also means shrugging off the pressure to produce a showstopper. 'I love things to look beautiful,' she says, 'but for me a cake is a cake. It's there to be eaten. And first and foremost, it needs to taste good. In my first book, there are lots of brown cakes, lots of un-iced cakes – but some of those are my favourites because they're the ones that are really delicious.'

To let baking come back down to earth, Tilly nudges us to see resourcefulness as inspiration. Each of her recipes begins with staples you can easily reach into the pantry for – but through some everyday magic they end up tasting anything but plain. Some days this might mean drawing from what she can't ignore (the rhubarb possessing her garden, for instance), while on others it's using up the easily overlooked (a tin of passionfruit lurking at the back of the cupboard). Sometimes it's as simple as pouring a butter cake mixture into a bundt tin for a change. There's always a reason to bake, hidden in the plain sight of every day.

ON TAKING TEA CAKES ONE STEP FURTHER

'I'm always trying to work tea into my baking. I love fragrance in baked goods and particularly herbal notes, so it's a good challenge for me. I use ground-up tea in quite a few recipes. Blitz it or use a mortar and pestle to grind the tea first, and then you can incorporate it straight into your batter for things like an Earl Grey bundt. Smoky teas, like lapsang souchong, work really well with chocolate. Ground chai works beautifully in fruit cakes like an apple cake. You can also infuse the milk with tea and then put it in, even herbal teas, like I do for a chamomile tea cake.'

WORDS TO BAKE BY

'For me, baking has always been like my form of mindfulness or meditation. When I'm in the kitchen, there is just enough occupation of my hands and my head to put me in a neutral state. I find that really relaxing, particularly with young kids and trying to juggle work and life. I bake when I've got too many things to do. I bake when I should be doing something else. You take that time to do something for yourself, but you wind up bringing people back together, to sit down and share something special.'

Lemon, thyme and honey madeleines

MAKES 24
SPECIAL EQUIPMENT two 12-hole madeleine tins, pastry brush

125 g (4½ oz) unsalted butter, plus extra, softened, for greasing
2 tablespoons milk
1 tablespoon honey
165 g (5¾ oz) caster (superfine) sugar
finely grated zest of 2 lemons
1 tablespoon lemon thyme leaves, plus extra (optional) to serve
2 large eggs
125 g (4½ oz) plain (all-purpose) flour, plus extra for dusting
1 teaspoon baking powder
pinch of salt

To finish
40 g (1¼ oz) butter

There is something about little cakes that never ceases to delight. And madeleines would have to be one of the most delightful small cakes around. The simplicity and ease of making them (hello, melt and mix) only endears them to me even more. These little beauties combine the classic duo of lemon and honey with the lovely herbaceous flavour of lemon thyme. I love the process of rubbing the lemon zest and thyme into the caster sugar for this recipe, a technique I often employ in sweet baking, and one that not only ensures a deliciously fragrant cake but is also wildly therapeutic. Win-win!

Combine the butter, milk and honey in a small saucepan over low heat. Stir gently until the butter has melted and the honey has dissolved. Remove from the heat and set aside to cool.

Combine the caster sugar, lemon zest and lemon thyme leaves in a small bowl and use your clean fingertips to rub the zest and thyme through the sugar until fragrant. Set aside 3 heaped tablespoons (60 g/2¼ oz) of the sugar mixture to sprinkle over the cooked madeleines. Cover and refrigerate this until you are ready to bake your madeleines.

Transfer the remaining sugar mixture to a medium bowl, then add the eggs and whisk to combine. Sift in the flour, baking powder and salt and whisk until smooth. Finally, whisk in the cooled melted butter mixture, taking care not to overmix. Cover and refrigerate the batter for at least 2 hours.

Preheat the oven to 170°C/350°F fan-forced (190°C/375°F conventional) and brush two 12-hole madeleine tins well with the softened extra butter using a pastry brush. Dust with a little plain flour, tapping out any excess.

Spoon a scant tablespoon of batter into each madeleine hole, filling them about two-thirds full. Bake for 8–10 minutes or until the madeleines have risen and are deep golden around the edges.

To finish, while the cakes are cooking, melt the 40 g (1¼ oz) butter. Remove the reserved sugar mixture from the fridge and scatter through some extra lemon thyme leaves, if you like.

When the madeleines are cooked, allow them to cool for a minute or two in the tins before removing them one by one and brushing the tops with the melted butter using a pastry brush. Sprinkle the reserved sugar mixture over them, gently pressing it onto the surface of the cakes. Leave the madeleines on a wire rack to cool slightly before serving warm or at room temperature with a big pot of tea.

The madeleines are best eaten on the day they are made, but the uncooked batter will keep happily in the fridge for up to 2 days – so you can just bake as many at a time as you wish to eat.

Raymond Tan

Ondeh ondeh (79)

Pandan drømmekage (148)

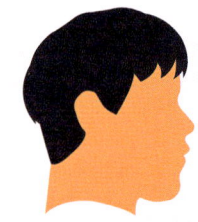

Founder, Raya Bakery

Melbourne, Vic
Wurundjeri Country

At Raya Bakery, Raymond Tan re-imagines his nostalgia for home into colourful creations that bring a South-East Asian influence to Western bakes – and vice versa. Fittingly, raya means 'celebration' in Malay. And first of all it's a celebration for the eyes: a Danish drømmekage takes on the classic Malaysian trifecta of pandan, coconut and gula Melaka (molasses-y palm sugar from the famous port town), and custard tarts are richly purpled by ube. At festival times, there are offerings of ornate mooncakes flavoured with bandung (a fragrant drink of rose syrup and condensed milk); red bean, lychee and pistachio for Lunar New Year; or Christmassy pink and cream chequerboard cookies laced with salted plum.

It can all be traced back to one fateful day when accounting student Raymond turned on his oven. 'We didn't have ovens in Malaysian houses,' he says. 'I've always loved cooking, but my baking began when I came to Melbourne and I realised there was an oven in every apartment, but I'd never turned one on.' His interest in baking was piqued by the drama of *MasterChef*. 'Baking seemed like the hardest thing – everyone seemed to flop,' he says. Instead of putting him off, it quite literally ignited something. Baking for family and friends turned into selling whole cakes (putting his skills from his accounting degree to use, he quickly realised he could break even). It all came with a sweet discovery: 'I realised that dessert is something that no one ever complains about. Every time you bring a dessert, that's what people remember the most. Those are the moments I wanted to make,' he says.

All the while, he'd been documenting his self-taught baking on a platform that was beginning to take off – Instagram – where he gained a big audience for the dramatic creations he'd whip up in his tiny home kitchen. 'I was comfortable working because I was just doing things for my friends and family. So you can't really go wrong with that, and I think that gave me the confidence to just keep doing it,' he says. Whirlwind years ensued as invitations to teach cake-decorating workshops flowed in from everywhere from London to Paris.

Back in Melbourne during COVID lockdowns, things began to change course. 'One of the reasons Raya came about was because I realised I don't want people to just look at my Instagram. I want people to taste my food,' he says. 'I really love it; it's more real.' Homesick for Malaysia, he turned his attention to the art of making kueh – the snack-sized canon of Malaysian desserts, brightly coloured, sometimes wrapped in banana-leaf parcels or rolled in coconut, and often made from glutinous rice. 'There weren't that many kuehs around at that time. I missed home,

> 'Every time you bring a dessert, that's what people remember the most. Those are the moments I wanted to make.'

there was no travel, so I tried to make them more home-like, what I remembered them to be.' His medley boxes – a staple at Raya today – were a hit. The success nudged him towards a thought that had been lingering at the back of his mind. 'I saw an opportunity to show my Malaysian background,' he says, 'Because you always hear that Malaysia is all about food but you don't hear so much about the sweets.' He has grand plans for kueh. 'Right now what we're doing is very traditional, but there's just so much that you can do with this thing alone.'

WORDS TO BAKE BY
'Don't be afraid to start. If I can do it, everyone can – even from the tiniest of kitchens – as long as you're passionate and serious about it. That's the most important ingredient, I think.'

NOTES ON STARTING OUT
'Over the years, I've learned that less is more. I like to keep things to three elements. The rule is to always stay simple. Baking is kind of like puzzling: if it doesn't work, it doesn't work. I always tell my team to experiment with whatever we have in the shop – and no matter what mistakes you make, remember that at the end of the day, it's just cake.'

Ondeh ondeh

Raymond Tan
Profiled on page 76

MAKES 40 balls
SPECIAL EQUIPMENT blender, steamer, gloves

200 g (7 oz) yellow sweet potato (white sweet potato will also work just fine)
1 g (1/32 oz) lye or alkaline water (see below)
130 g (4½ oz) pandan juice (see page 148)
1 g (1/32 oz) pandan essence
8 g (¼ oz) salt
180 g (6¼ oz) glutinous rice flour
10 g (¼ oz) tapioca flour
150 g (5½ oz) gula Melaka (palm sugar), blended with a few drops of water to form a paste
85 g (3 oz) finely grated fresh coconut (find it in the frozen section of Asian grocery stores)

Lye water
1 teaspoon bicarbonate of soda (baking soda)
1 tablespoon water

If you don't want to make your own lye water, you can find it in Asian grocery stores. The lye water prevents the pandan from discolouring and adds the bouncy texture and slight alkaline taste found in most pandan-flavoured kuehs.

When Raya first opened, people flocked to the store to get their hands on our vibrantly coloured Peranakan kuehs, which come in savoury and sweet versions and showcase different techniques and textures. A favourite in our store was our ondeh ondeh, bite-sized glutinous rice balls with bursting palm sugar centres, tossed in steamed and slightly salted grated fresh coconut. This little snack is commonly sold and eaten all over Malaysia and Singapore. And while 40 pieces might sound like a lot, they are highly addictive.

Peel the sweet potato and cut it into 2 cm (¾ inch) cubes, then place in a steamer. Bring a pot of water to a simmer over medium heat and set the steamer on top. Steam for about 20 minutes, or until tender when pierced with a fork.

If you are making your own lye water, bake the bicarbonate of soda in a 120°C/250°F fan-forced (140°C/275°F conventional) oven for 1 hour. Mix the baked bicarb with the water on a tray lined with foil (wear gloves, as the baked bicarb may cause skin irritation).

In a blender, purée the cooked sweet potato with the lye water, pandan juice, pandan essence and half the salt.

Combine the glutinous rice and tapioca flours in a large bowl and mix in the sweet potato purée. Mix until a dough forms, then knead the dough for about 10 minutes. If the dough is a little dry, add a few drops of water; if it's too soft and hard to work, add a few more tablespoons of glutinous rice flour. The dough should be smooth and not stick to your hands.

Divide the dough into 40 pieces of about 10 g (¼ oz) each. Gently flatten each dough ball with the palm of your hand. Place about ½ teaspoon of the gula Melaka paste in the centre, then bring up the sides of the dough to enclose the filling and re-form the ball.

Put the grated coconut in a bowl and place in a steamer set over a pot of simmering water. Steam for about 10 minutes, then fluff up the coconut with a fork and mix in the remaining salt.

Bring a medium pot of water to the boil. Working in batches, gently drop the filled dough balls into the boiling water and cook until they float to the surface, about 2 minutes. Leave them to sit in the boiling water for another 2 minutes to ensure the palm sugar is completely melted, then remove using a slotted spoon, drain in a strainer and roll in the coconut.

Gula Melaka (palm sugar) usually comes in a block, so cutting and grating it is normally the way to go, but I find blending it works best.

Maaryasha Werdiger

Mohn hamantaschen (poppyseed cookies) (83)

Plum streusel cake (150)

Founder and head baker, Zelda Bakery

Melbourne, Vic
Boonwurrung/Bunurong Country

For Maaryasha, sourdough was 'a hobby that was out of control'. She had been perfecting her practice at home for years, while raising three children, working as a paediatric physiotherapist – and leaving her microbakery dream safe in the back of her mind. Then: 'One day, I realised that it was me who was able to make my life better, and I gave myself permission to do so,' she says. 'I was allowed to change careers, or rather, to do something that was not expected of me. I think a lot of people have that moment.'

It's a familiar impasse: you can let your dream tug at your heels, or you can let it speed you on. 'It's like I was waiting to know *how* to have a bakery, but at the same time realising I wasn't going to *know* how. So I just started,' she says, and with that, she opened her sourdough microbakery, Zelda, from her garage. 'Immediately it was insane, with crowds of customers coming to the garage. Every few weeks I would stop for a week and try to improve it, and it kind of went like that for three years,' Maaryasha says. The customers kept coming, and she drew the attention of fellow local bakers.

Bolstered by their guidance (they included Michael James and other close friends she met in the early days of the Grainz initiative, see page 56), Maaryasha's confidence grew – not only to leave her career and commit fully to the craft, but to lead a team with her vision. She recalls one inspiring piece of advice: 'If you didn't know what you're doing, you wouldn't be here. But you do and you are.' And with that, she found a bakery space near her. 'It wasn't quite right,' she says, 'but I knew I could do it.' Working to limitations is part and parcel of Zelda, which as well as using only organic, sustainable and ethically sourced ingredients, keeps to the highest kosher standards.

Maaryasha grew up Jewish Orthodox. Eating within her family meant her mum's Italian pasta sauces ('a bit revolutionary for Ashkenazi Jews'), connecting with her Russian grandmother over Eastern European–style baking ('it was all Esther's poppyseed cake, Manya's strudel'), and herring, kugel and cholent on Shabbat ('all the food I didn't like!'). 'People ask if I'm a Jewish bakery, but it's more that I'm Jewish and this is a bakery and I just bake whatever I know,' she says. Her particular focus has been to expand the potential of kosher baking, which she sees as stuck in the eighties, with heavy reliance on margarine and a propensity for dry, yeasted cakes.

'The bakery is led by my obsession with nostalgia, of improving old food or giving people that sense of it. It's about being proud of my heritage, but also having fun,' she says. 'My parents keep a very strict level of kosher. I didn't want to ever own a shop that they couldn't eat at. So as long as I can do it, I'll do it,' she says. 'Now I realise it's not hard to make good kosher food. There are certain limitations – we have what we have and we make it work,' she explains. At Zelda, this means the cheese danish of her childhood gets the sourdough treatment, there's a weekly changing knish ('We do a butter and sour cream pastry for the knish, so it's a bit of

> 'I've always been baking for people. I always love that connection. I love making something that hits you, reminds you of something or helps you enjoy a moment or celebrate.'

nostalgia, but I think it's better'), and the once-loathed kosher poppyseed creations have been remade into the proudest-looking, puddingy-centred mohnstreuselkuchen. All alongside sourdough loaves, focaccias or whatever else is currently taking the team's and/or the community's fancy.

These days, Maaryasha has the space to appreciate what she's built. 'I often think that we wonder, "How did we get here?" without realising that actually, we've got ourselves there by making choices all along the way. It was everything that we did,' she says. 'That took me a long time to appreciate.'

ON BAKING FOR COMMUNITY

'I've always felt that I don't really fit into anything. But what I'm really into is community. I've always been baking cakes. I've always been baking for people. I always love that connection. I love making something that hits you, reminds you of something or helps you enjoy a moment or celebrate. When you're a community baker, you're in sync with the community. You can match their needs. You teach them, they teach you and then you're reflecting that back to them with what you're then baking. No one had any rye bread for many years and they had bad memories of it, so I started giving away a lot for free until people starting having this renewed faith in rye bread. I love being part of people's homes and connecting. It's a relationship. I feel energised by it.'

Mohn hamantaschen (poppyseed cookies)

Maaryasha Werdiger
Profiled on page 80

MAKES 24
SPECIAL EQUIPMENT stand mixer with paddle attachment, rolling pin, 8 cm (3¼ inch) round cookie cutter (or tumbler), spice or coffee grinder

Poppyseed filling
60 g (2¼ oz) unsalted butter
60 g (2¼ oz) honey
250 g (9 oz) milk (or cream if you're in the mood)
2 eggs
150 g (5½ oz) caster (superfine) sugar
½ teaspoon salt
½ vanilla bean paste
250 g (9 oz) freshly ground poppyseeds

Hamantaschen dough
1 egg
1 egg yolk
200 g (7 oz) unsalted butter, slightly softened (30 minutes out of fridge)
160 g (5¾ oz) caster (superfine) sugar
1 teaspoon salt
zest of 1 orange (optional)
1 teaspoon vanilla bean paste
330 g (11¾ oz) plain (all-purpose) flour, plus extra for dusting

Hamantaschen are triangular filled cookies eaten on the Jewish festival of Purim (a hamantasch is a singular cookie). They are given to friends and family in volumes. It is said they resemble Haman's ear but they do look more like his hat, truthfully. As a kid, I made hamantaschen in school, as did six of my siblings. Hamantaschen were everywhere during the festival and, honestly, they were dry and horrible, mostly made with margarine (that's a whole other story) and filled with fluorescent jam. Until one day, well into my adulthood, I came across a hamantaschen recipe where the dough was made with butter. I haven't looked back. Poppyseeds are the most traditional filling, particularly in communities with a strong Eastern European background, such as those in Melbourne, but these days jam is most common. At our bakery, we do fillings including halva, gianduja, pistachio, chocolate, prune and all sorts of jams. My personal favourite, though, is poppyseed and good raspberry jam together.

First make the poppyseed filling. You're essentially making a custard here. In a small saucepan over low heat, melt the butter and honey. Stir in the milk, then bring to the boil over medium heat. Watch closely, as it can boil over.

While the milk is coming up to temperature, in a separate bowl, lightly whisk the eggs, sugar, salt and vanilla until just combined. Once the milk has boiled, slowly pour the milk into the egg mixture, whisking as you pour, then pour the mixture back into the saucepan and return to medium heat, whisking constantly as the mixture thickens. This part may take 5 minutes or so. Keep whisking to prevent the custard sticking to the bottom.

Once the mixture has thickened, remove from the heat, add the poppyseeds and whisk together into a glossy poppyseed paste. Pour into a container, cover with biodegradable plastic wrap, with the wrap touching the surface of the custard to prevent a skin forming, and leave to cool.

The filling can be made several days in advance. It will keep in the fridge for 3–5 days and in the freezer for 1 month.

For the hamantaschen dough, beat the egg with the egg yolk in a small bowl. In a stand mixer with the paddle attachment, cream together the butter, sugar, salt, orange zest, if using, and vanilla on medium speed until combined. It does not need to be light and fluffy. With the mixer still running on medium speed, slowly add the beaten egg and yolk.

Reduce the speed to low and mix in the flour until just combined. An overmixed dough will make a less tender cookie. If the dough is still quite wet, add a little extra flour until it resembles a soft dough, but remember that the dough will harden while it rests in the fridge. >

The Coffee Company in Balaclava grinds poppyseeds for me on the spot. Whole poppyseeds can be bitter but when freshly ground they're not. We buy them ground in bulk and freeze immediately to prevent them going rancid, which they can do quickly. So try to source fresh poppyseeds; you can grind them using a spice or coffee grinder.

Bring the dough together into a ball, then divide into two smaller balls of about 350 g (12 oz) each. Flatten each ball into a thick disc, wrap in biodegradable plastic wrap and refrigerate for 30 minutes.

To shape the hamantaschen, remove the discs of dough from the fridge. If they are quite hard, leave them out for 10 minutes or until slightly malleable. Dust a work surface with flour and gently roll out the dough to about 5 mm (¼ inch) thick, dusting with extra flour as needed. Using an 8 cm (3¼ inch) round cookie cutter, or a tumbler of similar size, cut out circles of dough. This dough is a little fragile, so work fast and be gentle. If you need to put the dough back in the fridge for 5 minutes do so, as it will help with the final shaping.

Preheat the oven to 180°C/350°F fan-forced (200°C/400°F conventional) and line a baking tray with baking paper.

Using 2 teaspoons, drop a generous teaspoonful of filling in the centre of the dough circle, then shape three corners by pinching the dough together to form a triangle, leaving the middle exposed. Do not use too much filling or the cookies will burst.

Arrange on the baking tray and bake for 9–10 minutes, just until the edges have started browning but the cookies are still pale. An overbaked cookie is a dry cookie. Cool on the tray for 10 minutes, then enjoy straight away or transfer to a wire rack to cool completely.

The hamantaschen will keep for up to 1 week in an airtight container. The dough and the filling will each keep for up to 1 week in the fridge and 1 month in the freezer. The cookies can be shaped in advance and refrigerated or frozen before baking. To bake from frozen, add an extra minute to the cooking time. (I find they hold their shape well if they have been made in advance and baked straight from the freezer.)

This recipe makes enough filling for three batches of hamantaschen, because it just didn't feel right to go to all that effort for such a small amount of filling. It can also be swirled through brioche dough to make poppyseed babka, or baked in a sweet pastry for a poppyseed tart or whatever else you come up with.

Morning & *Afternoon Teas*

90 Glazed fruit buns

92 Baker Bleu babka

99 Beetroot and apple cake with wattleseed icing

100 Ricotta cassateddi

102 Chu flans

107 Pear frangipane slab tart

113 Bay gâteau d'émotion

115 Ginger and orange blossom cake

118 Peach and sour cream cake

122 Chocolate, amaretto and sour cherry tart

127 Lemon, polenta and raspberry tea cake

128 Lemon curd shortbread tart

134 Plum, frangipane and cream cheese galettes

139 Swedish semlor

142 Cinnamon braid

147 Buttermilk bundt with passionfruit icing

148 Pandan drømmekage

150 Plum streusel cake

Glazed fruit buns

Orlando Artavilla
Profiled on page 22

MAKES about 18
SPECIAL EQUIPMENT stand mixer with dough hook and whisk attachments, pastry brush, piping bag and plain no. 9 nozzle (optional)

Fruit buns
zest of 1 orange and 200 ml (7 fl oz) juice
500 g (1 lb 2 oz) bread flour (I use organic)
10 g (¼ oz) salt
50 g (1¾ oz) caster (superfine) sugar, plus extra to finish
1 teaspoon ground cinnamon
12.5 g (½ oz) fresh yeast or 4 g (⅛ oz) dried yeast
250 g (9 oz) sourdough starter
80 ml (2½ fl oz) lukewarm milk
2 large eggs, whisked and strained
200 g (7 oz) butter, softened
175 g (6 oz) sultanas (golden raisins)
icing (confectioners') sugar, for dusting (optional)

Egg wash
2 eggs
1 tablespoon milk

Sugar syrup
50 g (1¾ oz) caster (superfine) sugar
100 ml (3½ fl oz) water

Vanilla chantilly cream
540 g (1 lb 3 oz) whipping cream
1 vanilla bean, split lengthways and seeds scraped, or 1 teaspoon vanilla bean paste
200 g (7 oz) caster (superfine) or icing (confectioners') sugar

This recipe is from the early days of Candied Bakery. The buns have body, softness and a slight sweetness. I wanted to make something that wasn't too heavy without being too light, and I think I found the perfect medium. Fill them with freshly whipped chantilly cream, or enjoy that sticky, beautifully textured bun plain, as I do.

For the fruit buns, boil the orange juice and zest in a small saucepan over medium–low heat until slightly reduced, then set aside to cool.

Combine all the dry ingredients, plus the sourdough starter, in the bowl of a stand mixer. Mix just until combined, then add the milk, egg and the cooled orange juice and zest.

Fit the bowl to the stand mixer with the dough hook attachment and mix on low speed until the mixture is just clear of visible flecks of flour. With the mixer still running, add the butter in four stages. Once all the butter is incorporated, mix on high speed until the dough is just developed, about 10 minutes. (Use the window method to check: stretch a piece of the dough and see if it forms a thin window of dough rather than tearing.) Reduce the speed to slow, add the sultanas and mix until just incorporated.

Cover the bowl with a damp tea towel (dish towel) or biodegradable plastic wrap and set aside to rise at room temperature for 2–3 hours.

Grease a baking tray with butter or canola oil spray, or line with baking paper. Preheat the oven to 190°C/375°F fan-forced (210°C/400°F conventional). Don't use a steam setting.

Divide the dough into 18 pieces of about 85 g (3 oz) each. Mould each piece into a ball by rolling firmly between your hands – you want them as tight and smooth as possible without tearing the dough. Arrange the dough balls on the prepared baking tray, cover with a clean tea towel and leave in a warm place until almost doubled in size.

For the egg wash, beat the eggs with the milk. Brush each bun gently with the egg wash using a pastry brush, then place a teaspoon of extra caster sugar on top.

Bake the buns until golden, about 15 minutes.

For the sugar syrup, combine the sugar and water in a small heavy-based saucepan over low heat and stir well until the sugar dissolves. Bring to a gentle simmer and continue simmering, without stirring (or the sugar will crystallise), over low heat until reduced by one-third. Transfer the buns to a wire rack and brush the tops with the sugar syrup. Leave to cool.

For the chantilly cream, combine all the ingredients in a stand mixer with the whisk attachment and whisk until firm peaks form.

Serve the buns as is, or cut them in half and spread with chantilly cream, or put the cream in a piping bag fitted with a plain no. 9 nozzle, cut a small hole in the side of each bun and pipe the cream into the centre. If you like, lightly dust the tops with icing sugar to serve.

If you don't have sourdough starter, increase the fresh yeast to 20 g (¾ oz) or dried yeast to 6.5 g (⅛ oz), and cut the rising time to 90 minutes.

Baker Bleu babka

Gad Assayag
Profiled on page 26

SERVES 8
SPECIAL EQUIPMENT 22 cm (8½ inch) diameter bundt tin, stand mixer with dough hook attachment, stick blender (optional), rolling pin, pastry brush, angled palette knife

Brioche dough
265 g (9¼ oz) baker's flour
38 g (1¼ oz) caster (superfine) sugar
5 g (⅛ oz) salt
4 g (⅛ oz) dried yeast or
 12 g (½ oz) fresh yeast
80 g (2¾ oz) egg (from about
 2 eggs)
65 g (2¼ oz) milk
35 g (1¼ oz) sour cream
60 g (2¼ oz) unsalted butter,
 at room temperature (ideally
 18°C/64°F)

Chocolate hazelnut ganache
70 g (2½ oz) pouring cream
33 g (1¼ oz) brown sugar
2 g (1/16 oz) salt
15 g (½ oz) unsweetened cocoa
 powder, sifted
65 g (2¼ oz) dark chocolate,
 55%, roughly chopped
65 g (2¼ oz) hazelnut praline paste

Babka is the ultimate yeasted product – a cross between cake and bread that is appealing to eat at any time of the day. It has a soft texture that melts in the mouth, and it can be filled with various flavours. For me, it brings back memories of watching my great-grandmother make it, and of visiting bakeries in my hometown of Jerusalem and excitedly choosing between the different flavours on offer.

At Baker Bleu, babka has become one of our most popular weekend products. We use a light brioche dough with the most traditional filling, chocolate and hazelnut but almost any flavour goes. I prefer to make my own hazelnut praline, but you can use a quality praline from a specialty store. Rather than using a bundt tin, the dough can be made into different shapes, such as a large knotted ring; broken up into small individual portions; or baked in a loaf (bar) tin.

For the brioche dough, combine the flour, sugar, salt and yeast in the bowl of a stand mixer with the dough hook attachment and mix on medium speed for about 1 minute. Remove the bowl from the mixer.

In a separate bowl, break up the egg with a whisk, then whisk in the milk and sour cream. Using a spatula, fold the egg mixture into the flour mixture, ensuring there's no flour left at the bottom of the bowl.

Return the bowl to the stand mixer and mix on medium speed for 3 minutes, until the dough comes together. Divide the butter into three equal portions and, with the mixer running, add the butter one portion at a time and mix each for 4 minutes, ensuring it is well incorporated and scraping the side of the bowl before adding the next portion.

Test if the dough is ready by taking a small piece and stretching it. If it doesn't break and you can see through it, the dough is glossy and all the butter is well incorporated with no chunks, it's ready to be rested.

Lightly spray a large bowl with oil and transfer the dough to this bowl. Cover with biodegradable plastic wrap and refrigerate overnight.

For the chocolate hazelnut ganache, combine the cream, brown sugar and salt in a medium saucepan and bring to the boil over medium heat, stirring occasionally. Remove from the heat and add the cocoa powder, mixing until well combined.

Put the dark chocolate and hazelnut praline paste in a separate medium bowl and pour the cream and cocoa mixture over. Using a stick blender, blend for 3 minutes, until the mixture is shiny and elastic. (If you don't have a stick blender, use a whisk). Refrigerate overnight, then remove from the fridge the following morning and leave for 3 hours to bring to room temperature.

Sugar syrup
70 g (2½ oz) water
100 g (3½ oz) caster (superfine) sugar

To assemble
melted butter, cooled, for greasing
¼ cup (35 g) plain (all-purpose) flour, for dusting, plus extra as needed
80 g (2¾ oz) chocolate chips

Making the dough and filling a day in advance gives you a nice cold dough and spreadable filling, which ensures the shaping part goes smoothly. Rolling the dough thinly and spreading the filling evenly will ensure a super-chocolatey babka.

For the sugar syrup, combine the sugar and water in a small saucepan over medium–low heat and bring to a simmer, stirring regularly to dissolve the sugar but not stirring once bubbles start to form (or the sugar will crystallise). Remove from the heat and set aside.

Before you begin the shaping process, use a pastry brush to brush a 22 cm (8½ inch) bundt cake tin with melted butter, ensuring you get it into the details of the mould. Place in the freezer for 5 minutes, then apply a second coat of butter. Sprinkle the plain flour evenly into the tin, shake to coat completely, then turn upside down and discard the excess flour.

To shape and fill the babka, lightly dust a work surface with flour and, using a rolling pin, roll out the dough to a 30 × 22 cm (12 × 8½ inch) rectangle about 2 mm (¹⁄₁₆ inch) thick. A long side should be facing you.

Use an angled palette knife to spread the chocolate hazelnut ganache evenly over the dough, leaving a 2 cm (¾ inch) border. Sprinkle the chocolate chips evenly over the ganache.

Using both hands, roll up the dough like a roulade, starting from the long side closest to you, then even out the roll; it should be 23–26 cm (9–10½ cm) long. Cover with biodegradable plastic wrap, baking paper or a clean tea towel (dish towel) and refrigerate for 10 minutes to rest.

Cut the roll in half lengthways using a serrated knife or a pizza cutter. Cross the two pieces to form an 'X'. Twist them around each other two or three times on one side of the cross, ensuring the cut side is facing up. Repeat with the other side of the cross to create a total of five to seven even twists. The roll should be about 25 cm (10 inches) long. Connect the two edges to form a ring, ensuring the edges overlap slightly, then place carefully in the prepared tin.

Create a proving chamber in your oven by placing a pot with 2 cups (500 ml) of freshly boiled water in the bottom of your turned-off oven. Place a baking tray on the shelf directly above the water and put the babka on the shelf above this. Close the door and leave the babka to prove for 1–2 hours; it should rise by about a third.

Remove the proved babka and pot of water from the oven, and preheat the oven to 170°C/350°F fan-forced (190°C/375°F conventional). Return the babka to the oven and bake for 25–30 minutes, until the babka is golden and a skewer inserted in the dough comes out clean. Brush the warm babka generously with the sugar syrup until it becomes glossy and moist.

Cut into slices to serve.

Jo Barrett

Beetroot and apple cake with wattleseed icing (99)
Little Picket potato bread with roasted garlic butter and parsley (204)

Chef and co-founder, Wildpie

Anglesea, Vic
Waddawurung Country

When Jo Barrett bakes, it's determined by what's growing nearby. 'I think with baking, because a lot of it is sugar, flour and butter, you have such a blank canvas that fresh produce can heighten it, whether it's meats or fruits, vegetables, herbs,' explains Jo. 'There are all the techniques of laminating or enriching and the textures you can get from that, but then you add a deliciously ripe apricot brushed with some apricot jam and it becomes something amazing.'

It might be comforting to know that Jo, celebrated as much for her technical skill as her inspiring approach to sustainability, was once prone to thinking that sure, she could cook, but she couldn't bake. 'I definitely at the start fell into that category,' she admits. 'I thought, "I'm not even going to attempt that because I'd probably fail at it."' Cakes had been a conundrum, and family recipes a mystery (see opposite). But with her dream of one day leading a kitchen in her back pocket, Jo set out to get the most wide-ranging education she could. Baking and patisserie training at Michael James's Tivoli Road Bakery (see page 56) was formative – not just for growing her skills, but for the ethos she's known for today. 'It was probably the period when I had the most intense learning, and I guess that shaped me to be who I am now,' she says. 'I'd worked in kind of scary kitchens where you couldn't really ask questions, or if you made mistakes they weren't really met with the intention of trying to help. But Michael was incredibly generous with sharing knowledge and had all the answers – and I asked about 50,000 questions a day!'

And then, there was the whole world to be found in local grains and ingredients. 'It was this real ignition of something for me. It felt great inside to be working with proper ingredients, and I was very fulfilled, even though we were working with just one main ingredient every day. Baking is so intuitive. Your hands are in it. You can follow a recipe to a degree, but you have to have an understanding, and that's what I realised that I like about cooking,' explains Jo. 'It's knowing that if wheat is grown or milled a certain way and then transported and stored, it's going to have that kind of end product. It has changed everything for me. With baking, even though you're in a room, it really does connect you with nature.'

And after closing the two-year chapter on Little Picket, her quickly beloved restaurant at the Lorne Bowls Club on the Great Ocean Road, Jo's returning to bake with a new sustainable venture, Wildpie. 'Wild or

> 'With baking, even though you're in a room, it really does connect you with nature.'

feral species like venison, wallaby, boar and goat are all part of culling and population management programs in Australia, so my aim is to introduce the public to these free-ranging, organic proteins that we're leaving to waste as a delicious and approachable food – a pie, a dim-sim, a sausage roll,' she says.

NOTES ON TEXTURE

'I'm very much a textural kind of cook. So desserts for me are really textural and they need to have punchy flavours as well. One dessert we had on the menu at Little Picket was a really clear, acidic lemon jelly that got dressed in a little bit of Geraldton wax and then a meringue. We would just heat up the egg white and sugar so it was nice and hot and really dense and thick. We made it to order – it was just a few basic elements, but it was based on the idea that you'd get a warm, freshly whipped scoop of meringue. Usually you only get that while you're making it and you might be lucky enough to lick the bowl and go "Man, that's delicious," but then in half an hour, it's not like that any more. We're so lucky in the kitchen. I'm always trying to capture the things that you get to experience as a chef and present them to guests who would never get to try them otherwise. I really love capturing those little nuances that you may not notice.'

WORDS TO BAKE BY

'My nan was an amazing baker, but her recipes were very brief, so in the beginning, I was making these really tough cakes. She had really cursive writing and you couldn't read it properly. Then I would cook with her, but her recipe didn't really match up with what she was doing because it would just say, 'Cream the butter and the sugar.' But if you watched what she was doing, it wasn't really creaming it, she was just mixing it. I think it was because her hands were old and she had arthritis, but that kind of lack of mixing or the way she would handle the food had a massive effect on the texture.'

Beetroot and apple cake with wattleseed icing

Jo Barrett
Profiled on page 96

SERVES 12
SPECIAL EQUIPMENT 25 cm (10 inch) diameter bundt tin, stand mixer with whisk and paddle attachments

330 g (11¾ oz) plain (all-purpose) flour
16 g (½ oz) baking powder
10 g (¼ oz) bicarbonate of soda (baking soda)
15 g (½ oz) ground cinnamon
30 g (1 oz) unsweetened dark cocoa powder
185 g (6½ oz) egg (from about 3 large eggs)
420 g (14¾ oz) brown sugar
250 g (9 oz) extra virgin olive oil
560 g (1 lb 4 oz) peeled and coarsely grated beetroot (beets)
220 g (7¾ oz) peeled, cored and grated green apple

Wattleseed icing
125 g (4½ oz) butter, softened
320 g (11¼ oz) icing (confectioners') sugar, plus extra for dusting
1½ tablespoons pouring cream
1 teaspoon ground wattleseed, plus extra for sprinkling
¼ teaspoon ground cinnamon

I love this cake for its earthiness and moist texture. It's perfect served with sweet icing, but the dough can also be baked into muffins for a different breakfast or morning tea option.

Despite the amount of beetroot, you almost can't pick what the ingredients are once they are combined. I've used this recipe in the different places I have worked and in many different forms – as an element in a dessert, as a wedding cake, in breakfast hampers and in the bakery. It's extremely versatile. At different times of the year, replace the beetroot with parsnips or carrots and the cake changes dramatically while remaining delicious.

Preheat the oven to 160°C/325°F conventional (no fan). Lightly grease a 25 cm (10 inch) bundt tin with butter or spray with oil, and set aside.

Sift the flour, baking powder, bicarbonate of soda, cinnamon and cocoa powder into a bowl twice to make sure they are well combined.

Whisk the egg in a stand mixer with the whisk attachment on medium speed until it begins to foam, then add the brown sugar one-third at a time, whisking until each third is dissolved before adding the next.

When the mixture is thick and glossy, slowly drizzle in the olive oil until it is completely emulsified. Remove the bowl from the stand mixer and use a metal spoon to gently fold in the grated beetroot and apple. Once they are half folded through, gradually fold in the flour mixture. Fold until just combined, then pour into the prepared bundt tin.

Bake for 50 minutes or until a skewer inserted in the centre comes out clean. Leave in the tin for 15 minutes, then turn out onto a wire rack to cool completely.

For the wattleseed icing, cream the butter until pale in a stand mixer with the paddle attachment. Add the icing sugar and continue mixing until the sugar dissolves and the mixture is pale and fluffy. Mix in the cream and spices until combined, then set aside until ready to ice.

Once the cake has cooled, generously spread the wattleseed icing over the top. If you like, dust with a little extra icing sugar and some extra wattleseed.

Ricotta cassateddi

Marianna Di Bartolo
Profiled on page 40

MAKES 13 large or 26 small
SPECIAL EQUIPMENT stand mixer with dough hook attachment, rolling pin, pastry brush, sugar thermometer

You can halve the recipe, but given the work involved, I usually make this amount.

To bake the cassateddi instead of frying them, preheat the oven to 170°C/350°F fan-forced (190°C/375°F conventional), then drop the heat to 160°C/325°F fan-forced (180°C/350°F conventional) and bake for 20-25 minutes until golden, checking that the bases are also golden.

I've included this recipe as it's my favourite breakfast when I'm in Sicily – I always head off to my local pasticceria in my parents' hometown of Palazzolo Acreide. The cassateddi can be made as big as a calzone, as I find them there, or as small as a ravioli, as my mum likes to make them. They are sometimes baked (see the note below), but I can't go past a fried one. And yes – they are typically eaten in the morning as a light breakfast. The dough and filling can be made the day before.

For the dough, combine the flour, salt, sugar and lemon zest in the bowl of a stand mixer with the dough hook attachment.

In a small saucepan over low heat, heat the milk and water to lukewarm, then whisk in the yeast. Add the eggs and whisk well by hand. Turn the stand mixer on at low speed, add the egg mixture to the flour mixture and mix until everything comes together. Increase the speed to medium and mix for 10 minutes, until the dough comes away from the bowl and is silky smooth. Add the butter and mix until incorporated – this can take up to 5 minutes depending on the softness of the butter. The dough should be silky and smooth.

Transfer the dough to a lightly oiled bowl, cover with biodegradable plastic wrap or a damp tea towel (dish towel) and leave to rise at room temperature for 2–3 hours, until doubled in volume.

Lightly dust a work surface with flour and gently roll the dough into a ball. At this stage, you can wrap the well-dusted dough in biodegradable plastic wrap and refrigerate to use the following day.

For the filling, mix all the ingredients in a medium bowl.

Divide the dough into 13 pieces for large cassateddi or 26 pieces for smaller ravioli. Lightly dust the work surface with flour. Roll each piece into a tight ball by cupping the dough and rotating it in your hand. Lightly dust with flour and leave to sit for 5 minutes.

Using a rolling pin, roll each ball into a disc 12 cm (4½ inches) in diameter for large cassateddi or 6 cm (2½ inches) for small ravioli. Place 1 tablespoon of filling for large or 2 teaspoons for small on one half of each pastry, flattening slightly.

Make an egg wash by lightly beating the egg yolk with the water. Using a pastry brush, brush this on the edge of one half of each pastry, then fold over to create a ravioli/calzone half-circle. Press the edges together well with a fork to prevent the ricotta from oozing out during cooking. Place the cassateddi on a floured tray, leaving at least 5 cm (2 inches) between them. Lightly dust with flour and cover with a clean tea towel.

Leave in a warm place until almost doubled in volume, 60–90 minutes. One way of testing is to lightly press a fingertip into the pastry; if it leaves an indentation, it is ready. If it bounces back, leave it a little longer.

Half-fill a large heavy-based saucepan with canola oil. (If using a deep-fryer, heat to 180°C/350°F.) Heat the oil over medium heat for 5 minutes, then test by dropping in a small piece of bread – it should colour within 1 minute. Fry the pastries in batches until golden, taking care they don't get too dark. Drain on paper towel. Leave for a minute, then dust with extra caster sugar.

If you wish to use dried yeast, you'll need 5 g/ ⅛ oz. Heat 100 ml (3½ fl oz) of the liquid in the recipe until lukewarm, then dissolve the yeast in it.

quality canola oil,
  for deep-frying

Dough

350 g (12 oz) 00 flour or plain
  (all-purpose) flour, plus extra
  for dusting
6 g (¼ oz) salt
40 g (1½ oz) caster (superfine)
  sugar, plus extra for dusting
finely grated zest of ½ lemon
50 ml (1¾ fl oz) milk
50 ml (1¾ fl oz) water
10 g (¼ oz) fresh yeast
2 eggs
90 g (3¼ oz) unsalted butter,
  at room temperature, diced

Filling

600 g (1 lb 5 oz) ricotta, strained
  to remove excess liquid
60 g (2¼ oz) caster (superfine)
  sugar
⅛ teaspoon ground cinnamon

Egg wash

1 egg yolk
1 tablespoon water

Chu flans

Ryan and Seren Chu
Profiled on page 30

MAKES 10

SPECIAL EQUIPMENT ten 8 cm (3¼ inch) diameter non-stick fluted brioche moulds, stand mixer with dough hook attachment, rolling pin, 11 cm (4¼ inch) diameter cookie cutter, sugar thermometer (optional)

Poolish
1 g (1/32 oz) dried yeast
142 g (5 oz) water
167 g (5¾ oz) baker's flour

Croissant dough
150 g (5½ oz) water
310 g (11 oz) poolish (see above)
750 g (1 lb 10 oz) baker's flour, plus extra for dusting
132 g (4¾ oz) milk
95 g (3¼ oz) caster (superfine) sugar
22 g (¾ oz) salt
7.5 g (¼ oz) instant yeast
60 g (2¼ oz) unsalted butter, softened, plus 500 g (1 lb 2 oz) chilled

Ryan: When I was growing up, weekend dim sum lunches always ended with egg tarts for dessert. On our regular family trips to Hong Kong, the egg tarts from local bakeries only reinforced my enjoyment. It's a fascinating pastry to me, as it was inspired by the Western custard tart or Portuguese pastel de nata, and the Cantonese version became very popular with the working-class Hong Kong population. My version of the egg tart uses a croissant pastry for extra depth of flavour in the crust, and a silky vanilla custard filling. Poolish is a liquid pre-ferment that enhances the flavour profile of bread or croissant doughs, improves dough extensibility and shelf life, and ensures the desired Maillard browning reaction.

For the poolish, pour the yeast and water into a medium bowl and let the yeast hydrate for 5 minutes. Whisk the yeast and water together, then add the flour and mix until the mixture has the consistency of pancake batter. Leave at room temperature (the ideal range is 20–24°C/68–75°F) for 12 hours or until the dough doubles in size.

For the croissant dough, pour the water into the bowl of your stand mixer, add the poolish, and mix to break up the poolish. Add the flour, milk, sugar, salt and yeast and the 60 g (2¼ oz) softened butter.

Fix your bowl to the stand mixer with the dough hook attachment and mix slowly until everything is incorporated, then stop the mixer and scrape the bowl to make sure nothing is stuck to the side. Continue to mix slowly, then gradually increase to medium speed and mix until a cohesive and tacky dough forms.

Take the dough out of the bowl and place it on a greased baking tray. Shape into a rectangle, cover loosely with biodegradable plastic wrap and leave to rest at room temperature for 1 hour or until doubled in volume.

Unwrap the dough and squash the gas out, maintaining the rectangular shape, and wrap it up again in biodegradable plastic wrap. Refrigerate the dough to ferment overnight.

Lightly dust a work surface with flour. To laminate the croissant dough (i.e. form it into thin layers with butter between them), use a rolling pin to roll the dough out to a 70 × 25 cm (27½ × 10 inch) rectangle about 8 mm (⅜ inch) thick. Have a short edge facing you.

Sandwich the chilled butter between two sheets of baking paper and hit it with a rolling pin until it is flattened to a 40 × 15 cm (16 × 6 inch) rectangle about 8 mm (⅜ inch) thick. Place the chilled butter in the centre of the rolled-out dough. Fold the left-hand edge towards the right so the edge lands about two-thirds of the way across (this addition to the usual book fold helps to create less stress in the dough, which in turn will help you roll it out more evenly). Fold the right-hand side of the dough towards the left so the two edges meet. Fold the left-hand edge of the dough to meet the right-hand edge of the dough. You have now completed a 'book fold'. Refrigerate the dough for 20 minutes.

Crème pâtissière

65 g (2¼ oz) egg yolk (from about 4 eggs)
132 g (4¾ oz) caster (superfine) sugar
18 g (¾ oz) plain (all-purpose) flour
27 g (1 oz) cornflour (cornstarch)
407 g (14¼ oz) milk
10 g (¼ oz) vanilla bean paste
40 g (1½ oz) unsalted butter, softened

Roll the dough out to a 70 × 25 cm (27½ × 10 inch) rectangle about 8 mm (⅜ inch) thick. With a short side facing you, fold in the left-hand third of the dough, then fold the right-hand third over so that the right-hand edge meets the left-hand fold. You have now completed a 'letter fold'. Refrigerate the dough for 20 minutes, then repeat the letter fold step and refrigerate for a further 20 minutes.

Roll out the dough to 3 mm (⅛ inch) thick. Wrap in biodegradable plastic wrap and refrigerate for 1 hour.

For the crème pâtissière, use a hand whisk to whisk the egg yolk, sugar, flour and cornflour in a bowl until thick and pale. Heat the milk and vanilla in a medium saucepan over medium–low heat until almost boiling. Gradually whisk the hot milk into the egg mixture, then pour the egg mixture back into the saucepan and whisk constantly over medium heat until the custard comes to the boil. Boil for 1 minute.

Transfer to a bowl and cover with biodegradable plastic wrap, with the wrap touching the surface of the custard to prevent a skin forming. Cool to 50°C/120°F, then whisk in the butter by hand until smooth.

Cover with biodegradable plastic wrap, with the wrap touching the surface, and refrigerate to cool completely. Before using, whisk by hand until smooth.

Preheat your oven to 240°C/475°F fan-forced (or for conventional as high as it will go). If your ten 8 cm (3¼ inch) fluted brioche moulds aren't non-stick, grease them lightly with butter or oil spray.

To assemble the tarts, using an 11 cm (4¼ inch) diameter cookie cutter, cut 10 circles out of the rested dough.

Place each circle on top of a brioche mould and, with clean fingers, gently push the dough into the corners of the mould. Leave to rest in a warm place (25–27°C/77–80°F is ideal) and after about 30 minutes, when the tart dough has increased in volume by about a quarter, gently push it down to knock out the gas.

Using a ladle, fill each mould with crème pâtissière to just below the rim. Give the filled moulds a gentle tap on the bench to settle the mixture into the pastry casing.

Bake for 20 minutes or until deep golden brown.

Sophie Hansen

Pear frangipane slab tart (opposite)
Fig, chocolate and sweet dukkah sundaes (267)

Sophie Hansen's baking captures the year-round joys of living on a farm outside of Orange. 'Simple, seasonal and generous,' are the three words she uses to describe her approach to cooking – and baking particularly. In a region famed for its orchards and vineyards, seasonal produce tends to make itself known. Fruit is often a front-running ingredient in Sophie's baking. She uses it to cut through sweetness, and loves stone fruit especially for the bursts of acidity it brings to sweet bakes.

For all its blessings, living in a food bowl also means working with what Sophie calls 'seasons of glut', which in practice means both relying on passed-down knowledge and coming up with new tricks for using, preserving and saving what's on hand, for right now and all the way into the leaner months.

Working with the ebb and flow of the seasons means the style of baking is both resourceful and responsive – there's a reason recipes in the style of the Country Women's Association still reign. 'It's the idea of just knowing what you're cooking is going to work, knowing that it's going to be a crowd-pleaser and going to give everybody a boost in their day when they need it,' she says.

Morning tea is still the way of life – and a source of energy in more ways than one. 'It's like that moment of breaking bread together – or breaking cake,' Sophie says. 'Even just this morning, I took banana bread up to the guys in the paddock and everyone just stopped work for ten minutes and had a hot coffee from the thermos and had some cake. And I could just tell it gave everyone a real lift.' But you're only going to bake like this when it gives back to you, too. 'My cakes aren't fiddly. I want them to be comforting to bake as well as to eat,' she says.

Food writer and cookbook author

Orange, NSW
Wiradjuri Country

'Baking should be a joyful experience, from the making of it to the sharing of it. And if you're stressed about it, that's like completely the opposite of what it should be.'

WORDS TO BAKE BY

'Share what you know and be generous with it, because it comes back to you. We all have things we can share, knowledge gleaned from years of experience. I think it's because baking isn't necessarily a "need", it's a "want", a pleasure and a joy. We do it to be generous, spread some cheer and share our time, skills and produce. And it doesn't have to be anything earth-shattering or super tricky or technical. Look, I can't do a lot of things (macarons are a struggle, for example), but I can pass on a good pastry recipe – and maybe that will become somebody's favourite and they'll make all kinds of lovely tarts out of it.'

NOTES ON BASIC RECIPES

'I have the quantities for a few basic recipes stuck up on my fridge (butter cake, pastry, muesli bars, that kind of thing), and this makes it really easy to make something quickly and riff on it depending on what's in season and/or handy. If I want to make a cake, then I generally want to have it coming out of the oven within the hour. I don't have all day to build something amazing. I'm in awe of bakers who create those spectacularly beautiful decorated cakes, but that's not how I bake day to day. I prefer to throw whatever fruit I have into the batter and know that it will work out because it always has. Having those back-pocket recipes you're comfortable with and can just riff on is the key for me.'

Pear frangipane slab tart

SERVES 4–6
SPECIAL EQUIPMENT food processor, rolling pin, pastry brush

Pastry
300 g (10½ oz) plain (all-purpose) flour, plus extra for dusting
pinch of salt
⅓ cup (40 g) icing (confectioners') sugar
225 g (8 oz) chilled unsalted butter, finely diced
¼ cup (60 ml) chilled water

Frangipane
1½ cups (240 g) raw almonds, freshly toasted
160 g (5¾ oz) butter, softened
½ cup (110 g) caster (superfine) sugar
2 eggs
2 tablespoons plain (all-purpose) flour
1 teaspoon vanilla extract
pinch of salt

Poached pears
4 cups (1 litre) cold water
2 cups (440 g) caster (superfine) sugar, plus 3 tablespoons extra for dusting
2 cinnamon sticks
1 teaspoon vanilla paste
4 beurré bosc pears (or other firm pears), peeled, halved and cored

Egg wash
1 egg
1 tablespoon pouring cream

This gorgeous tart is one of my favourite things to make, take and share. You can use any fruit, but pears are particularly beautiful. And you can make it in any shape, but a big slab like this is so easy to make and then cut into squares to share around. I hope you try and love it too.

For the pastry, combine the flour, salt and icing sugar on a clean work surface. Bring into a small mound and make a well in the centre. Fill this with the butter and a splash of the chilled water. Use the heel of your hands to bring the mixture together, working the butter into the flour, adding more water as needed. Keep working and smooshing with the heel of your hand until you have a rough dough. Shape into a disc, cover with biodegradable plastic wrap and refrigerate to rest for 30 minutes. You could also make the pastry in a food processor.

For the frangipane, tip the almonds into a food processor and blitz to a coarse crumb. Add the remaining ingredients and blitz until you have a lovely paste. Refrigerate until ready to assemble.

Preheat your oven to 200°C/400°F fan-forced (220°C/425°F conventional). Line a baking tray with baking paper and lightly dust your work surface with flour.

For the poached pears, combine the water, sugar, cinnamon and vanilla in a large saucepan over medium–high heat. Bring to the boil, then reduce to a simmer. Add the pears, cover with a circle of baking paper (to prevent discolouration), then poach for 10–15 minutes or until the pears are tender. Leave to cool in the pan.

To assemble, using a rolling pin, gently roll out your chilled pastry dough to a 30 × 25 cm (12 × 10 inch) rectangle about 3 mm (⅛ inch) thick. Carefully transfer the dough to your prepared baking tray.

Spread the base of your pastry with the frangipane mix, leaving a 4–5 cm (1½–2 inch) border all around – the frangipane layer should be about 1.5 cm (⅝ inch) thick. Top the frangipane with the drained pear halves, gently removing the stalks if they are still attached. Now bring the pastry edges in, pinching and folding them together at each corner.

For the egg wash, mix the egg and cream and use a pastry brush to brush this over the pastry edges. Sprinkle the pears with the extra caster sugar and bake for 30 minutes or until the pastry is golden. Serve warm or at room temperature, with cream or ice cream.

Gillian Bell

Bay gâteau d'émotion (113)

Ginger and orange blossom cake (115)

Wedding-cake maker and social worker

Killarney, Qld
Gidhabal Country

When Gillian Bell answers the phone, she's on the road to a wedding in northern New South Wales, living out her catchphrase: 'Has whisk, will travel.' The wedding is tomorrow, but a question mark has loomed over it. Fires have enveloped the countryside in the past few days, taking homes with them but thankfully sparing lives. 'This is sort of my wedding cake life,' Gillian explains, 'on the road or paddling off to all these different places and situations. It's all part of the adventure. But I'm beyond an optimist. I just think, "It'll happen."' And this time, she's proven right, again.

'Believe it or not, the heavens have just opened up,' she says as a steady patter of rain sounds down the line. There is, however, still a question mark hanging over the cake. This part, at least, is by design. Gillian only begins to bake the cake at midnight on the day of the festivities. Only after she arrives to meet the couple, equipped with her hand whisk (there are no mixers here) and her cake tins ('filled with socks and things to stop them banging around and rumbling in my case'), and takes in the surroundings does she begin. It's less about reaching for a fitting recipe and more about telling a story. 'I bake like that for myself, too. It's always got a sort of a narrative to it for me,' she says. 'If I can't feel poetry in something, I'm not interested in it.'

This goes back to the beginning: as a child in England, Gillian escaped the 'chaos' of life in a large family by running off into the paddocks, climbing up trees, and getting lost in stories about capable girls off on adventures – always equipped with provisions of the just-plucked blackberry or Victoria-sponge kind. 'We didn't have cookbooks at home in those days, so I just used to experiment and think, "How can I create that cake I read about? How can I get the perfume of that fruit growing on the tree into my cake?" So in some respects that made me an intuitive baker rather than a recipe-follower.'

For a springtime wedding in New York State, Gillian wove in the lilacs that were in bloom all around her ('I knew then that every year for their anniversary, they'd see those flowers and smell their perfume'). For another couple, to pay homage to a groom who worked out at sea, she added savoury seaweed ('There just had to be something of that ozoney, fresh sea spray'). She's baked wedding cakes on barbecues, in steamers and on yachts. If she's in need of an ingredient, she might turn up on a stranger's doorstep with a request.

Usually, people are all too happy to go on an adventure with her – to mark an occasion and to give themselves over to it. 'It's memory-making, and it's about the richness of life,' she explains. 'I can only say that in all the years, in all my baking life, I've seen that it can be transformational for people. It's about going on a journey that is so simple but so rich. I think in some respects we've lost some of that in our lives. And somehow me coming along making a cake in the way that I do is almost an invitation into experiencing some of that magic – it's almost for me like a door into Narnia. They can join me in that imaginative world, and they are the protagonists in their own story.'

NOTES ON BAKING WITH GOODWILL

'I'm very mindful of the mood I'm in, of where my mind is at when I start to make someone's wedding cake. I like to do it when everybody's slumbering. I sort of see myself then as the only person in the world. So there's a zone. I always mix my cakes by hand, and I stir in good wishes, good thoughts. I really quite believe that somehow it comes through. Food is so primal for me. It's so attached to who we are as people and our emotional energy that to create a cake of love, you've got to be in a certain mindset. So I say to people, "Find that place in your head, put on some music, do whatever you can to get to that place."'

WORDS TO BAKE BY

'When I have the chance to teach baking, I say to people, "Okay, we're not going to put a timer on. We're just going to go by how it smells and sounds. We need to learn to trust our senses again. It's a cake – it isn't about putting a rocket on the moon – so enjoy it more." Because if it's not fun when you do it, you won't do it very often – or if at all – again. The number of people who tell me, "I can't bake"! I say, "Everyone can bake. It's just that you don't know how to – or you don't have the confidence. You can make a cake in anything, you know, you can make a cake in a big bean tin. So relax, let go."'

'I always mix my cakes by hand, and I stir in good wishes, good thoughts. I really quite believe that somehow it comes through.'

Bay gâteau d'émotion

Gillian Bell
Profiled on page 110

SERVES 8–10
SPECIAL EQUIPMENT 20 cm (8 inch) diameter deep cake tin (preferably springform), stand mixer with whisk attachment

butter, for preparing tin

Bay-infused sugar
8 bay leaves
230 g (8 oz) caster (superfine) sugar

Cake
600 g (1 lb 5 oz) pouring cream
300 g (10½ oz) milk
230 g (8 oz) bay-infused caster sugar (above)
20 fresh bay leaves
50 g (1¾ oz) self-raising flour
50 g (1¾ oz) cornflour (cornstarch)
75 g (2¾ oz) plain (all-purpose) flour
5 eggs, at room temperature
4 leaves titanium-strength gelatine

I've been known to cry over cake. To an embarrassing degree. My feelings rise to the surface then bubble over like a saucepan of scalding milk. The name for this cake, gâteau d'émotion, was coined by my French host, in a lavender field, at the height of a hot, languorous summer cooking in France. It's not just about tears but a sense of place, a memory, a feeling that needs expression. Some people paint; I bake cakes that seek to capture emotions and sensory memories.

This particular gâteau d'émotion was created one summer in Bourgogne when I was asked to cook in a chateau. Wandering through the gardens, I was brought to a halt by the exquisite fragrance of bay coming from a very old laurel tree. I decided to create this cake to honour the tree and the joy its fragrance gave me that summer. And now I re-create this cake using the bay laurel leaves from the tree in my own garden, or those of a client. Consider planting your own bay laurel, in your garden or in a pot. The aim with this cake is to capture the flavour and fragrance of bay laurel by infusing your ingredients: some for the sugar, some for the cream and milk, and some to line the base of your cake tin. You will need a couple of handfuls of fresh, unsprayed bay leaves.

For the bay-infused sugar, crush the bay leaves with your hands and warm the caster sugar in a low oven or the microwave. Combine the bay leaves and caster sugar in a large screw-top jar. The warmth of the sugar will help the bay infuse. Leave overnight.

For the cake, combine your cream, milk, 60 g (2¼ oz) of the bay-infused sugar and bay leaves from the jar and warm over low heat until hot but not boiling. Remove the pan from the heat and set aside to cool. As it cools, you will see the cream mixture start to coagulate. This is to be expected.

Preheat your oven to 180°C/350°F conventional (no fan), and line the side and base of a 20 cm (8 inch) deep round cake tin with baking paper. Using tiny dots of butter, stick the bay leaves to the base of the tin, covering it generously with a single layer of leaves. (If you have a springform tin, use that. It makes it easier to release the cake but don't fuss over it. All will be fine.) Cut a 20 cm (8 inch) circle of baking paper.

Sift the flours together into a medium bowl and set aside.

Warm the ovenproof bowl of a stand mixer in the preheating oven. Now crack your eggs into the bowl and add the remaining bay-infused caster sugar. (The warmth of the bowl will increase the volume of the whipped eggs.) Fit the stand mixer with the whisk attachment and whip the egg and sugar mixture on medium–high speed until it forms a thick, pale-cream foam and when you lift your whisk it leaves a ribbon of foam sitting on the surface of your mixture. If the ribbon doesn't form, whisk the mixture for a few more minutes until you reach the ribbon stage. >

Decant the egg foam from your mixer bowl into a larger, wider mixing bowl. Sift the combined flours again but this time over the surface of the egg foam. Using a large spoon or spatula, gently fold the flour into the mixture until the flour is completely incorporated. Take your time. Dream of the beautiful cake that you're creating for yourself or your loved ones. Enjoy every moment of making it. Now gently pour the cake batter into the prepared tin, covering the bay leaves. Gently place the circle of baking paper on the surface of the batter and use your fingertips to gently smooth it out and adhere it to the surface. Place the tin on the middle shelf of the oven and bake for 20–25 minutes. The cake is ready when the surface is golden and the cake springs back when gently pressed in the centre. Lift the baking paper circle enough for you to test the cake with a skewer or your index finger. The skewer should come out clean.

Remove the cake from the oven and leave in the tin. Gently peel the baking paper circle off the surface, then place it back on top of the cake.

Gently reheat the cream mixture to warm but not hot and scoop out the bay leaves. While this is heating, bloom your gelatine by soaking in a wide pan or tray of cold water. Try to spread the leaves over the surface of the water so they're not overlapping, then press them below the surface of the water. Blooming will only take a few minutes, so have your heated cream ready and do not stray. When the gelatine is soft enough to crumple in your hands like cellophane, lift it out of the water and gently wring out the excess with your hands. Plunge it into the warm cream and let it dissolve for a few minutes. Stir with a small whisk or fork to ensure it is fully dissolved.

Lift the baking paper circle and pour the cream/gelatine mixture over the top of your cake, still in the tin, pouring in concentric circles from the outside towards the centre. Don't ignore the very edges of your cake and don't worry if mixture pours down between the baking paper lining the tin and the sides. The cake will absorb it. (If your cake is slightly sunken in the middle, it's not a problem and it's not your fault. It's to do with the dimensions of your tin. You can easily fill it with buttercream or fruit or whatever filling you choose and nobody will love it any the less.) Finally, cover the tin with a plate and refrigerate for at least 4 hours or overnight for the cream mixture to set.

To serve, release the cake from its tin. You may need to run a knife around the edge of the tin between the paper and the tin to help release it. Tip it out, bay-leaf side up, and gently peel off the base paper and the leaves. They will leave some marks. You may wish to leave them in place and serve your cake with a simple dusting of icing sugar and the bay leaves for decoration. Whatever takes your fancy at the time. Otherwise, invert the cake.

If you wish to fill the cake, slice it in half horizontally. If your cake has sunk in the middle, you can swap the top and bottom halves, with the sunken surface now in the centre of the cake.

> *Fill with cream, fruit, preserves — whatever takes your fancy — but let the bay take the lead role and don't let your chorus upstage it. Now, go forth and create your own gâteaux d'émotion using your own senses and memories to inform your creations.*

Morning & Afternoon Teas

Ginger and orange blossom cake

Gillian Bell
Profiled on page 110

SERVES 10–12
SPECIAL EQUIPMENT 23 cm (9 inch) diameter deep cake tin or two 20 cm (8 inch) diameter shallow cake tins, stand mixer with paddle attachment, hand-held electric beaters (optional)

1¼ cups (310 ml) stout
1½ cups (375 ml) dark treacle (not golden syrup)
1 teaspoon bicarbonate of soda (baking soda)
2½ cups (375 g) self-raising flour
1½ teaspoons ground cinnamon
1 teaspoon ground allspice
1 teaspoon freshly grated nutmeg
½ teaspoon fine salt
4 eggs
1 cup (220 g) dark brown sugar
¾ cup (165 g) caster (superfine) sugar
1 cup (250 ml) vegetable oil
3 tablespoons finely grated fresh ginger or 2 heaped teaspoons ground ginger
about ¼ cup (60 ml) orange blossom water (optional)
icing (confectioners') sugar, for dusting (optional)

I was first inspired to bake by the story books I read as a child. I would escape my numerous siblings up a tree or behind a hedgerow, where I would spend peaceful hours reading and dreaming. The books were full of adventure, picnics and provisions. The children in the books always had a cake in a tin that seemed to save the day or was eagerly shared as they debriefed after another successful mission. Adventures always make you very hungry.

Cakes have filled my life with happiness and adventure, and a good ginger cake often featured in the storybooks and has to be among my favourites, especially as autumn approaches. As a child, I only had access to powdered ginger and you may only have that, too. But nowadays I like to finely grate fresh ginger for my cakes. Ginger is at its best when it's harvested, around early autumn. The skin will be pale and tissue-thin, and the flesh juicy and non-fibrous. You can freeze it and use it as you need it.

Here I've paired the ginger with orange blossom, because I really love its taste and fragrance. It was far too dreamy for the England of my childhood. If you're not keen, choose something else you like. Chocolate, perhaps? Or there's a quiet dignity in the simplicity of plain ginger. I use stout (a type of beer) in this recipe for its flavour – it's boiled before it goes into the cake, so all alcohol is removed.

You're about to make a cake that will spread happiness and goodwill. Which is to be encouraged. As is sharing.

Preheat your oven to 175°C/350°F conventional (no fan) and fully line one 23 cm (9 inch) deep round cake tin or two 20 cm (8 inch) sandwich tins with baking paper.

In a large saucepan, combine the stout and treacle (you'll need the largest saucepan you have, or the mixture will froth and rise and threaten to boil over). Bring to the boil over medium heat, stirring carefully but constantly to keep the treacle from burning on the bottom of your pan. When it boils, remove from the heat and stir the bicarbonate of soda into the mix. It will immediately froth up and rise in the pan, threatening to bubble over. Whisk quickly and constantly until the danger passes and the mixture settles down. Set aside to cool to room temperature while you move on.

In a very large wide bowl, sift together the flour, cinnamon, allspice, nutmeg and salt.

Using a stand mixer with the paddle attachment, beat the eggs, brown sugar and caster sugar on medium–high speed. Beat until the mixture becomes pale, then reduce the speed to low and slowly add the vegetable oil, beating until completely incorporated. >

Remove the bowl from the mixer and carefully add the cooled stout and treacle mixture, along with the ginger. (If you think your mixer bowl isn't going to be large enough for your batter and the stout mixture, stop and transfer the batter to a larger bowl.) Gradually add the stout mixture to the flour mixture, using a spatula, hand-held electric beaters on low speed or a large spoon to combine. Don't overmix – stop once they have come together and there is no sign of the flour. Pour into your prepared tin/s. For one deep cake, bake for at least 1 hour before testing to see if it's cooked. For two shallow cakes, bake for about 50 minutes. A skewer inserted into the middle that comes out batter-free means your cake is ready.

When your cake is straight out of the oven, drizzle the orange blossom water, if using, across the whole top of the cake. Be generous. Let that soak in for about 10 minutes, then tip the cake out of its tin onto a wire rack to cool completely. You can ice it, fill it, sprinkle icing sugar on it or drizzle ginger juice on it. Whatever you like. And this cake is a keeper. Stored in an airtight container, it will get stickier and even more delicious – if that's possible. It even freezes well. And it's great served with lashings of hot custard, as you'd expect. Bring on the chilly weather! x

Dear baker, please be prepared for your cake to sink in the middle after it comes out of the oven. The best ginger cakes always do.

It's a minor price to pay for a sticky, fragrant, rich ginger flavour that only gets better with time. And it has to be to be worthy of a place in a children's story book.

Peach and sour cream cake

Alisha Henderson
Profiled on page 48

SERVES 8–12
SPECIAL EQUIPMENT 20 cm (8 inch) diameter springform tin, stand mixer with whisk attachment, food processor, sugar thermometer (optional)

Cake
- 200 g (7 oz) salted butter, softened and diced
- 1¼ cups (280 g) light brown sugar
- 2 cups (300 g) self-raising flour
- ½ teaspoons bicarbonate of soda (baking soda)
- 2 teaspoons ground cinnamon
- 3 eggs, lightly beaten
- ½ cup (125 g) sour cream
- 825 g (1 lb 13 oz) tinned sliced peaches, drained and roughly chopped

Crème diplomat
- 48 g (1¾ oz) cornflour (cornstarch)
- 115 g (4 oz) caster (superfine) sugar
- 135 g (4¾ oz) egg yolk (from about 7 eggs)
- seeds of 1 split and scraped vanilla pod or 1 tablespoon vanilla bean paste
- pinch of salt
- 550 ml (19 fl oz) milk
- 30 g (1 oz) unsalted butter
- 350 ml (12 fl oz) whipping cream

This makes 4 cups (1 litre) of crème diplomat. You can make the base a day ahead, then whip in the cream before serving.

Even though I spend my days making 'fancy' cakes, this is the humble home-baked cake I request for my own birthday every year. I first tried a peach and sour cream cake at my godmother's house as a child, and instantly fell in love with the juicy chunks of peach dotted within a moist, brown-sugary cake crumb. I like to serve this one warm with crème diplomat, which makes it feel a touch more distinguished. For me, crème diplomat is an 'If it ain't broke don't fix it' sort of recipe. It's a thick custard with whipped cream folded through at the end – very traditional but totally delicious.

Preheat the oven to 170°C/350°F fan-forced (190°C/375°F conventional). Line the base of a 20 cm (8 inch) springform tin with baking paper and grease the ring.

For the cake, in a food processor, combine the butter, ¾ cup (165 g) of the sugar, the flour and bicarbonate of soda and half the cinnamon. Blitz for about 30 seconds, until combined and crumbly in texture. Add the eggs and sour cream and pulse for 15 seconds, until all the ingredients are combined. Using a spoon, stir in the peaches until evenly distributed through the batter.

Spoon the mixture into the cake tin and smooth the top. Mix together the remaining sugar and cinnamon and sprinkle evenly over the top of the cake (you can add a little more brown sugar if you wish, for extra crunch).

Bake for about 45 minutes or until a skewer inserted in the centre comes out clean. Cool in the tin for 15 minutes, then remove from the tin and leave on a wire rack to cool completely.

For the crème diplomat, mix together the cornflour, sugar, egg yolk, vanilla seeds and salt in a large mixing bowl.

Heat the milk in a medium saucepan over low heat until scalded – you will know it's done once you see steam and some tiny bubbles. Remove from the heat and, whisking constantly, pour the milk over the egg mixture to temper it. Pour the combined mixture back into the saucepan and place over medium–low heat. Keep whisking constantly for about 5 minutes, until the mixture bubbles and thickens, showing signs of sticking to the bottom of the pan. Take care not to overcook it or you will scramble the mixture. (If you have a thermometer handy, you'll know the mixture is ready when it reaches 82°C/180°F.)

Place a sieve over the mixing bowl and strain the custard through it to remove any lumps. Stir in the butter until combined. Cover with biodegradable plastic wrap, with the wrap directly touching the surface, and refrigerate overnight or for at least 2 hours.

Before serving, whip the cream using a stand mixer with the whisk attachment until medium-stiff peaks form. Fold the whipped cream into the custard mixture – this is your crème diplomat ready for serving.

The cake will keep for 4 days in an airtight container – you can heat your slices in the microwave during that time.

Nadine Ingram

Chocolate, amaretto and sour cherry tart (122)

Baker, cookbook author and founder of Flour and Stone

Sydney, NSW
Gadigal Country

Nadine Ingram bakes from life. By her hand, a recipe is not just a recipe, but something that has lived first. 'It's easiest to make a cake around something that's happened to me,' she explains. 'Everything has to have meaning for me, and a lot of the stories that I tell through the cake, well they all have meaning.' Storied as they are, her recipes become a kind of conversation – first with herself, and then with you, the eater. 'It's honesty I'm after. It's that something that you can't even put into words,' she says. It is best baked.

This is the effect of the lemon drizzle cake, one of the bestsellers at Nadine's much-beloved Woolloo-mooloo bakery Flour and Stone. It's a cake that settles you at her table and invites you home (it's also the topic of her rousing TED Talk, 'On the healing power of cake'). 'When somebody looks at a cake like the lemon drizzle and it's got that thin veil of white icing over the top, they know that they can trust that cake and they can trust the person that made it because it's not embellished with the unnecessary,' she says. 'It's like us, when we go into a room and we're talking in front of people we don't know, sometimes we put up this façade and we try to hide our real selves by speaking like other people do and embellishing everything with formal language. The cakes are a departure from that. They're just really pared back. You know, "This is me and this is who I am."'

That you feel at home in her bakery is intentional – and it extends from the shop floor to the kitchen. 'I've always worked hard at creating that extension of my home. I think that kitchens naturally, regardless of the culture, are an environment that does foster family and community,' she says. 'I think that consistently, the one thing that binds everyone together is the support and knowing that people are there to help them – and to be able to accept that – and know they're not alone.'

The kitchen has always been a place of nurturing for Nadine. When she was a child in the New South Wales Hunter Valley, her grandparents often found her farmwork lacking. She was sent inside (in any case her preference: 'The interior landscape is vastly underrated,' she says) and discovered a kind of haven for herself in the kitchen. Pulling a tray of proudly puffed scones from the oven to present to her family, she found a way she could contribute something. 'I think baking has always been a way to express myself, but it has literally been a way to connect with people,' she muses. 'And I know it sounds corny, but to make people love me. I think when you bake for people, it's a gift of love. It's that reward that you get back in turn from baking that drives you forward. I think that's all anyone ever hopes to do – to love and be loved. And if you can do it through your craft, it's not even a job. It's the luckiest thing in the world to be able to make a living out of something you love doing that much.'

'I think baking is one of those things that you can't ever really be perfect at. What it teaches you about is the imperfect and how beautiful that can be.'

NOTES ON IMPERFECTION

'I think we just need to slow down for long enough, to be able to take the time to bake. There seems to be a big focus around being perfect at everything. And I think baking is one of those things that you can't ever really be perfect at. What it teaches you about is the imperfect and how beautiful that can be. If you want to get to that level, you need to try things more than once to improve. I think a lot of our culture these days says you've got to get it right the first time and you've just got to be the best at it. I don't understand that. Baking teaches you how to break those habits. If you try to make things perfect all the time, it's not really an extension of yourself. Because no one's perfect. I'll test recipes eight times and they're still not right. And just trying to get it to how I want it to be is such a manipulation of reality, because sometimes things will turn out how they're going to turn out and you have absolutely no control over it. Even with all the skills in the world.'

WORDS TO BAKE BY

'Baking is a chance for people to connect with their bodies. It's like a meditation. And I think these days more than ever, that's why baking is becoming so popular. First it's physical, it's hand–eye, and then it becomes emotional through the process of creating something with your hands. We're all meant to do that, every single one of us. We're all creative in some way, and so it's that process, that physical process that inspires the emotional, that puts us back in touch with ourselves.'

Chocolate, amaretto and sour cherry tart

Nadine Ingram
Profiled on page 120

SERVES 10–12
SPECIAL EQUIPMENT 26 cm (10½ inch) diameter tart (flan) tin, stand mixer with paddle and whisk attachments, rolling pin, baking weights (such as baking beads), angled palette knife, kitchen scissors

Almond and emmer sable
175 g (6 oz) unsalted butter, softened, plus extra for greasing
70 g (2½ oz) icing (confectioners') sugar, sifted
50 g (1¾ oz) demerara sugar
2 egg yolks
200 g (7 oz) emmer or spelt flour, plus extra (optional) for dusting
80 g (2¾ oz) raw almonds, toasted and finely ground
¼ teaspoon sea salt

For the romance between the cherry and almond trees kindled by the first flowers of spring.

And the petals that do not wither, fortified by all kisses under their branches.

They are the keepers of all the whispered stories akin to those told among the stalks of ancient wheat.

For the almond and emmer sable, cream the butter and sugars in the bowl of a stand mixer with the paddle attachment on low speed for no more than 2 minutes. The mixture should be pale but not too fluffy. (This step can also be done with a wooden spoon, since it is not essential to aerate the butter. In fact, overbeating the butter may make the sable very crumbly and too fragile once baked. Remember, you are not making a cake here, you are making pastry.)

Scrape down the side of the bowl using a spatula, to ensure the butter is being creamed evenly with the sugar. Add the egg yolks one at a time, mixing until combined before adding the next, then remove the bowl from the stand mixer. Sift in the flour, add the ground almonds and salt and fold through using a spatula. (When making sable, this step is always done by hand so as not to overwork the gluten in the flour, which will toughen the pastry.) The texture will now seem more like a paste, due to the high butter-to-flour ratio. Ensure there are no remaining streaks of butter by scraping all the way to the bottom of the bowl with your spatula.

Cut two pieces of baking paper at least 32 cm (12½ inches) square. Lay one baking paper square on your work surface and scoop the pastry into the centre. (If your paper is not wide enough, use two sheets side by side, overlapping the edges.) Put the second sheet on top of the pastry and, using your hands, pat the pastry into a disc to create the beginnings of the shape you need to line the tart tin. Using a rolling pin, roll the pastry out evenly between the two sheets, regularly rotating it 90 degrees as you go, to achieve a sheet of pastry 30 cm (12 inches) in diameter and 5 mm (¼ inch) thick. Refrigerate for 30 minutes to rest and set.

Lightly grease a 26 cm (10½ inch) diameter tart (flan) tin with butter and dust with flour, or give it a light spray with oil. Test the pliability of the pastry by bending it gently. The process of bringing the pastry to the ideal temperature for lining the tart tin can be ambiguous, given the variables, such as room temperature and the amount of air you've incorporated into the pastry, so a little intuition is required here. It could need as long as 15 minutes out of the fridge before you attempt the lining process. In any case, remember this pastry is high in butter, so don't worry, it can be coaxed into shape easily with a little persuasion by you.

Chocolate mousse

300 g (10½ oz) quality dark chocolate, at least 60%
170 g (6 oz) unsalted butter
3 eggs
3 egg yolks
50 g (1¾ oz) caster (superfine) sugar
30 ml (1 fl oz) amaretto

Topping

40 g (1½ oz) unsweetened cocoa powder, for dusting
100 g (3½ oz) raw almonds, toasted and sliced
250 g (9 oz) frozen sour cherries
200 g (7 oz) thick (double) cream, to serve

Remove the top sheet of baking paper, then invert the pastry over the tart tin. Gently peel off the second sheet of paper. Using clean hands, carefully tuck the pastry into the tart tin all the way round – to prevent the surplus pastry from tearing over the rim. Then go round again, this time focusing on settling the pastry more securely into the groove where the base of the tart tin meets the side. Finally, the third time round, press the pastry into the sides of the tin to create that beautiful right angle between the base and sides. Using kitchen scissors, neaten up the rim of the pastry shell by cutting it evenly 5–7 mm (¼ inch) above the rim of the tin. (The idea here is to allow a bit more height for all the fillings and ensure a favourable proportion of custard, pastry, fruit and jelly.) Pop the pastry case in the freezer for 15 minutes to set hard.

Meanwhile, preheat the oven to 150°C/300°F fan-forced (170°C/350°F conventional). Cut a 30 cm (12 inch) diameter circle of baking paper or foil to set inside the tart tin for blind baking. Line the inside of the frozen pastry with the prepared baking paper, tucking it tightly into the right angle you've created. Fill the case with baking beads or other baking weights. Ensure the paper or foil is not hanging over the edge or it will place pressure on the fragile pastry as it bakes, which may cause it to break and leave you with less height on your finished case. Blind bake for 35 minutes, then leave to set with the weights still in for 15 minutes. Gently remove the weights and paper.

Reduce the oven temperature to 140°C/275°F fan-forced (160°C/325°F conventional).

For the chocolate mousse, chop the chocolate and butter into small pieces and place in a medium–large heatproof bowl set over a saucepan of barely simmering water, ensuring the bowl does not touch the water, stirring occasionally until melted and combined. Keep warm so it doesn't seize when added to the eggs.

Meanwhile, combine the eggs, egg yolks and sugar in a stand mixer with the whisk attachment and whisk on medium for 7–10 minutes, until pale and fluffy and doubled in volume. Add the egg mixture to the chocolate all at once and gently fold through until there are no more streaks in the mousse. Fold the amaretto through.

Pour the mousse into the pastry shell and smooth the surface gently with an angled palette knife until it is flat. Sift a light dusting of cocoa on top, then scatter the almonds and sour cherries evenly over that. Bake for 25 minutes. Test the chocolate mousse for readiness by pressing the centre with your finger. If it springs back slightly, it's cooked. If the outside edges of the chocolate mousse are starting to soufflé (rise), reduce the oven temperature to 120°C/250°F fan-forced (140°C/275°F conventional). The slower the better at this stage, otherwise the edge of the mousse will crack and the centre will be undercooked. Once the tart is cooked, turn off the oven and leave the door ajar for a further 5 minutes. Remove from the oven and cool in the tin for a minimum of 2 hours before removing the tin and cutting. If you are in a hurry, you can speed things up by chilling the tart in the fridge for 15 minutes, no longer.

Serve with thick cream.

Lemon, polenta and raspberry tea cake

Michael James
Profiled on page 56

SERVES 6–8

SPECIAL EQUIPMENT 25 × 10 cm (10 × 4 inch) loaf (bar) tin, stand mixer with paddle attachment, food processor, angled palette knife

Feel encouraged to use your choice of berries or maybe a lemon icing, or try with ground hazelnuts.

- 250 g (9 oz) unsalted butter, at room temperature
- 225 g (8 oz) raw caster (superfine) sugar
- zest of 2 lemons
- 1 vanilla bean, split lengthways and seeds scraped or 1 teaspoon vanilla bean paste
- 170 g (6 oz) egg (from about 4 eggs), at room temperature
- 110 g (3¾ oz) fine polenta
- 275 g almond meal (see recipe introduction)
- 50 g (1¾ oz) rice flour
- 1 teaspoon baking powder
- ¼ teaspoon fine sea salt
- 50 g (1¾ oz) lemon juice
- 125 g (4½ oz) fresh or frozen raspberries, or 50 g (1¾ oz) dried raspberries
- 1 teaspoon cornflour (cornstarch)

Raspberry icing
- 125 g (4½ oz) fresh, frozen or dried raspberries
- 110 g (3¾ oz) icing (confectioners') sugar
- 1 teaspoon lemon juice

This is a standard tea cake transformed with Italian-inspired flavours: almonds, polenta, lemons and seasonal berries. The flavoursome grittiness of the polenta and tender textured nuttiness from the ground almonds makes for a flavourful gluten-free afternoon-tea treat. Making your own freshly ground nut meal really enhances the flavours. Pop whole nuts in the fridge or freezer for an hour and then use a food processor to blitz them, taking care not to over-blitz or you will end up with nut butter. The cake is easy to make and very forgiving with the baking time, as it won't dry out like a floury cake. This was on permanent rotation when we had Tivoli Road Bakery, and a real favourite with customers – and also staff vying for the trimmings.

Preheat the oven to 160°C/325°F fan-forced (180°C/350°F conventional). Grease a 25 × 10 cm (10 × 4 inch) loaf (bar) tin with butter or oil spray and line it with baking paper.

In a stand mixer with the paddle attachment, beat the butter, sugar, lemon zest and vanilla seeds for about 10 minutes, until pale and creamy. In a small bowl, lightly beat the egg. In several stages, add the egg to the creamed butter mixture, mixing well between additions until fully incorporated. Scrape down the side of the bowl to ensure everything is thoroughly mixed.

In a separate bowl, combine the polenta, almond meal and rice flour with the baking powder and salt and whisk with a fork to knock out any lumps and mix well. Add the dry mixture to the mixer bowl and mix on low speed until just incorporated. With the mixer still running, slowly pour in the lemon juice and mix until just combined.

In a small bowl, gently toss your fresh raspberries with the cornflour.

Pour half the cake mixture into your prepared tin and scatter half of the raspberries over the top. Add the remaining cake mixture, using a spatula to gently smooth out the top, then scatter the remaining raspberries over the top. Bake for 50 minutes, then rotate the tin and bake for a further 10–15 minutes, or until the top is a lovely golden colour all over and is firm to the touch. As this is gluten-free and very moist, it's not a good idea to test it with a cake skewer, as it will come out with crumbs. Cool in the tin for about 10 minutes before turning out onto a wire rack to cool completely.

Meanwhile, make the raspberry icing. Blend the raspberries in a food processor, then pass the pulp through a fine sieve over a small saucepan to remove the seeds. Place over medium heat and reduce until you have about 1½ tablespoons (30 g/1 oz) of purée. Set aside to cool.

Sift the icing sugar into a bowl and add most of the raspberry purée. Stir it in and check the consistency – you want it to be thin enough to spread but not so liquid that it won't set. Adjust the consistency by adding a little lemon juice or icing sugar as required.

Immediately pour the icing over your cooled cake, use an angled palette knife to spread it all over the top, then leave to set.

Store in an airtight container for up to 5 days.

Lemon curd shortbread tart

Belinda Jeffery
Profiled on page 60

SERVES 8–12
SPECIAL EQUIPMENT 25 cm (10 inch) diameter loose-based tart (flan) tin, food processor, angled palette knife, fine palette knife, heatproof jug

Shortbread pastry
2 cups (300 g) plain (all-purpose) flour, plus extra for dusting
1 teaspoon baking powder
⅛ teaspoon salt
250 g (9 oz) room-temperature unsalted butter, roughly chopped
1 cup (220 g) caster (superfine) sugar
2 egg yolks
2 teaspoons vanilla extract

Lemon curd
3 eggs
90 g (3¼ oz) caster (superfine) sugar
½ cup (125 ml) freshly squeezed lemon juice, strained
90 g (3¼ oz) unsalted butter, melted
finely grated zest of 1 large lemon

This 'tart' is one of the most popular in my cooking classes. The combination of tangy, not-too-sweet lemon curd and short, buttery pastry is wonderful. I quite often make a batch of the lemon curd on its own, as I adore it spread on my breakfast toast. It's also fabulous for sandwiching cake or meringue layers together, topping little pavlovas, or folding into cream and plopping onto scones. You can make the curd a week or so ahead, if you like.

For the shortbread pastry, combine the flour, baking powder and salt in a food processor fitted with the steel blade and whiz them together so they're thoroughly mixed. Tip them into a bowl and set aside.

Put the butter in the food processor along with the caster sugar and whiz for about 40 seconds or until the mixture is pale and creamy (you may need to stop the machine and scrape down the side once or twice). Add the egg yolks and vanilla, then process again for 15 seconds or until well combined. Add the flour mixture and pulse in short bursts until a ball of pastry forms around the blade (try not to overdo this or the pastry may be a bit tough).

Very lightly dust a work surface with flour. Turn the pastry out onto the work surface and shape it into two equal logs (if the pastry seems too soft, refrigerate it for a little while so it firms up enough to handle comfortably). Wrap each log in baking paper, then refrigerate them for at least 3 hours (or overnight), until really firm.

Meanwhile, make the lemon curd. Combine the eggs and caster sugar in a medium heavy-based saucepan and whisk them together until thoroughly mixed but not too frothy. Whisking gently, mix in the lemon juice and the melted butter.

Set the pan over medium–low heat. Cook the mixture, stirring constantly with a flat-based wooden spoon or sauce whisk, until it thickens to a lovely custard-like consistency. As you stir, try to use a figure-of-eight motion to cover the entire base of the pan so the curd doesn't catch and burn. The most important thing of all is not to let it boil, or it may curdle. As soon as it's ready, remove the curd from the heat and strain through a fine sieve into a heatproof jug. Stir in the lemon zest, then cover the jug loosely with a sheet of baking paper and leave to cool. Once cool, cover the jug with biodegradable plastic wrap and pop in the fridge. The curd will keep well for up to 10 days.

Preheat your oven to 160°C/325°F fan-forced (180°C/350°F conventional). Very lightly butter a 25 cm (10 inch) loose-based tart (flan) tin.

To assemble the tart, remove one pastry log from the fridge. Coarsely grate the pastry onto a plate. I tend to do this in batches, as the grater fills quickly and the pastry strands will squash if they become too compacted. As you finish each batch, carefully transfer the grated dough to the prepared tin. When you have finished grating, gently pat the dough strands out evenly over the base of the tin, trying not to squash them down too much.

To serve
icing (confectioners') sugar, for dusting
200 g (7 oz) lightly whipped cream or thick (double) cream, to serve

Dollop the lemon curd evenly over the grated pastry. Smooth it out into a thin layer using an angled palette knife, leaving a 1 cm (½ inch) border around the edges. Grate the remaining pastry log the same way as before and scatter it over the lemon curd. Give it the lightest pat down to even it out.

Carefully transfer the tin to the oven (watch out you don't pop the base up – unfortunately, it's quite easily done) and bake the tart for about 45 minutes, until deepish golden brown. Check after half an hour, as it can go quicker in some ovens. Remove it from the oven and cool completely in the tin.

To serve, carefully remove the tart from the tin and place on a serving plate. Sometimes the tart may feel as though it's sticking to the tin and doesn't want to release from the base. If you find this happens, check underneath the tin to see if a bit of mixture has run out and stuck the base and side of the tin together. If it has, use a fine palette knife to scrape away any crusted-on bits of pastry and the tart should release.

Dust the tart with icing sugar and serve with softly whipped cream. It's equally lovely served simply with a cup of tea or coffee or as dessert with thick cream.

Dougal Muffet

Plum, frangipane and cream cheese galettes (134)
Burnt fenugreek and sesame loaf (215)

Head baker and founder/co-owner of A.P Bakery

Sydney, NSW
Gadigal Country

Working in kitchens as a uni student in Sydney, Dougal Muffet found salvation in the bread section. 'It literally started from being the most junior person and not wanting to be told what to do all day. No one was really excelling in the bread station, and I thought, "I'm going to go down this rabbit hole."' It led him back home to Forbes, New South Wales, to his wheat-farming family. 'Baking opened up this whole huge world of cooking that overlapped with my childhood and my parents,' he says. 'All of a sudden I was calling my mum and dad every day, talking about how we were going to grow certain varieties.' Together, they sourced heirloom seeds from the Australian Grains Genebank and began to experiment by planting test plots that grew into commercial-sized crops. 'I would love a clone of me to be out there growing wheat and filling silos and then making bread with it. That's kind of like the dream one day – to be able to do it all,' he says.

But for now, his hands are full as head baker at Sydney's celebrated A.P (All Purpose) Bakery, famed for an ever-changing menu of what can only be crudely described as flavour bombs – think puffed focaccias imprinted with zucchini flowers, saltbush and Goldstreet Dairy Cawdor Curd, stratified pies filled with Sri Lankan black chicken curry, and jewel-toned blackberry, brown butter and pistachio tarts. Developed with an eye for produce, it's a menu that showcases Matt Lindsay (one of A.P's four co-founders) and Dougal's experience as chefs. And it's feel-good stuff. 'There are so many good people opening bakeries, and people who aren't typical bakers,' Dougal says. 'A lot of them have come through the pathway that I have, working in restaurants, and found their love for this. Everyone's just got this crazy-different approach. It's just really diverse now. It's fun.'

At A.P, bread is at the heart of things, and their approach is to mill on site, using sustainable grain that Dougal sources from local producers. 'Apart from the fact that I love knowing where our grain's coming from, I love knowing the farmer's name and I love knowing varieties of wheat,' he says. 'I just feel it makes us more responsible for the product that we're making because we're more involved in the process. We're talking about how it's feeling, we're talking about how it's coming out of the oven more, we're just more absorbed by it because we're taking more control of the whole process.'

And that goes for everyone. 'Working in bakeries is such a team effort. When you're in the middle of a big bake and it's all coming together, it's just so rewarding, because so many different people have all put in over a week to make all of that happen. And when it works, it's such a beautiful thing.'

'When you're in the middle of a big bake and it's all coming together, it's just so rewarding. And when it works, it's such a beautiful thing.'

ON GRIT AND GRAIN

'We mill all the whole grain that we use in-house. What we're doing is kind of the fun pointy end of it, but the really fulfilling stuff – and the gut-wrenching stuff – was when we were growing small plots and working with the Genebank. We had a mouse plague one year, a wet year the next year. All the local farmers had a massive year and I was freaking out, but it wasn't my livelihood on the line. I don't know how farmers do it. My hat goes off to them. It's such a wild job, but it's also so rewarding. I'm fascinated with farming and natural systems, and there are some amazing people out in New South Wales in particular, doing some really cool stuff growing wheat in as close to a natural system as possible with as minimal interference as possible [see page 282].'

WORDS TO BAKE BY

'A very useful skill to have for baking, especially bread, is to polish up on your percentages. Baker's maths is a formulation of all the ingredients in your loaf in relation to the total flour weight, which is always taken as 100 per cent. Reading a recipe in grams only, it's hard to get a feel for what the loaf is going to be, whereas reading the formula in its percentages, you can instantly recognise what kind of bread you're making. It's also extremely handy when it comes to creating your own recipes: write it out in baker's maths first, thinking about what kind of bread you want to make, then formulate. Over time you'll get a real feel for what the percentages represent. Fear not if maths isn't your strong point; I recall sitting down with my mum in my late twenties to polish up on percentages. There's hope for all of us ...'

Plum, frangipane and cream cheese galettes

Dougal Muffet
Profiled on page 132

MAKES 12 small
SPECIAL EQUIPMENT stand mixer with paddle attachment, heavy rolling pin, pastry brush

Brisée pastry
465 g (1 lb) plain (all-purpose) flour
35 g (1¼ oz) caster (superfine) sugar
18 g (¾ oz) salt
340 g (12 oz) chilled unsalted butter, cut into 1 cm (½ inch) dice
240 g (8½ oz) cold water
5 g (⅛ oz) apple cider vinegar

Frangipane
200 g (7 oz) cool unsalted butter (between fridge and room temperature)
200 g (7 oz) raw (demerara) sugar, plus extra for sprinkling
175 g (6 oz) egg (from about 4 eggs), gently whisked
300 g (10½ oz) almond meal

Cream cheese mix
330 g (11¾ oz) cream cheese
120 g (4¼ oz) icing (confectioners') sugar
1 vanilla bean, split lengthways and seeds scraped
pinch of ground cardamom

Galettes are a humble, rustic pastry that everyone loves. They are the perfect platform that can easily adapt to seasonal ingredient changes. We used in-season blood plums, but you can substitute any other fruit that is beautiful and abundant (cherries, rhubarb, poached quinces and pears are all lovely). I love using this ratio at home, as you can shoot from the hip. Here, though, I've made a brisée recipe that's a little shorter and more tender.

For the brisée pastry, put the flour, sugar, salt and butter in your stand mixer bowl and refrigerate for 1 hour. Fit the bowl to the stand mixer with the paddle attachment and mix on low speed until the butter pieces are pea-sized. Add the cold water and vinegar at the same time, mixing on low speed only until there are no longer any dry flecks. You want pieces of butter in your rolled dough, so little streaked lumps of butter now are great.

Remove your dough from the bowl, press it into a disc and wrap it tightly in biodegradable plastic wrap. Refrigerate to rest for at least 1 hour.

For the frangipane, combine the butter and sugar in the stand mixer bowl and cream with the paddle attachment on medium–low speed until somewhat homogenous. Don't beat it – aerating the ingredients here will leave you with some unpleasant textures after baking.

With the mixer on medium speed, gradually add the egg, taking your time or the mixture will split. If you start to get nervous towards the end of adding the egg, stop. (Gut feeling is always right; the moment before you split an emulsion, you know you should have stopped.)

Remove the bowl from the mixer and gently fold through the almond meal. If it does split, don't stress. For this application, a broken frangipane will still get the job done deliciously.

For the cream cheese mix, combine the cream cheese and icing sugar in the bowl of the stand mixer and mix with the paddle attachment on low speed until almost homogenous. Add the vanilla seeds and cardamom and mix until smooth and glossy.

To assemble, cut each plum half into six wedges. Take your pastry from the fridge. I like to work with it straight out of the fridge because it's much more manageable but, to make your life easier, give it a serious beating with a heavy rolling pin to make it more malleable.

Roll out the pastry to 3–4 mm (⅛–³⁄₁₆ inch) thick and cut into 12 cm (4½ inch) diameter rounds (use a cutter or cut around a bowl or plate that's about the right size). Make four angled cuts in the disc at roughly 1, 4, 7 and 10 o'clock, leaving space in the middle for the fillings.

Place 35 g (1¼ oz) or a small scoop of frangipane in the centre of each pastry disc. Top with 20 g (¾ oz) or a smaller scoop of the cream cheese mix. Arrange about six plum wedges on top, then fold the pastry up and over at the sides. Give it a little press down – you want the pastry to collapse inwards as it bakes, so I like to set it up for success here. >

To assemble and finish

6 small plums, halved and stones removed

1 egg

1 tablespoon water

fennel seeds, gently toasted then ground

flaky sea salt

Freezing helps with the structure of the tarts. Going into a hot oven while frozen gives the pastry a chance to cook and firm a little before the internal ingredients start to disrupt it.

Freeze for 1 hour or overnight.

Preheat the oven to 200°C/400°F fan-forced (220°C/425°F conventional) and line a baking tray with baking paper.

Arrange the frozen tarts on the prepared tray. Make an egg wash by beating together the egg and water. Use a pastry brush to brush the tops of the galettes with the egg wash, then sprinkle with extra raw sugar over. Bake for 10 minutes, then reduce the temperature to 170°C/350°F fan-forced (190°C/375°F conventional) and bake for a further 10 minutes.

Sprinkle each galette with ground fennel seed and a few nice big sea salt flakes. Cool on the tray.

Eat the galettes as is or with cultured cream or ice cream.

Once made up, the galettes can be left in the freezer for up to 3 weeks and baked from frozen at any time.

Dougal Muffet

Gregorio Montalbán Sánchez

Swedish semlor (opposite)

Cinnamon braid (142)

Baker, chef and founder of The Invy Baker

Inverloch, Vic
Boonwurrung/Bunurong Country

If you were on a journey to find the best cinnamon bun in Australia, you'd have to make a stop in the coastal Victorian town of Inverloch. Here you'll find expertly knotted Swedish-style buns made by chef-turned-baker Gregorio Montalbán Sánchez, better known as Grego – or The Invy Baker. Originally from Granada, Spain, Grego fell for Scandinavian baking when he and his family moved to Sweden in 2019, following a job opportunity for his wife, Hanna. Walking down the cobbled streets in Lund, the charming university town they called home, he spied richly dark loaves of sourdough gracing the windows of local bakery and cheesemonger, Ostabengtson. 'Visually, it was just "Wow". And I thought, "I have to learn how to do this."' They weren't hiring, but Grego managed to convince them to enlist him as a volunteer, which he squeezed in around another part-time job. "In a short period of time I learned a lot about processes, schedules and equipment in bakeries, and the importance of using local, quality ingredients. I was also inspired by their fearlessness in pushing the colour of their loaves – they are baked really dark and beautiful.'

After Grego and the family moved to Inverloch with newfound inspiration, an idea began to take shape. The Bass Coast and South Gippsland were surprisingly lacking in quality bread, and Grego was looking to put his new training to work. In a garage built for the purpose, he set up a microbakery and – inspired this time by Scandinavia's cycling culture – made a plan to deliver Swedish-inspired bakes to the community on a cargo bike. It also offered a change in lifestyle he'd been looking for. 'By baking from home and setting my own schedules, I get to spend more time with the family compared to my past jobs as a chef.'

The philosophy is one of micro but mighty – a flexible format for the baker, a gem for the local community. 'I can't do too much since I'm just one baker,' he says, 'but it's also got to do with my belief in the micro-bakery idea, where you just focus on doing a few things well. I think that's what makes it unique. I love knowing and talking with the people who enjoy my product. By keeping it small, I get all the benefits of genuine relationships with the people in my community and with other local businesses.'

ON THE IMPORTANCE OF AN AFTERNOON BREAK

'Baking in Sweden plays an important role in daily life, workplaces and in people's homes. Swedes use the word fika to refer to a quick break at work or catching up with a friend to stop, take a pause and reconnect over a cup of coffee and a sweet treat (often a cardamom or cinnamon bun or a even a slice of cake), and it's truly embedded in their culture. Many people have a batch of cinnamon buns in their freezer, ready to pop in the oven for guests when they arrive. I love this, and I believe that in the fast-paced world we live in we should all find time for fika.'

WORDS TO BAKE BY

'Never give up! I learn something new every day, and instead of letting it frustrate me (too much) I learn from each and every batch of dough. I have learned that the more times you do something, the more skills you gain to deal with the never-ending changes in temperatures, humidity and, of course, the ingredients themselves. Each loaf or pastry shouldn't be identical, it should be a reflection of the moment in time in which it was made.'

Swedish semlor

MAKES 12

SPECIAL EQUIPMENT stand mixer with dough hook attachment, pastry brush, sugar thermometer, piping bag and large star nozzle (optional)

Almond paste
200 g (7 oz) almond meal
180 g (6¼ oz) icing (confectioners') sugar, plus extra for dusting
1 egg white
100 g (3½ oz) milk

Cardamom buns
150 g (5½ oz) milk
100 g (3½ oz) water
140 g (5 oz) unsalted butter
40 g (1½ oz) fresh yeast or 20 g (¾ oz) dried yeast
600 g (1 lb 5 oz) plain (all-purpose) flour
80 g (2¾ oz) caster (superfine) sugar
25 g (1 oz) milk powder
10 g (¼ oz) ground black cardamom seeds
pinch of salt
90 g (3¼ oz) egg (from about 2 eggs)
600 ml (21 fl oz) whipping cream, whipped

Egg wash
1 egg yolk
1 teaspoon milk
pinch of salt

Counters in Scandinavian cafes are commonly piled high with delectable buns, pastries and cakes. Of all the pastries I was determined to perfect, it was the semla (or semlor, plural). These light, cardamom-infused buns filled with soft almond paste and topped with whipped cream are surprisingly easy to make and part of an unforgettable fika experience (see opposite). They are traditionally eaten on Shrove Tuesday, and Swedes eat around six million of them on this day each year. If the marzipan flavour of the almond paste is not your thing, you can also fill these buns with jam and cream, which is how they are made in Norway and Finland.

For the almond paste, mix the almond meal and icing sugar in a medium bowl. Mix in the egg white and milk to create a smooth paste. Set aside.

To make the cardamom buns, heat the milk, water and butter in a medium saucepan over medium heat until the butter melts. Leave to cool to about 25°C/75°F, then add the yeast and mix until dispersed.

In a stand mixer with the dough hook attachment, mix the dry ingredients on medium speed, then add the egg and the milk, water and butter mixture, mixing to create a soft, smooth and elastic dough. Do a quick 'window' test by stretching a section of the dough and between your fingers to make sure the gluten has developed. It should stretch to create a paper-thin layer without breaking. If not, mix for another few minutes.

Turn the dough out into a large lightly greased bowl and cover with biodegradable plastic wrap. Leave to rest at room temperature for 1 hour. Remove the plastic wrap and punch the dough down in the middle to reduce its volume, then cover again with the plastic wrap and refrigerate for a minimum of 6 hours, or overnight.

Line a baking tray with baking paper. Cut the dough into 12 even pieces. Roll each piece into a ball using clean palms and place them all on the prepared baking tray at least 4 cm (1½ inches) apart. Cover the buns with a clean damp tea towel (dish towel) and leave to rise at room temperature (ideally at 22–23°C/72–73°F) for 1½ hours, or until doubled in size. When ready, the buns should jiggle nicely when you move the tray.

Preheat the oven to 190°C/375°F fan-forced (210°C/400°F conventional).

Prepare the egg wash while waiting for the buns to rise by mixing all the ingredients in a small bowl. When the buns are ready to bake, use a pastry brush to brush each one with the egg wash, place the tray in the oven and immediately turn the temperature down to 170°C/350°F fan-forced (190°C/375°F conventional). Bake for 12 minutes or until golden brown. Transfer the buns to a wire rack to cool. >

Caramelised almond topping
50 g (1¾ oz) caster (superfine) sugar
100 g (3½ oz) slivered almonds

Meanwhile, make the caramelised almond topping. Heat a small frying pan over high heat, then add the sugar, making sure to spread it out evenly across the pan. Once the sugar starts to dissolve and turn lightly golden, add the slivered almonds. Start stirring the almonds slowly and remove the pan from the heat. Continue stirring the almond mix for 1–2 minutes, then spread it out on a sheet of baking paper to cool.

To assemble, once the buns have cooled completely, cut a small lid from the top of each one using a sharp knife. Scoop a large spoonful of the almond paste onto each bun, followed by a generous amount of whipped cream – piping the whipped cream using a large star nozzle gives a more finished look. Scatter the caramelised almonds over the cream, then replace the lid of the bun. Dust lightly with extra icing sugar. Time for fika!

Cinnamon braid

Gregorio Montalbán Sánchez
Profiled on page 138

SERVES 6–8
SPECIAL EQUIPMENT stand mixer with dough hook and paddle attachments, rolling pin, pastry brush

Sweet dough
275 g (9¾ oz) 00 flour, plus extra for dusting
50 g (1¾ oz) caster (superfine) sugar
1 teaspoon ground black cardamom seeds
12 g (½ oz) fresh yeast or 6 g (¼ oz) dried yeast
115 g (4 oz) water
50 g (1¾ oz) chilled unsalted butter, diced
½ teaspoon salt

Vanilla syrup
100 g (3½ oz) caster (superfine) sugar
100 ml (3½ fl oz) water
2 vanilla beans, split lengthways and seeds scraped

Cinnamon filling
2 teaspoons ground cinnamon
1 tablespoon water
50 g (1¾ oz) unsalted butter, softened
50 g (1¾ oz) caster (superfine) sugar
20 g (¾ oz) almond meal
2 teaspoons vanilla syrup (see above)

I make hundreds of Swedish cinnamon and cardamom buns each week in my home-based microbakery. This is a fun take on my bun recipe, instead making a single braid for sharing. The sweet, yeasted cardamom-speckled and enriched dough has a cinnamon filling and soft almond paste in the centre. It's perfect for cutting into thick slices and sharing with family and friends.

For the sweet dough, combine the flour, sugar and cardamom in a stand mixer with the dough hook attachment. In a separate bowl, mix the fresh yeast into the water until dispersed, then add to the flour mixture and mix on low speed for 2–3 minutes. Add the butter and continue mixing on low speed for a further 5 minutes until the dough is smooth and coming away from the side of the bowl. Finally, add the salt and mix for a further 5 minutes, until the dough is soft and elastic. You can also check to see if the dough is ready by doing a 'window' test. Stretch a small amount of dough between your fingers until there is a thin film of dough in the middle. If you can stretch it to the point that light passes through it without it tearing, it is ready.

Turn the dough out onto a work surface dusted with flour and fold the dough over two or three times to create tension in the dough. Place in a bowl greased with oil, cover with biodegradable plastic wrap, then refrigerate to rest for 4–6 hours, or overnight.

To make the vanilla syrup, combine the caster sugar and water in a small saucepan. Add the vanilla beans and seeds and bring to the boil without stirring. Remove from the heat, swirl to ensure the sugar is dissolved, and set aside to cool. (This syrup, strained, can be stored in a glass bottle in the fridge and is great to use in other recipes, such as cakes, muffins and even cocktails.)

To prepare the cinnamon filling, start by mixing the cinnamon and water in a small bowl to create a paste. Place the butter in the bowl of the stand mixer, this time fitted with the paddle attachment, and mix on low speed for 1 minute, or until smooth. Continue mixing, while gradually adding the sugar to the butter, followed by the almond meal, strained vanilla syrup and cinnamon paste. Take care not to overmix – 1–2 minutes on low speed is enough.

Almond paste
100 g (3½ oz) almond meal
90 g (3¼ oz) icing (confectioners') sugar
1 egg white
15 g (½ oz) milk

Topping
vanilla syrup (see opposite)
20 g (¾ oz) almond flakes
20 g (¾ oz) pearl sugar

To make the almond paste, mix the almond meal and icing sugar in a small bowl. Mix in the egg white and milk to create a smooth paste.

To assemble, take your dough out of the fridge and place on a lightly floured work surface. Using a rolling pin, roll out the cold dough into a 30 × 15 cm (12 × 6 inch) rectangle. Spread the cinnamon filling over the entire surface of the dough, taking care not to leave any gaps.

With a short edge of the dough facing you, use a spoon to spread the almond mixture in a vertical strip 3 cm (1¼ inches) wide down the centre of your rectangle. Using a sharp knife, cut the dough horizontally on either side of the almond paste into 5 mm (¼ inch) strips (or wider if you prefer; in the photos they are 5 cm/2 inches). Now's the fun part! Take the first strip on one side and fold it over the centre. Now take the first strip from the opposite side and fold it over the top. Continue crisscrossing the strips across the almond paste all the way down to create your braid. Transfer the braid to a baking tray lined with baking paper, cover with a clean damp tea towel (dish towel) and leave to rise for 1 hour or until almost doubled in size.

Preheat the oven to 170°C/350°F fan-forced (190°C/375°F conventional).

Use a pastry brush to brush the top and sides of the braid with vanilla syrup, then scatter almond flakes and pearl sugar over the top. Bake for 15–20 minutes or until golden. Transfer the braid to a wire rack to cool, then cut into 2–3 cm (¾–1¼ inch) slices to serve.

Buttermilk bundt with passionfruit icing

Tilly Pamment
Profiled on page 72

SERVES 10
SPECIAL EQUIPMENT large 10 cup (2.5 litre) bundt tin, stand mixer with paddle attachment

plain (all-purpose) flour, for dusting

Cake
225 g (8 oz) unsalted butter, softened, plus extra for greasing
275 g (9¾ oz) caster (superfine) sugar
3 teaspoons vanilla bean paste
4 large eggs, lightly beaten
250 g (9 oz) self-raising flour
pinch of bicarbonate of soda (baking soda)
⅛ teaspoon fine salt
185 ml (6 fl oz) buttermilk, at room temperature

Passionfruit icing
180 g (6¼ oz) icing (confectioners') sugar, sifted
2 tablespoons fresh passionfruit pulp

There is both great comfort and generosity to be found in a good plain cake. We return to it again and again in my house. When I don't know what else to make, this is what I always bake. The choice of icing may vary – sometimes a fruity glaze or just a dusting of icing sugar – but my personal favourite, and one that feels particularly Australian, is passionfruit icing. The sharp fruitiness is the perfect foil for the soft, sweet cake beneath. I'm also particularly fond of what buttermilk and a bundt tin can bring to a simple cake. Buttermilk adds a lovely soft crumb and slight lactic-acid tang. I always have a carton of it in my fridge, thereby ensuring a cake or batch of pikelets is never far away, and I often use it in recipes in place of regular milk. And a bundt tin? Well, it can elevate the plainest of cakes into an aesthetic masterpiece, so what's not to love there?

Preheat the oven to 160°C/325°F fan-forced (180°C/350°F conventional) and grease a large 10 cup (2.5 litre) bundt tin well with extra softened butter. Dust with a little plain flour, tapping out any excess.

For the cake, combine the butter, sugar and vanilla in the bowl of a stand mixer with the paddle attachment and cream until very light and fluffy. This will take several minutes, depending on how soft your butter is, but it's important to continue until the mixture is very pale and light. Add the eggs, one at a time, beating well after each addition.

Sift the self-raising flour, bicarbonate of soda and salt into a medium bowl, and whisk gently to combine. Add half the flour mixture to the creamed butter, stirring gently until just combined, then add half the buttermilk. Once incorporated, follow with the remaining flour, then the remaining buttermilk, stirring gently until the batter is smooth. Don't be inclined to overmix. I do this step by hand, rather than in the mixer.

Spoon the batter into the prepared tin, smoothing the top and tapping the tin on the bench a few times to remove any air bubbles. Bake for 30–35 minutes, until golden and cooked through – a skewer inserted in the centre should come out clean. Cool in the tin for 10 minutes before carefully turning out onto a wire rack to cool completely.

Make the passionfruit icing while the cake is cooling by combining the icing sugar and passionfruit pulp in a small bowl. Stir until smooth, then check the consistency – you want it to be a nice pourable thickness so that it drips down the cake, but not so runny that it all slides off. Add a little extra passionfruit pulp or icing sugar if necessary. Transfer the cooled cake to a serving plate and pour the icing over it, letting it drip down the sides. Slice and serve straight away or wait for the icing to set if you prefer.

This cake is best eaten on the day it is made, but it keeps happily in an airtight container in a cool place for 2–3 days. I like to reheat slices gently if serving on day two or three.

Pandan drømmekage

Raymond Tan
Profiled on page 76

SERVES 8–10
SPECIAL EQUIPMENT 23 cm (9 inch) square or round cake tin, stand mixer with whisk attachment, pastry brush

For making pandan juice, the preferred ratio of pandan leaves to water is 1:1. To be on the safe side, the quantity in the ingredients list makes a little more than you will need.

melted butter, for greasing

Pandan juice
125 g (4½ oz) pandan leaves
125 g (4½ oz) water

Cake
225 g (8 oz) plain (all-purpose) flour
22 g (¾ oz) baking powder
2 g (¹⁄₁₆ oz) salt
150 g (5½) oz pandan juice
150 g (5½ oz) coconut cream
3 g (⅛ oz) pandan essence
3 large eggs
200 g (7 oz) caster (superfine) sugar
150 g (5½ oz) vegetable oil

Coconut topping
150 g (5½ oz) butter
135 g (4¾ oz) dark brown sugar
135 g (4¾ oz) gula Melaka (palm sugar)
75 g (2¾ oz) milk
8 g (¼ oz) salt
85 g (3 oz) desiccated coconut
50 g (1¾ oz) shredded coconut

As a tourist to the Freetown Christiania commune in Copenhagen, I came across the drømmekage, which translates literally to 'dream cake'. Traditionally, this Danish cake is a fluffy vanilla sponge topped with sweet, sticky caramelised coconut. At Raya, we of course put our Malaysian twist on this cake, replacing the vanilla with freshly squeezed pandan juice and making the caramelised coconut with palm sugar. We hope the Danes approve.

Preheat the oven to 180°C/350°F fan-forced (200°C/400°F conventional). Use a pastry brush to brush the bottom and side of a 23 cm (9 inch) square or round cake tin with melted butter and line the bottom with baking paper.

For the pandan juice, wash and cut the pandan leaves to about 2.5 cm (1 inch) long pieces and blend with the water. Strain through a fine-mesh sieve or cheesecloth. Always stir the pandan juice before using, as it tends to have sediment.

For the cake, sift the flour, baking powder and salt into a medium bowl. In a separate medium bowl, mix the pandan juice, coconut cream and pandan essence.

In a stand mixer with the whisk attachment, whisk the eggs and sugar on medium speed until pale yellow. Turn the speed to low and gradually add the vegetable oil until emulsified. Gently fold in the flour mixture, alternating with the pandan juice mixture, until just combined.

Pour into the prepared tin and bake for 45 minutes, or until a wooden skewer inserted in the centre of the cake comes out clean.

Prepare the coconut topping while the cake is baking. Melt the butter with the dark brown sugar, gula Melaka and milk in a medium saucepan over low heat until the sugar is just dissolved. Fold in the salt and desiccated and shredded coconut and stir until the coconut is completely coated. Remove from the heat and set aside to cool slightly.

Once the cake is cooked, spoon the coconut mixture over the top and spread out evenly. Bake for a further 10–15 minutes, until the coconut is toasted and crisp. Cool in the tin for 30 minutes before cutting and serving.

Plum streusel cake

Maaryasha Werdiger
Profiled on page 80

SERVES 8–10 generously
SPECIAL EQUIPMENT 22 cm (8½ inch) round or square cake tin, stand mixer with paddle attachment

Streusel
100 g (3½ oz) unsalted butter, slightly softened (30 minutes out of fridge)
50 g (1¾ oz) caster (superfine) sugar
50 g (1¾ oz) brown sugar
100 g (3½ oz) plain (all-purpose) flour
¼ teaspoon salt

If I was forced to choose one cake to serve my friends for the rest of my life, it would be a plum streusel cake. Growing up, there was always a streusel cake at my grandmother's house, and it was probably one of the first cakes I learned to make. Streusel is German for a crumbly cake topping made with flour, butter and sugar, and it's one of my favourite foods. A streusel cake can be made with or without fruit, with apples, pears, blueberries, raspberries, apricots or peaches – but, honestly, plums are the best. They are a wonderful mix of sweet, tart and juicy and, when baked, can become almost jam-like. Our plum streusel at the bakery is a little different, slightly more complex, with added nuts and various other grains, such as oats. I wanted you to have a recipe that isn't too complex, that doesn't exclude your friend with a nut allergy, that is moist and that lasts a good few days before going dry. Once this comes out of the oven, switch on the coffee machine and invite your friends over.

Preheat the oven to 180°C/350°F fan-forced (200°C/400°F). Line a 22 cm (8½ inch) round or square cake tin with baking paper.

To make the streusel, finely dice the butter. Combine the remaining ingredients in a medium bowl then, using clean fingertips, rub the malleable butter into the sugar and flour mixture until it resembles large coarse breadcrumbs of various sizes. If there are still chunks of butter remaining, it's okay as long as most of the butter has been mixed into the dry ingredients. Set aside.

For the cake, sift together the flours, baking power and bicarbonate of soda. Set aside.

Using a stand mixer with the paddle attachment, beat the butter, sugars, orange zest, cardamom (if using), salt and vanilla on medium–high speed until pale and fluffy. Depending on your butter, this can take 2–5 minutes. With the mixer running on high speed, gradually add the eggs, beating well after each addition and stopping intermittently to scrape down the side to ensure the batter is evenly mixed. (In my experience, if the butter isn't too soft initially, and the whisked egg is added slowly, a fluffy emulsion will develop, leaving you with a beautiful batter. If at this stage the mixture splits, do not fear. While the final crumb may not be quite the same, your cake will still be delicious.) Once all the egg has been added, reduce the speed to low.

While the paddle is on low speed, add the flour mixture into the batter in 3–4 batches, alternating with the sour cream. Don't add all the sour cream at once, please! Once the flour is just incorporated, switch off the mixer – do not overmix or you will have a breadier cake. (The batter is thicker than usual, but with the butter as well as the sour cream, along with the moisture from the plums, this cake will not be dry.)

Pour the batter into the prepared tin and smooth out the top. Sprinkle the cinnamon over the top and arrange the plums evenly over that, without worrying about making a nice pattern. Push the plums into the batter slightly. Now cover the entire top with the streusel.

Cake

- 215 g (7½ oz) plain (all-purpose) flour
- 100 g (3½ oz) whole-wheat flour
- 2 teaspoons baking powder
- ½ teaspoon bicarbonate of soda (baking soda)
- 180 g (6¼ oz) unsalted butter, slightly softened (30 minutes out of fridge)
- 180 g (6¼ oz) caster (superfine) sugar
- 45 g (1½ oz) brown sugar
- zest of 1 orange
- ½ teaspoon ground cardamom (optional)
- 1 teaspoon salt
- 1 teaspoon vanilla bean paste
- 2 room-temperature eggs, beaten
- 250 g (9 oz) sour cream
- ½ teaspoon ground cinnamon
- 4 ripe medium plums, cut into quarters and stones removed
- icing (confectioners') sugar, for dusting (optional)

You can replace the sour cream with milk, cream, yoghurt or orange juice. They should all work and will all change the final result in slightly different ways. Sour cream makes for a tender, denser crumb and you won't regret it.

Bake for about 1 hour and 15 minutes, checking the cake at the 45-minute mark and again at the 60-minute mark. This is quite a big and dense cake and looks can be deceiving, so test it by inserting a skewer in the centre. If the top is getting dark before the middle is done, cover the cake with foil for the remainder of the baking time.

Cool in the tin and store wrapped in foil at room temperature for 2–3 days. (It freezes well too. Just give it half a day to thaw at room temperature.)

Serve with a dusting of icing sugar, if you like.

You can replace the flour mix with all plain, or all whole-wheat, or even replace the whole-wheat portion with other grain flours, such as spelt. There should be enough moisture from the remaining ingredients to ensure this cake won't be dry.

Special *Occasions*

160 Inception cake

164 Hibiscus cake

167 Miss Trixie's classic chocolate cake

172 Hazelnut and apple cake with sour cream frosting
and apple caramel

176 Preserved lemon layer cake with blackberry
and olive oil buttercream

182 Layered rhubarb meringue cake

187 Chocolate cherry choux

191 Strawberry, chocolate and balsamic lamington stack

Rosemary Andrews

Inception cake (160)

Negroni chocolate tart (243)

Founder and head pastry chef, Mietta

Melbourne, Vic
Wurundjeri Country

Rosemary Andrews boxes up joy. As a child, she noticed the contagious effect of baked goods – it was there when her mum shared community fundraising bakes, in the special treat of a trip to the cake shop, and unmissable in her grandmother's afternoon teas, complete with passionfruit sponges and pink lamingtons on diamond cake stands. And along her way to becoming the renowned pastry chef she is today, this joy has remained in sight. 'I love how happy desserts and baking can make people,' she says. 'This was reinforced in COVID lockdown, how important a slice of cake could be to someone to cheer them up in a difficult time. Baking something for someone else, with your time, really can show how much you care. Sweets are like a love language, in all cultures. In times of need, people give the gift of food or particular cakes, and it can be an act of love.'

On the heels of her much-loved cake boxes, in 2023 Rosemary launched her own cake boutique, Mietta, in the inner south-eastern Melbourne suburb of Malvern. She is known for her artistic touch and imaginative creations that include bouncy, two-texture cheesecakes, many-layered honey cakes and the utter chocolatey delight of a Negroni chocolate tart (see page 243) or an Inception cake (see page 160) inspired by that famous scene in Roald Dahl's *Matilda*. In her own words, she says, 'I would describe my particular approach to baking as finding the best ingredients I can, and figuring out how to showcase them in their original beauty, whether that's the way you slice strawberries on a sponge or the quality of chocolate you use. It really makes a significant difference to the taste.' Rosemary credits this to her time working with some of the best chefs in Australia – and a lot of hard work. In early 2021, Rosemary helmed the dessert trolley at Ben Shewry's Attica Summer Camp, and her work went deservedly viral. She keeps herself interested with experimenting. 'I try my best to educate my palate and try new flavours,' she says. 'I do like the classics, like a classic lemon tart. However, I try to jazz them up, whether that's with zest, spices or flavours from other countries to cater for all audiences, ages and cultures.'

For all the technical heights she's baked to, she's grounded by an age-old adage. 'In cookery school, we learn the KISS – keep it simple, stupid – method, which I really relate to now after many years of experience. All the details create an artwork, but it's important that it's delicious, too.' Equally, Rosemary works towards highlighting the pastry profession and keeping it alive. It was she, after all, who suggested the idea that brought about this book, to shine a spotlight on the talent, creativity and wisdom in the baking community around us. Pastry chefs, she says, 'are like gold to find' in restaurants these days, with many (herself included) moving into or opening their own cake shops and bakeries for a better work–life balance. 'We learn lessons every day in baking, but my most challenging one is definitely Mietta, which is a work in progress. When you work for yourself and need to think about the business side, it can be challenging as a chef, as we express our emotions through food.' But the rewards are plenty: 'If all the flavours are there, it's delicious and you make people happy through what you create or have made – that's the most important part.'

NOTES ON PERFECT COOKIES

'The secret to getting cookies perfectly round every time? A cookie scoop – an ice-cream scoop works perfectly. Be adventurous; instead of brown sugar try muscovado sugar or molasses – the flavour changes in recipes to a more in-depth caramel.'

WORDS TO BAKE BY

'My advice to aspiring pastry chefs would be to keep going; work positively towards your ambitions and goals. The only person who's going to get you to where you want to be is you – and you can do anything if you truly desire it. With ambition and resilience, you will get to where you see your potential to be. They say hard work pays off, so keep working hard to the level you want to achieve and rewards will follow.'

'Baking something for someone else, with your time, really can show how much you care. Sweets are like a love language, in all cultures.'

Inception cake

Rosemary Andrews
Profiled on page 158

SERVES 12–14

SPECIAL EQUIPMENT two 23 cm (9 inch) diameter cake tins, sugar thermometer, angled palette knife, palette knife, fine chinois (fine-mesh conical sieve) or similar, cake board or plate

Chocolate glaze
35 g (1¼ oz) gold-strength leaf gelatine
150 g (5½ oz) milk
1.2 kg (2 lb 10 oz) thick (double) cream
900 g (2 lb) caster (superfine) sugar
300 g (10½ oz) cacao powder
300 g (10½ oz) dark chocolate, 66% or 70%, roughly chopped
5 g (⅛ oz) toasted wattleseed powder
2 pinches of sea salt

Cake
260 g (9¼ oz) dark chocolate, 66%, chopped
655 g (1 lb 7 oz) brown sugar
15 g (½ oz) muscovado sugar
440 g (15½ oz) unsalted butter, roughly diced
640 g (1 lb 6½ oz) water
290 g (10¼ oz) egg (from about 6 eggs)
250 g (9 oz) cake flour
250 g (9 oz) plain (all-purpose) flour
10 g (¼ oz) unsweetened cocoa powder
23 g (¾ oz) bicarbonate of soda (baking soda)
2 pinches of sea salt

To decorate (optional)
gold leaf

Inception. It's mysterious and rich, sweet yet bitter – like the road of a journey. The taste and quality ingredients (I like to use Valhrona chocolate and cocoa) shine through each layer. This cake represents the inception of a plan or the beginning of new ones, or celebrations of a new year. Like the experiences you stack up on your way to success, there's a moment of happiness in each layer, through balanced bitter and sweetness. At Mietta, we bake each layer individually to create an eight-layered cake, but in this recipe for home bakers we make two full cakes, and cut each cake into four layers – they'll be a little thicker than ours, but the process will be simplified.

For the chocolate glaze, first leave the gelatine to soak in a bowl of cold water.
Combine the milk and cream in a large saucepan and bring to the boil over medium heat. Whisk in the caster sugar, cacao powder, dark chocolate, wattleseed and salt, then continue whisking until melted. Bring to the boil while whisking vigorously, then remove from the heat and cool to 60°C/140°F. Squeeze out the gelatine and whisk it in. Pour the mixture through a chinois or other fine-mesh sieve into a storage container. Seal and refrigerate until set, about 6 hours or overnight.

For the cake, grease two 23 cm (9 inch) diameter cake tins with canola oil spray, then line each with baking paper. Preheat the oven to 140°C/275°F fan-forced (160°C/325°F conventional).
In a large bowl, combine the dark chocolate, brown sugar and muscovado sugar. Combine the butter and water in a large saucepan, stir over high heat until melted, then pour into the chocolate and sugar mixture and whisk until combined. Cool to below 50°C/120°F. Meanwhile, sift the dry ingredients. Once the chocolate mixture is cool, whisk in the egg, followed by the dry ingredients.
Divide the mixture evenly between the cake tins, smooth out the top with a palette knife and bake for 45–60 minutes or until cooked through. The tops of the cakes should be soft and spring back.
Leave the cakes to cool for at least 2 hours or until cooled completely.
Using a sharp serrated 25 cm (10 inch) knife, carefully cut each cake into four layers, ensuring you keep a level hand and using your other hand to hold the cake firmly to avoid any slips or wonky angles. You may still need to trim the top of each cake to ensure it's flat.

To assemble, set aside a quarter of the glaze mixture and whisk the remainder until fluffy and spreadable. Place one cake on a stable surface. Spread 100 g (3½ oz) of the glaze on top, then place another cake on top. Repeat until all the layers are assembled. Using an angled palette knife or dough scraper, spread a thin layer of the ganache over the top and sides of the stack as a crumb coat.
Heat the remaining glaze to 40°C/100°F in a small saucepan over low heat, then pour over the cake to create a shiny glaze. Remove any excess glaze and transfer the cake to a cake board. Decorate the edges with gold leaf, if using. Refrigerate to set. For the best texture, leave out at room temperature for 3 hours before cutting into 12–14 slices to serve.

Nornie Bero

Hibiscus cake (164)

Founder and chef at
Big Esso by Mabu Mabu,
and author

Melbourne, Vic
Wurundjeri Country

If you've ever been lucky enough to hear Nornie Bero speak, you'll know she's a born storyteller. And if you've been even luckier and have tasted her food, you'll know there's always a tale there too. 'When I make something, I always try to make it about home,' she says.

Home is Mer Island, in the Torres Strait. Some of her earliest memories are of baking – of being just big enough to peer over the stovetop to glimpse her dad making pumpkin buns and damper doughs. 'I'd wake up with him and see him make everything and help him out,' she recalls. 'Then I'd do the deliveries before school started.' He'd pay her in marbles that she'd collect in an old powdered milk tin and clack around in matches with the other kids. 'The best things about it were, one, that we did a lot of baking in an underground oven. And two, I learned all these great things from my aunties and my dad – about how we use cassava and yams, how to squeeze them and then turn them into flour – about the natural forms that you get to work with.'

Just as she'd be out on the reef every morning, gathering food to cook for the day, she learned from the properties of the ingredients around her. 'Growing up like that, you can develop that as a kid – that was the funnest process,' she says, 'And when I became a chef, I thought, "I can't believe I have all these beautiful memories". I didn't grow up with food dyes and food colourings, so it was just about, "What do you use to give you natural colours that's at your fingertips?" Pumpkins, yams and hibiscus, all these things.'

Today, a chef and business owner, Nornie is a trailblazer on a mission to get Australian native ingredients into everyone's kitchen. Through Mabu Mabu, she sells a pantry-span of native ingredients (sourced directly from farmers) and condiments, and in her Federation Square restaurant, Big Esso, she reinterprets dishes from home. 'I get to bring some of my traditional island cooking that no one has ever had, but also those beautiful bits of mainland ingredients, and from all over,' she says of her work.

Her recipes continue to provide inspiration for how to celebrate and get the most out of native ingredients. For anyone struggling to source them, her advice is to ask – and keep asking. 'We're doing a lot of firsts with native ingredients. There's not many recipes that you can just look up. I tell my team that as some of the leaders of making recipes that use native ingredients fully, we should represent them and honour them – as well as their story and the people who give them to us.'

'We're doing a lot of firsts with native ingredients. We should represent them and honour them – as well as their story and the people who give them to us.'

NOTES ON PEPPERBERRY AND WATTLESEED

'My top two native ingredients for baking are pepperberry and wattleseed. Pepperberry gives you that beautiful clove-y flavour that is so unique to us, but also the slow burn of spice. It'll give you its natural colour too – it leaks purple tinges. If you're making something like chai-spice cake, use pepperberry as an alternative to give you this beautiful spiciness. Then wattleseeds. There are about 165 edible wattle [*Acacia*] species out there that range in colour. So the lighter the seed is, the more malty it is, and the darker it is, the more bitter-chocolatey it is. A nice middle-ground brown will give you those hazelnut sort of coffee flavours that really work in baking. If you use the seed on its own, it will expand when you bite into it – you'll get all those flavours that it sucks up with the liquid. But to get more out of it, you grind it down into a powdered form that has a much more intense flavour. You'll get this poppyseed effect and it'll give your cake a tinge of sourdoughy, chocolatey colours, depending on how much flour you use.'

WORDS TO BAKE BY

'The biggest thing about baking is being patient. When you're baking something for a long period of time, cover it. I've noticed that when people make things like Christmas puddings they let it brown and it dries out on the top. Use baking paper or foil to cover it, let it rise up nicely and cook through but stay moist. Remember that old-school way? Then take off the covering and get that colour on at the end. That's how you get the depth. Just be patient.'

Hibiscus cake

Nornie Bero
Profiled on page 162

SERVES 12

SPECIAL EQUIPMENT 25 cm (10 inch) diameter cake tin, stand mixer with paddle and whisk attachments or hand-held electric beaters, palette knife

butter, for greasing

Cake
6 egg yolks
55 g (2 oz) caster (superfine) sugar
½ teaspoon salt
85 g (3 oz) milk
55 ml (1¾ fl oz) vegetable oil
½ teaspoon pepperberry
1 tablespoon dried hibiscus flowers, ground
finely grated zest of 1 lemon
115 g (4 oz) plain (all-purpose) flour
2 tablespoons cornflour (cornstarch)

Meringue
6 egg whites
60 g (2¼ oz) caster (superfine) sugar

Strawberry gum cream frosting
300 g (10½ oz) cream cheese, at room temperature
150 g (5½ oz) unsalted butter, softened
½ teaspoon pepperberry
1 teaspoon vanilla extract
½ teaspoon ground strawberry gum
150 g (5½ oz) icing (confectioners') sugar

To decorate (optional)
fresh figs and blackberries

I love hibiscus. It reminds me of home a lot, especially of my grandma – aba – who used to wear them every day. We call them kukuwams in our language – the women on Mer Island always have kukuwam in their hair. There are different types and they grow really naturally up in the Straits. Every time I go home and see them, I think to myself, 'This is home.' Making this hibiscus cake is a way for me to bring in that island flavour from home and the bright colours that my aba, aunties and uncles all like to wear – all the rainbow, all in one. It represents, I think, the smile that we try to carry with us.

The hibiscus gives its natural colour and vibrancy, and its unique zesty tartness, which makes for an absolutely delicious cake.

Preheat the oven to 160°C/325°F fan-forced (180°C/350°F conventional). Grease a 25 cm (10 inch) diameter cake tin with butter and line it with baking paper.

To make the cake, cream the egg yolks, caster sugar and salt in a stand mixer with the paddle attachment, or using hand-held electric beaters, on low–medium speed until the mixture turns pale yellow. Add the milk, oil, pepperberry, ground hibiscus and lemon zest. Mix well.

Sift in the flour and cornflour, mix on low–medium speed to combine and set aside.

If you don't have another mixer bowl or hand-held electric beaters, transfer the cake batter to a separate bowl and wash the mixer bowl well.

For the meringue, using the stand mixer with the whisk attachment, whisk the egg whites on medium–high speed until fluffy, then add the sugar and whisk until soft peaks form.

With the mixer on low, or whisking by hand, mix half the meringue into the cake batter until partially combined. Using a spatula, gently fold in the rest of the meringue.

Spoon the mixture into the prepared tin and bake for 35 minutes, or until a skewer inserted in the centre comes out clean. Leave in the tin for 10–15 minutes, then turn out onto a wire rack to cool completely.

For the strawberry gum cream frosting, using a stand mixer with the paddle attachment or hand-held electric beaters, beat the cream cheese and butter on high speed until smooth and creamy. Add the pepperberry, vanilla, strawberry gum and sugar and beat on low speed for 30 seconds, then on high speed for 2 minutes. If you'd like your frosting thicker, add a little more icing sugar.

Cover the cake with the strawberry gum cream frosting, spreading it out with a palette knife but keeping it rough and organic. Decorate with fresh figs and blackberries if you have them.

Miss Trixie's classic chocolate cake

Alice Bennett
Profiled on page 36

SERVES 15–20
SPECIAL EQUIPMENT three 15 cm (6 inch) diameter cake tins, stand mixer with paddle and whisk attachments, dough scraper, angled palette knife, piping bag and open star nozzle, cake board or plate

Cake
80 g (2¾ oz) unsweetened cocoa powder, sifted
190 g (6¾ oz) dark chocolate, 70%, roughly chopped
1 teaspoon instant coffee
175 ml (6 fl oz) boiling water
230 g (8 oz) sour cream, at room temperature
210 g (7½ oz) plain (all-purpose) flour
1 teaspoon bicarbonate of soda (baking soda)
1 teaspoon salt
175 g (6 oz) unsalted butter, softened
360 g (12¾ oz) brown sugar
5 eggs, at room temperature

Salted vanilla Swiss meringue buttercream
200 g (7 oz) egg white (from about 7 eggs)
375 g (13 oz) caster (superfine) sugar
500 g (1 lb 2 oz) unsalted butter, softened
1 teaspoon vanilla extract
1 teaspoon fine salt
yellow food colouring (optional)

I like a chocolate cake that is addictive, one you go back to for another sliver, another bite. It needs to be rich, but not as dense as a mud cake. This cake has a gorgeous crumb, and is moist and super versatile. You can pair it with various flavoured buttercreams and fillings, but I've opted for a classic (slightly salty) vanilla buttercream. Just be sure to use the best-quality chocolate you can get your hands on for the cake and the best-quality vanilla bean extract or paste for your buttercream.

For the cake, preheat your oven to 135°C/275°F fan-forced (155°C/300°F conventional). Line three 15 cm (6 inch) diameter cake tins with baking paper and spray the paper liberally with oil.

Combine your cocoa powder, chocolate, coffee powder and boiling water in a glass or metal bowl and whisk to combine. Allow to cool slightly, then whisk through your sour cream. Set aside.

Sift your flour, bicarbonate of soda and salt into a separate bowl and whisk to combine. Set aside.

Using a stand mixer with the paddle attachment, beat together your butter and brown sugar on medium speed. Once combined, add your eggs, one at a time, beating well after each addition. It may curdle a bit, but don't stress. Add half of your chocolate mixture and half of your flour mixture and beat to combine. Repeat with your remaining chocolate mixture and flour.

Evenly divide the batter between your three cake tins and bake for 40 minutes, until a skewer poked into the centre of the cakes comes out clean. Leave your cakes in the tins for 15 minutes before turning out onto wire racks to cool completely.

Wash out your mixer bowl if you only have one.

For the salted vanilla Swiss meringue buttercream, make a bain-marie by bringing a half-pot of water to the boil, then turning down the heat to keep it at a simmer. In a heatproof mixing bowl (I like to use the stainless-steel bowl from my stand mixer), combine your egg white and sugar. Place the bowl over the simmering water, ensuring the bowl is not directly touching the water. You just want the steam from the simmering water to make the bowl hot.

Using a hand whisk, whisk the sugar and egg white together – you don't need to whisk constantly, but I like to keep my eyes on it. Whisk until all the sugar has dissolved and the egg white feels syrupy – rub a small amount of the mixture between forefinger and thumb to see if there are any remaining sugar granules. Once there are none, take the bowl off the heat.

Fit the bowl to your stand mixer with the whisk attachment or transfer your egg white syrup to the bowl of your stand mixer and beat on high speed until the mixture has come down to room temperature, about 30 minutes. The egg white needs to be stiff and luscious, resembling a pure white meringue mixture. Add your butter and beat until combined (see the note on page 168). Continue to beat until a smooth buttercream forms. Quickly beat in the vanilla and salt. >

To decorate (optional)
4–6 maraschino cherries

To assemble the cake, if needed, carefully trim the top of each cake with a bread knife to flatten. Divide your buttercream between two bowls. Add yellow food colouring to one half if you'd like and set aside. Leave the other half as is for crumb coating your cake.

Place a schmear of uncoloured buttercream on a cake board or plate and press the first cake layer on the board. Spread a thick layer of buttercream on the cake, then place the next cake layer on top. Repeat with the final cake layer.

Using an angled palette knife, gently start to spread buttercream over the top and side of the cake. The first layer of buttercream only needs to be thin. This is called the crumb coat and is designed to catch any loose crumbs and fix them in place. You should still be able to see your cake through the buttercream. Refrigerate or freeze the cake for 15–25 minutes.

Take the cake out and slather on a layer of coloured buttercream. Using a dough scraper, smooth out the edges and remove any excess buttercream. Continue to smooth and patch over any holes. You should have enough buttercream left over for piping.

Once the cake is completely covered, spoon the remaining buttercream into a piping bag fitted with an open star nozzle. Pipe around the bottom edge and the top of the cake, and decorate with maraschino cherries if using.

When beating the butter into your meringue, it will look as though the mixture is splitting. It's not. It's just because your meringue and butter aren't friends to start off with. They'll eventually learn to get along and form a great buttercream bond as you continue to beat them together.

Alice Bennett

Natasha Brownfield

Hazelnut and apple cake with sour cream frosting and apple caramel (172)
Tomato, herb and quark tart (206)

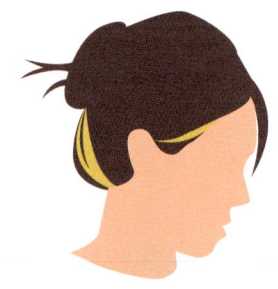

Founder and head pastry chef, Teeter Bakery

Perth, WA
Whadjuk Country

Natasha Brownfield bakes her way. 'I think sometimes I'm a bit of a cowboy – but it seems to have gotten me this far,' she says. Far indeed – she has a huge fan in Natalie Paull (page 4), and today is the owner of Teeter, her East Perth bakery that instantly made a name for itself with its signature fruity chiffons (think mandarin and olive oil) and pastries that swoon with local produce, such as figs from 'Betsy and family'; or pithiviers packed with greens from the farm across the railway. But back to the cowboy notion: 'It probably stems from my approach to baking. So many pastry chefs love pastry for its calculated methods and the precision, but I've never been into it for the rigidity – or at least that's not why I love it.'

Natasha has worked in kitchens of all types, from her early days as a teenage apprentice in what she calls 'a literal cake factory', to pasticcerias, neighbourhood bakeries and high-end wine bars in Melbourne, Perth and New Zealand. 'I've jumped around a bit. A few years ago I definitely was trying to work out where I actually fit. I've never worked under a hatted chef or the best bakery in Perth. I never thought I could be a perfectionist enough for these environments,' she says. 'I always wanted to have more fun than for it to be really serious practice, and I think maybe that's why I wanted to do it my own way.'

The dream remained her earliest one: to make pastries and celebration cakes. And that's what she does now at Teeter, which opens as an online cake shop for part of the week and in person for the rest. It's an inviting cornershop in a former gelateria with a jacaranda out front – and the sense of warmth continues in its kitchen that gives people chances. 'There's this expectation that you need to have the experience up your sleeve to get a job or get your foot in the door,' says Natasha. Not so here. Among the team are a former engineer and passionate home baker who Natasha trained from scratch and who now leads the cake section.

Baking, she knows, is one continuous experience. 'I feel like a lot of my recipes just feel pretty intuitive. So much of baking is feel and the experience of doing it over and over again – all the effort. I think of pastry cheffing as constant troubleshooting.' And this means plenty of time to choose your own adventure. 'You're never going to be getting something right all the time. Maybe it's not quite what the recipe said, but what can we do with this so it's going to be delicious? I hate to waste anything. I feel like we can always pull something together that's going to be delicious, no matter what mistakes have happened' (case in point, see the apple cores put to use in a caramel on page 172). Flexibility will always be at the heart of Teeter. 'We change most things every two weeks. The idea of "What can we work with?", that's how I stay excited. I kind of get an idea right then and there.'

WORDS TO BAKE BY

'Perhaps, given my approach, some would be wise to take my baking advice with a grain of salt, so I will add this: while precision is highly important in baking, don't be afraid of making mistakes – handle them with imagination, confidence and intuition, and always troubleshoot before tossing. This is often where you may find your flair or create something entirely new and enjoyable. If not, then you have learned what to look out for next time you strive to perfect the recipe. Baking is a constant practice.'

Hazelnut and apple cake with sour cream frosting and apple caramel

Natasha Brownfield
Profiled on page 170

SERVES 8–10
SPECIAL EQUIPMENT three 22 cm (8½ inch) diameter springform cake tins, stand mixer with whisk and paddle attachments, food processor (optional), two small heavy-based saucepans

Cake

140 g (5 oz) hazelnuts, plus extra, roasted and shaved, to garnish
3 green apples
¼ lemon
85 g (3 oz) egg (from about 2 eggs)
45 g (1½ oz) egg yolk (from about 3 eggs)
¼ teaspoon vanilla bean paste
300 g (10½ oz) caster (superfine) sugar
300 g (10½ oz) grapeseed or rice bran oil
95 g (3¼ oz) egg white (from about 4 eggs)
240 g (8½ oz) plain (all-purpose) flour
4 g (⅛ oz) baking powder
4 g (⅛ oz) ground cinnamon
2 g (1/16 oz) bicarbonate of soda (baking soda)

This cake is an adaptation of my carrot and pecan layer cake, which was loved for its sponginess and shiny crackly crust. Here, earthy toasted hazelnut and tart green apple are suspended in a lightly spiced sponge. It's layered with a silky cream cheese and sour cream frosting, influenced by one of our bakers, Gabrielle, who made something similar for her honey cakes in Lithuania. It's then finished with a sharp, apple-infused caramel. Once set in the fridge overnight, the cake layers marry together and the flavours become more pronounced, making it a perfect and homely layer cake that cuts like a dream into generous towering wedges.

For the cake, preheat the oven to 170°C/350°F fan-forced (190°C/375°F conventional), then roast the hazelnuts on a dry baking tray for 15 minutes or until golden. Allow to cool, then pinch or rub the skins off with your hands. Crush in a food processor or with the blade of a knife, leaving some larger pieces for texture. Reduce the oven temperature to 160°C/325°F fan-forced (180°C/350°F conventional).

Core and grate the apples. Squeeze the lemon quarter over the grated apple to stop it browning. Set the cores aside for the caramel.

Line the base and sides of three 22 cm (8½ inch) diameter cake tins with baking paper.

Using a stand mixer with the whisk attachment, whip the whole egg and the egg yolk with the vanilla and half the caster sugar on medium–high speed until thick and fluffy. With the motor still running, slowly pour in the oil. The mixture should be super thick and glossy. Transfer to a new bowl and set aside. Thoroughly wash and dry the whisk attachment and mixer bowl (or use a second mixer bowl if you have one).

In your stand mixer with the whisk attachment, whip the egg white on medium–high speed, gradually adding the remaining caster sugar, one-third at a time, until the mixture forms stiff glossy peaks. This will take at least 5 minutes. Gently fold this meringue into the yolky batter.

Stir through the apple and hazelnuts.

Sift in the dry ingredients and gently fold everything together, then divide the batter evenly between the tins and smooth out the tops.

Bake for 16 minutes, then rotate and bake for a further 2–4 minutes. The cake layers are ready once they spring back upon touch. The surface should be blond and beautifully crinkled. Cool in the tin for 30 minutes before gently turning out onto a wire rack to cool completely.

The apple caramel can be made as far as a week ahead and stored in the fridge. To use, you will need to warm the caramel slightly and whisk to emulsify to the desired consistency.

Apple caramel

3 reserved green apple cores
110 g (3¾ oz) pouring cream
150 g (5½ oz) caster (superfine) sugar
100 g (3½ oz) butter, diced
¼ teaspoon sea salt

Sour cream frosting

140 g (5 oz) cream cheese, at room temperature
140 g (5 oz) caster (superfine) sugar
270 g (9½ oz) best-quality sour cream
270 g (9½ oz) pouring cream
⅛ teaspoon vanilla bean paste

To make the apple caramel, warm the apple cores and cream in a small heavy-based saucepan over low heat for the apple to infuse the cream. Remove from the heat.

In a second small heavy-based saucepan over medium–high heat, warm the sugar until it begins to dissolve and caramelise. Don't be afraid to take it quite dark or to stir with a spoon or spatula to melt away any lumps of sugar. Once the sugar is fully dissolved and turns deep amber, add the apple cores from the cream, along with the butter and salt, and whisk quickly over medium heat to emulsify. Add the warmed cream, whisking to combine, then leave the mixture to boil for 5 minutes, letting the apple cook down a little to release more of its flavour. Stir occasionally so that it doesn't catch on the bottom. Strain into a bowl and set aside to cool to room temperature.

To make the sour cream frosting, beat the cream cheese and sugar on medium speed in the stand mixer with the paddle attachment, stopping regularly to scrape down the side with a spatula, until completely softened. Change to the whisk attachment and add the remaining ingredients, whipping together on medium speed until soft yet stable peaks form. Set aside at room temperature.

To assemble the cake, place the first sponge layer on a serving plate and top with one-third of the frosting. Drizzle a generous quarter of the strained caramel over the frosting. Repeat with the next two layers of sponge. Decorate the top with the extra shaved hazelnuts and more caramel.

Refrigerate for 2–3 hours or overnight for the cake layers to settle for perfect portioning, then bring back to room temperature before serving – 30 minutes should do. You want to eat the cake with the chill off to enjoy its full flavour.

Patchanida Chimkire

Preserved lemon layer cake with blackberry and olive oil buttercream (176)

Pandan, coconut and mango chiffon roll (257)

Pastry chef and founder, Mali Bakes

Melbourne, Vic
Wurundjeri Country

Mali Bakes creations are a feast for the eyes. Cakes, multi-tiered, shaped like hearts or mightily mini, are festooned with rows of piped ruffles, ribbons and flowers. And the pomp continues in the colour schemes. There are some in the dream-like pastels of a Wes Anderson film; a monochromatic chartreuse number like a hit of sherbet; and a cream-tinted wedding cake in Trevi Fountain chic, complete with cherubs. They are artworks with literal cherries on top.

Patchanida, a chef, started Mali Bakes from home in 2020, bringing together her love of baking with her eye for colour and aesthetics. Learning from a vintage Wilton cookbook, she applies her love of precision and symmetry – which, she thinks, harks back to hours of doodling Thai patterning, equally symmetrical and botanical, in the margins of her notebooks at school. 'I find beauty in the precision. When I'm doing something that's a bit more abstract, it's quite hard for me to see the bigger picture. But when I do things that need to be so exact, I find it easier.'

Mali Bakes is now a burgeoning event-cake business in Melbourne's inner-northern Thornbury with a tight-knit team of pastry chefs. The flavours are as va-va-voom as the exteriors. 'I want people to just be blown away,' says Patchanida, keen to disprove drab expectations of aesthetic custom cakes. 'There's something for everyone, because everyone's different.' Her own tastes lean towards a balance of contrasts, a preference she attributes to traditional Thai dishes like sticky mango rice, where the twang of sweet, tangy mango chimes in tune with savoury, slightly salted rice. 'I come from a family of sweet tooths. I didn't grow up baking, because we don't have much of a baking culture in Thailand, but always enjoyed traditional Thai sweets, which have this interesting dimension to them,' she says. Her flavours are a lesson in balanced decadence – think preserved lemon, blackberry and olive oil (page 176); or pandan chiffon with mango and toasted coconut cream (page 257).

Everyone in the team is involved in creating elements of these showstoppers. 'We have super-experienced pastry chefs in the kitchen, and I try to draw from each of their strengths.' For Patchanida, the most joyful thing is creativity – including the joy that comes from letting everyone express theirs. 'It's such an exciting experience, for you to have an idea, to define it and then to do it. It's so important for all of us to have that opportunity.'

'I come from a family of sweet tooths. I didn't grow up baking, but always enjoyed traditional Thai sweets, which have this interesting dimension to them.'

NOTES ON PIPING

'I prefer using ultra-soft buttercream for smoothly covering the cake. For piping, though, it's best to use a slightly firmer buttercream to maintain better shape and hold. Keep a small pot of water on the stovetop for easily adjusting the softness of your buttercream – simply place the buttercream bowl over the simmering water.'

WORDS TO BAKE BY

'We learn from each other in the kitchen. If someone makes a mistake, then we work to help each other fix the problem. I know what it's like to feel so small in the kitchen that you work in. We all had gatekeepers in every kitchen we worked in, who wouldn't tell you exactly what you needed to do, but would watch you work, and then once you make a mistake, they would criticise everything you did. We don't have that. Everyone's happy to share their experience. We just want to see everyone do well. Pastry is so tricky. Once you make a mistake, you can't always really fix things, so why wouldn't you want people feeling good while they're working?'

Preserved lemon layer cake with blackberry and olive oil buttercream

Patchanida Chimkire
Profiled on page 174

SERVES 8–10
SPECIAL EQUIPMENT two 20 cm (8 inch) diameter cake tins, stand mixer with paddle and whisk attachments, blender or food processor, sugar thermometer, angled palette knife, cake turntable

Cake
70 g (2½ oz) preserved lemon
135 g (4¾ oz) plain yoghurt
zest of 2 lemons and 20 g (¾ oz) juice
300 g (10½ oz) plain (all-purpose) flour
300 g (10½ oz) caster (superfine) sugar
9 g (¼ oz) baking powder
2 g (1/16 oz) bicarbonate of soda (baking soda)
2 g (1/16 oz) salt
190 g (6¾ oz) egg (from about 4 eggs)
170 g (6 oz) unsalted butter, at room temperature
35 g (1¼ oz) vegetable oil

This cake was inspired by Claire Saffitz's preserved lemon cake. I fell in love with the idea of using preserved lemon – which is better known for its use in savoury dishes – on a sweet cake. Pairing the tangy lemon curd with a rich olive oil and blackberry Italian meringue buttercream, we were able to bring these supposedly disparate elements together. The preserved lemon highlights the sweeter citrus notes of the cake without overpowering the senses. It's become a favourite at Mali Bakes, both to bake and to enjoy. The recipe uses the reverse creaming method, where softened butter is added to all the dry ingredients first and the liquids are added last, resulting in a more uniformly textured crumb. Needless to say, a quality extra virgin olive oil is essential for this cake. And if you're using bought preserved lemons, look for a variety with no added herbs and/or spices. A little tip: I like finishing the cake with fresh blackberries, a dollop of lemon curd, and some fresh edible flowers.

Preheat the oven to 160°C/325°F fan-forced (180°C/350°F conventional). Grease two 20 cm (8 inch) diameter cake tins with butter or oil spray and line the bases with baking paper.

For the cake, cut the preserved lemon in quarters, remove the flesh and finely chop the rind. In a food processor, blend the preserved lemon rind with the yoghurt and lemon juice until the mixture is smooth and the lemon rind almost invisible.

Sift the flour, caster sugar, baking powder, bicarbonate of soda and salt into the bowl of a stand mixer with the paddle attachment. Add the lemon zest and mix on low speed until well combined, about 1 minute.

Add the egg to the preserved lemon and yoghurt mixture and beat lightly with a fork. Set aside.

With the mixer on the lowest speed, incorporate the butter and vegetable oil into the flour mixture until the texture is crumb-like. Increase the speed to medium and mix for about 30 seconds, until the batter comes together and is slightly pale. Reduce the speed to low and slowly add the egg and yoghurt mixture in a steady stream. Thoroughly scrape down the side of the bowl.

Turn the mixer to high speed (cover the top with tea towels/dish towels if the batter reaches higher than a third of the bowl) and mix for 30 seconds, until the batter is smooth and fluffy. Divide equally between the prepared cake tins. Bake for 35 minutes or until a skewer inserted in the centre comes out clean.

Cool in the tins for 5 minutes, then turn out onto wire racks to cool completely. If preparing the cakes a day before, wrap them well with biodegradable plastic wrap. The cakes will remain fresh at steady room temperature for 1–2 days or in the freezer for 2 weeks. (If freezing, remove from the freezer on the morning of assembling the cake.)

Thoroughly clean and dry the mixer bowl if you only have one.

Lemon curd

120 g (4¼ oz) egg yolk (from about 6 eggs), at room temperature
225 g (8 oz) caster (superfine) sugar
1 g (1/32 oz) salt
zest of 2 lemons and 150 g (5½ oz) juice
90 g (3¼ oz) chilled unsalted butter, diced

Blackberry purée

130 g (4½ oz) fresh or frozen blackberries
40 g (1½ oz) caster (superfine) sugar
6 g (¼ oz) lemon juice

Olive oil and blackberry buttercream

200 g (7 oz) caster (superfine) sugar
100 g (3½ oz) water
200 g (7 oz) chilled egg white (from about 7 eggs)
2 g (1/16 oz) cream of tartar
4 g (⅛ oz) salt
450 g (1 lb) unsalted butter, softened and diced
zest of 1 lemon
50 g (1¾ oz) lemon juice
100 g (3½ oz) blackberry purée (see above)
25 g (1 oz) extra virgin olive oil

For the lemon curd, using a heatproof bowl that fits snugly over a saucepan while staying well clear of the bottom, whisk together the egg yolk, sugar and salt until well combined. Make a bain-marie by bringing water to a simmer in the saucepan and placing the bowl over it, ensuring the water doesn't touch the bottom of the bowl. Gradually add the lemon juice, whisking constantly to combine. Stir in the lemon zest and continue whisking as the mixture thickens. Once it has a custard-like consistency and sticks to the back of a spoon or has reached 75°C/165°F (this may take 10–15 minutes), remove the bowl from the heat.

Add the butter, stirring until it is completely melted and the curd is smooth. Strain through a fine-mesh sieve into a clean bowl. Cool to room temperature, then cover and refrigerate for at least 1 hour. The curd will continue to thicken as it cools.

For the blackberry purée, combine all the ingredients in a small saucepan over medium heat. Stir to coat the blackberries with the sugar. Cook, stirring occasionally, until the blackberries release their juices and become soft, 5–7 minutes. Use a potato masher or the back of a spoon to mash the berries and extract as much juice as possible. Cook for a further 5–7 minutes, allowing the mixture to thicken slightly. Remove from the heat and set aside for a few minutes to cool slightly.

Transfer the blackberry mixture to a blender or food processor and blend until smooth. Strain through a fine-mesh sieve into a bowl. Press down on the remaining blackberry solids to extract as much liquid as possible. Set aside to cool completely.

For the olive oil and blackberry buttercream, combine the caster sugar and water in a small saucepan and make sure there are no lumps of dry sugar (as this will cause the syrup to crystallise). Place the saucepan over medium heat and avoid stirring, to prevent the sugar from crystallising.

While the sugar syrup is heating, combine the egg white, cream of tartar and salt in the clean, dry mixer bowl and fit the whisk attachment to the stand mixer. Once the sugar syrup reaches 110°C/230°F, start whipping the egg white on high speed until it forms a light foam. Once the sugar syrup reaches 115°C/239°F, with the mixer on high speed, carefully pour the sugar syrup into the egg white in a thin, steady stream, taking care that it doesn't hit the whisk and scald you.

Continue whipping on high speed until stiff peaks form and the bowl is cool to the touch. Reduce the speed to medium and gradually add the butter, ensuring each piece is fully incorporated before adding the next. Add the lemon zest and juice, blackberry purée and olive oil. Whip on high speed for about 3 minutes or until smooth and creamy. >

To decorate (optional)
fresh blackberries
edible flower petals

To assemble the cake, trim the top of each cake evenly and halve each horizontally to get four thin layers. Use the bottom layer of one cake as the bottom and the bottom of the other as the top layer for the assembled cake. Place the bottom layer, cut side up, on a cake turntable.

Apply about a spatula full of buttercream, and spread it thinly over the top of the cake. It's okay if it extends slightly beyond the edges. Spread two generous tablespoons of lemon curd over the buttercream using a clean angled palette knife. Repeat this process twice with the next two cake layers, then add the top layer, with the cut side down.

Spread half the remaining buttercream over the cake, starting from the sides and spreading into a thin layer with the angled palette knife to cover the entire cake. This is known as a crumb coat, and will help seal in any loose crumbs, resulting in a clean finish when the final coat of buttercream is applied. Refrigerate the cake for 5 minutes before coating the entire cake with crumb-free buttercream. Decorate with fresh blackberries, a dollop of lemon curd and edible flower petals, if using.

Cherie Hausler

Layered rhubarb meringue cake (182)

Cook, baker, author and founder of All The Things

Barossa Valley, SA
Peramangk Country

For Cherie Hausler, the Barossa Valley is baked into all things. As she writes in her cookbook *A Plant-Based Farmhouse*, 'I honestly thought I could outrun my small-town upbringing when I left for bigger adventures – and I almost did, until I needed to find common ground with a new work colleague or flatmate, when the offer of a pot of tea or a homemade cake seemed to speak the language of instant community in a way I had completely underestimated.' For many years, she lived an itinerant life across Australia, London and Bangkok, but vestiges of a country upbringing followed her – from vegetables gardened in every possible nook, to generous gatherings that belied apartment living.

These days, in a farmhouse in the Barossa, Cherie produces bakes that look like they've been conjured by nature itself – which is not far from the truth. They are plant-based and inspired by the wealth of local produce – much of it gathered from her garden. One day might bring in a chocolate, rye and brown sugar cake cloaked in a cloud of woozy burnished meringue and roasted quince, another sourdough bagels enriched with fragrant home-milled flour and home-grown sultanas. 'I love cakes that are full of fragrance, that you can smell as you come to the table – all of your senses are excited to eat this thing. It's just a really nice conversation piece, when you let nature take the lead,' she says.

When Cherie travels interstate to teach workshops, something of the Barossa inevitably ends up in her suitcase. On one occasion, a Barossa-lemon tart arrived at the table festooned with a 'ute-load' of just-bloomed jasmine from a vine she spotted nearby. It sparked a conversation – which her bakes tend to do – and that's how she found her way into plant-based baking.

During her eleven years of trading at a farmers' market in the Barossa, conversations and requests from regulars led Cherie to tinker with alternative flour bases and, despite a self-confessed 'love affair with gluten', she developed a feeling for alternative flours and plant-based bakes. Instead of restrictions, Cherie saw opportunity. 'The things people were asking would send me on a different adventure. I've gathered my own experience in what I love eating but also what feels good to eat. Plus, she adds, 'The language of cake is universal.' Instant community, if you like.

ON TAKING DECORATING CUES FROM NATURE

'Something pops up in my garden and I think to myself, "That would look amazing on a cake". It's mostly about the flowers or the foliage. If I'm driving home and I see all these briar roses just shining their little gem-like flowers on the side of the road, I'll pull over – I've always got secateurs in the car. And the same thing goes whatever the season. In the Barossa, you look around in autumn and the leaves are doing that Technicolor-Dreamcoat scenario, so it doesn't take much to pick some lengths of all of these leaves and just wrap them around a cake, leave it a bit wild, and bring that to the table. It's almost like the floral arrangement arrives at the same time the cake does. It becomes a talking point, some fanfare. If you were to serve it plain, it doesn't have the same effect.'

'I love cakes that are full of fragrance – all of your senses are excited to eat this thing. It's just a really nice conversation piece, when you let nature take the lead.'

WORDS TO BAKE BY

'There's a whole new world that can be introduced to baking if you just look outside white wheat. You can make flour out of anything you like. I make a bespoke flour almost every week, and I literally throw in whole lentils, kukicha green tea, chamomile flowers, brown rice and chickpeas – whatever I have – and I blitz all of those up. You don't need to start thinking about making cakes with these dense, heavy flours that make you feel like you're being punished as you eat, but if you use this kind of mix as ten per cent of your overall bake, not only are you adding that phenomenal nutrition, but the flavour and the fragrance are so different from just using plain flour. You walk around and it all feels a little witchy, grabbing a few bits of this and a few bits of that. And then you go, "Wow, this is just based on intuition and what you have in your pantry," and it's just so fantastic to bring that diversity of fibre into your gut.'

Layered rhubarb meringue cake

Cherie Hausler
Profiled on page 180

SERVES 8–10
SPECIAL EQUIPMENT three 20 cm (8 inch) diameter springform cake tins, stand mixer with whisk attachment, mini kitchen blowtorch (optional)

Cake

- 4 cups (600 g) unbleached plain (all-purpose) flour
- 3 teaspoons bicarbonate of soda (baking soda)
- 3 teaspoons ground cinnamon
- 2 cups (320 g) rapadura sugar
- 300 g (10½ oz) soy milk
- 225 g (8 oz) extra virgin olive oil, plus extra for greasing
- 2 teaspoons vanilla bean paste
- zest and juice of 1 lemon
- 385 g (13½ oz) fresh rhubarb, cut into 1 cm (½ inch) slices

Meringue icing

- 240 g (8½ oz) cold aquafaba, drained from tinned chickpeas
- 265 g (9¼ oz) raw (demerara) sugar
- 3 g (⅛ oz) cream of tartar

To decorate
unsprayed flowers

If ever I'm in need of a showstopper cake, I just add meringue. In this case it's the literal (vegan) icing on the cake. It manages to take a simple cake that I might make for a morning tea with girlfriends into something that will happily sit all puffed up with pride at any special occasion. I absolutely love how toasted meringue makes its own art on a cake, but I can never resist adding an extra layer of decoration with fresh flowers too – why not, we're celebrating. Choose whatever flowers take your fancy, or if you have a garden that is in bloom, grab a cup of tea and some secateurs and wander through to see what smells and looks really beautiful on the day. Some of my favourites are almond blossom or heady, open heirloom roses, or even a single oversized dahlia looks stunning against the caramelised meringue. Remember to go for unsprayed flowers, even if you have no intention of eating them.

Rhubarb is one of our vegie garden staples that seems to like the spot it's found itself in, and so it generously offers up multicoloured stalks every season. This cake gives me the perfect use for homegrown produce, outside of jam and crumble making, which I love, but cake will always win the rhubarb stakes for me.

There are two further notes with this cake: the meringue is so easy to make, and – surprise – there's no egg whites in it. Read on.

Preheat the oven to 180°C/350°F fan-forced (200°C/400°F conventional). Line the base of three 20 cm (8 inch) springform cake tins with baking paper and grease the sides with extra virgin olive oil.

For the cake, sift the flour and bicarbonate of soda into a medium bowl. Add the cinnamon and rapadura sugar to the flour and stir through with a wooden spoon. Make a well in the middle of the dry ingredients with the back of the wooden spoon. Add the soy milk, olive oil, vanilla, and lemon juice and zest. Mix until completely blended into a smooth batter. Add the rhubarb and gently stir through one final time, taking care not to break up the rhubarb too much as you fold it into the batter.

Divide the cake batter equally between the prepared tins. Bake for 35–40 minutes, or until a skewer inserted in the centre of the cakes comes out clean. Cool in the tins for 10 minutes, then turn out onto a wire rack to cool completely.

To make the meringue icing, pour the cold aquafaba into the very clean, dry bowl of a stand mixer with the whisk attachment. Add the raw sugar and cream of tartar. Whisk the mixture on low speed for exactly 2 minutes. This will give the sugar a chance to dissolve into the aquafaba.

Increase the speed to medium and continue mixing for another 2 minutes. Finally, increase the speed all the way to high and whisk for 6 minutes. (You will likely have more meringue than you need for the cake, but it's better to be on the generous side when it comes to icing, I think. You cannot overbeat aquafaba in the same way you can egg whites, so if you leave it mixing for longer, that's fine, just don't under-mix it. The timing is, however, really important to the success of meringue. I make it just before I am going to ice the cakes and serve them; aquafaba is better if used closest to the time of eating.)

To assemble, place one cooled cake on a cake plate, bottom side facing up to give a nice flat surface. Top with a generous amount of the meringue, then add the cake. Repeat the process, then add a final layer of meringue to ice the top of the layered cake, creating peaks as high as you dare. You can also coat the whole cake in a layer of meringue, if you like.

If you have a mini kitchen blowtorch, you can use it to toast the layers of meringue icing until golden. Remember, it's not egg white, so it's perfectly safe to eat raw. Decorate with unsprayed flowers and serve immediately.

Chocolate cherry choux

Emelia Jackson
Profiled on page 52

MAKES 25
SPECIAL EQUIPMENT stand mixer with paddle attachment, rolling pin, 3 cm (1¼ inch) round cookie cutter, piping bags, 1 cm (½ inch) round piping nozzle and star piping nozzle

Craquelin
100 g (3½ oz) caster (superfine) sugar
100 g (3½ oz) unsalted butter, softened
100 g (3½ oz) plain (all-purpose) flour

Choux pastry
225 g (8 oz) water
100 g (3½ oz) unsalted butter
1 teaspoon caster (superfine) sugar
1 teaspoon fine salt
140 g (5 oz) plain (all-purpose) flour
265 g (9¼ oz) egg (from about 6 eggs)

This is my no-fail, use-for-everything choux recipe, developed through years of experimentation and tweaks. There are a few key steps for achieving the perfect choux. Many recipes call for milk, but I prefer just using water for the dough – it means there are fewer ingredients to measure, and the higher water content provides the perfect amount of steam for a tall rise. Choux buns can be baked and frozen for up to eight weeks – just allow them to thaw for 15 minutes before filling.

The craquelin is a secondary pastry – consisting of equal quantities of sugar, butter and flour – that essentially melts over the top of your choux pastry. It insulates the choux, giving you the perfect symmetrical rise. It's also delicious – a sweet, crackly coating that stays crisp even when the choux softens from its filling. The best thing about a craquelin (other than the taste)? It gives you the perfect choux every time. To understand the role of the craquelin, bake some choux with craquelin and some without, and you will see the massive difference it makes.

For the craquelin, mix the sugar, butter and flour together in a small bowl until the mixture has a paste-like consistency. (Or use a stand mixer if you are making a bulk batch. The equal quantities of the three ingredients means they can be easily multiplied.)

Using a rolling pin, roll the craquelin dough between two sheets of baking paper to 2.5 mm (⅛ inch) thick. Freeze for about 15 minutes to set. Using a 3 cm (1¼ inch) round cookie cutter, cut the dough into discs and then return to the freezer.

Preheat the oven to 160°C/325°F fan-forced (180°C/350°F conventional) and line two baking trays with baking paper or silicone baking mats.

For the choux pastry, combine the water, butter, sugar and salt in a medium saucepan and bring to a rapid boil over medium–high heat. Stir in the flour and cook this roux for 5–7 minutes, until a thick crust forms on the base of the pan (this ensures the flour is well hydrated, giving you the best and most consistent results).

Transfer the hot roux to the bowl of a stand mixer with the paddle attachment. Mix on medium speed for 3–5 minutes, until all of the steam dissipates – this ensures any excess moisture that could weigh down the choux evaporates and you are left with the lightest pastry. With the mixer running, add the egg, a little at a time, and mix until the dough comes together into a silky, shiny batter. It should just fall off a spatula when you lift the batter out of the bowl – not too thick and not too thin.

Transfer the choux to a piping bag fitted with a 1 cm (½ inch) round piping nozzle. Pipe the choux into 3 cm (1¼ inch) rounds, leaving plenty of space between them. Top each round with a disc of craquelin. >

Dark chocolate whipped ganache
1 large sheet leaf gelatine
600 ml (21 fl oz) whipping cream
1 teaspoon vanilla bean paste
pinch of salt
200 g (7 oz) dark chocolate, at least 54%, chopped

Bake for at least 45 minutes before opening the oven door. Choux pastry rises due to the build-up of steam in the oven, so if you open the door too soon, you risk the choux collapsing. I often find, especially in Australia, people don't bake their pastries for long enough. We want them to be dark – for a caramelised, complex flavour – rather than pale with flavour notes of flour. (And if they're not cooked enough, they can collapse while cooling, so please, please, pretty please cook your choux until they are dark golden brown.)

Once the choux are a deep golden, caramelised brown all over, remove from the oven and cool on the trays.

For the dark chocolate whipped ganache, soak the gelatine in a small bowl of iced water for 5 minutes to bloom. Once softened, squeeze out any excess water and set aside.

Meanwhile, combine the cream, vanilla and salt in a small saucepan over medium heat. Bring to a simmer, then remove from the heat. Add the gelatine and stir until completely melted. Put the chocolate in a bowl and pour in the hot cream. Once the chocolate has melted, whisk until well combined. Refrigerate overnight or until completely chilled.

Using a stand mixer with the whisk attachment, whisk the chilled ganache until stiff peaks form. Be careful not to over-whisk, as it can split quite easily (especially with particularly dark chocolate). If the ganache does split, you will need to melt it again and then let it chill before whisking. Spoon the whipped ganache into a piping bag fitted with a star nozzle and refrigerate until needed.

Morello cherry jam

680 g (1 lb 8 oz) pitted morello cherries in syrup

150 g (5½ oz) caster (superfine) sugar

1 vanilla bean, split lengthways and seeds scraped

juice of 1 lemon

To assemble (optional)

20 fresh cherries

If you need a shortcut, you can buy a quality cherry jam instead.

To make the morello cherry jam, pour the cherries with their syrup into a medium saucepan and sprinkle the sugar over the top. Add the vanilla bean and seeds and the lemon juice, then bring to the boil over medium–high heat. Reduce the heat to medium–low and simmer, stirring occasionally to prevent burning, for 45 minutes or until the jam is sticky and reduced.

Remove the vanilla bean. Pour the jam into a sterilised jar or clean airtight container and allow it to cool completely. (It can be stored in the fridge for a couple of weeks and is great on Greek-style yoghurt.)

To assemble, take a sharp serrated paring knife and cut the top off each choux bun. Fill the bottom of each choux with 1–2 teaspoons of morello cherry jam. Pipe the whipped ganache over the cherry compote so that it is tall, then put the top of the choux back on. Pipe a little more of the whipped ganache on top and press in a fresh cherry, if using, to garnish.

These are best eaten the day they are filled.

Emelia Jackson

Darren Purchese

Strawberry, chocolate and balsamic lamington stack (opposite)
Basque cheesecake (270)

Chef, author and
co-creator of
Studio Kitchen

Melbourne, Vic
Wurundjeri Country

Hear the name Darren Purchese and you'll immediately think of extravagant creations worthy of a *MasterChef* pressure test (and yes, he's often set them). But these days he's more interested in paring things back. 'My food's getting a little bit less fussy as I get older. I started off working in all the places, doing all the fancy stuff, and I really enjoyed that,' he says. 'But I think I get more joy now from encouraging people to bake more at home.'

In 2023, Darren and his wife and collaborator, fellow chef Cath Claringbold, closed their pastry institution Burch & Purchese, which they had opened in 2011 just as dessert mania began to explode in Australia. 'The two of us going to work early in the morning and the smell of Basque cheesecake never got tiring,' says Cath. 'All of those early bakes, things like canelé and cookies, they would set you up for the day. Because you knew people would be coming in just because they loved them. That was really rewarding.'

But with time, their simpler baking dream began to take over. 'We were missing the joy of baking other things. We've come full circle and we're happy for it, aren't we?' says Darren, who goes on to explain the joy of an old-school ginger fluff sponge he and Cath whipped up the other day, which is a possibility now that seven-day weeks are a thing of the past. Nowadays, they run Studio Kitchen, a website where they share their hefty back catalogue of recipes and new inspiration (plus a reliable smattering of 'my old tricky stuff' says Darren).

And as a judge on *The Great Australian Bake Off*, Darren is spreading his words of encouragement to home bakers through-out the country. 'I just love people cooking. I really appreciate anyone who takes time and effort to make something. I appreciate that more than a fancy dish. It means more to me.'

IT'S NOT WHAT YOU BAKE, BUT WHO YOU'RE BAKING IT FOR

'Baking always brings people together and it always sparks something. Cath and I make a lot of our content at home. And what do we do with it? We drop it off at the cafe downstairs or at a neighbour's, and that sparks a conversation and then a connection and then you start up relationships with people. We just want to encourage as many people as possible to get in the kitchen and bake – and preferably bake for someone. Make it with love and think about the person you're baking it for. And that's it. It's that simple.'

WORDS TO BAKE BY

'I always plan my baking in advance by deciding on a recipe and working it through in my head. I'll make and prepare components in advance to ensure I have enough time on the day to assemble my creation. When deciding on flavours for my bakes, I love to incorporate as many local and fresh ingredients as I can, and this often gives me inspiration when designing dishes.'

Strawberry, chocolate and balsamic lamington stack

SERVES 12

SPECIAL EQUIPMENT two 22 cm (8½ inch) diameter springform cake tins (or one tin, used twice), stand mixer with whisk attachment, blender, stick blender (optional), sugar or digital thermometer, angled palette knife, piping bag and wide plain nozzle

Strawberry, chocolate and balsamic vinegar jam
250 g (9 oz) ripe strawberries
175 g (6 oz) caster (superfine) sugar
2.5 g (¹⁄₁₆ oz) pectin powder (e.g. Jamsetta)
25 g (1 oz) glucose syrup
20 g (¾ fl oz) balsamic vinegar
40 g (1½ oz) dark chocolate, at least 55%, buttons or coarsely chopped

Lamington sponge
225 g (8 oz) unsalted butter, plus extra for greasing
270 g (9½ oz) egg white (from about 9 eggs)
5 g (⅛ oz) cream of tartar
270 g (9½ oz) caster (superfine) sugar
210 g (7½ oz) plain (all-purpose) flour
8 g (¼ oz) baking powder
3 g (⅛ oz) sea salt
180 g (6¼ oz) egg yolk (from about 9 eggs)
5 g (⅛ oz) vanilla bean paste

Nothing says celebration like this impressive lamington layer cake. It has all the fun and delicious joy of lamingtons but on a much grander scale. Things get lively once you taste the unique piquancy of the strawberry, chocolate and balsamic vinegar jam, with the luxurious mascarpone cream that cuts through the richness and acidity. There are a few steps involved, so get ahead by making the jam a day or two ahead of time. You can even make the first phase of the white chocolate, vanilla and mascarpone cream the day before assembly, ready for whisking on the day.

For the strawberry, chocolate and balsamic vinegar jam, finely chop the strawberries, then crush with a fork or pulse quickly in a blender. You don't want to purée the fruit – we are after a blend of juices and small chunks. Mix the sugar with the pectin in a medium bowl and combine this and the strawberries in a large heavy-based saucepan over medium–high heat. Add the glucose and continue cooking, stirring regularly with a heat-resistant spatula to ensure the jam doesn't stick or burn. We are trying to cook the jam quickly to retain the vibrancy of the fruit. Once the jam comes to the boil, add the vinegar. Continue to cook and stir the jam, taking care of splatters, until it reaches 103°C/217°F (using a digital or sugar thermometer to measure the temperature accurately). Remove from the heat.

Put the chocolate in a heat-resistant bowl and pour 100 g (3½ oz) of the hot jam over it. Use a spatula to mix well and melt the chocolate. At this stage, you can use a stick blender to fully emulsify the chocolate and jam. Return this mixture to the remaining jam and mix well with a spatula. Pour the jam into sterilised jars or airtight containers. Seal and leave to cool.

For the lamington sponge, grease two 22 cm (8½ inch) diameter springform cake tins with butter and neatly line the bases and sides with baking paper. If you only have one tin, then halve the sponge quantities and make twice, reusing the tin for the second batch. Preheat your oven to 190°C/375°F fan-forced (210°C/400°F conventional).

Melt the butter in a small saucepan over medium–low heat and set aside to cool. Combine the egg white and cream of tartar in a stand mixer with the whisk attachment and whip together on medium speed until stiff. With the mixer still running, gradually add the sugar, 1 tablespoon at a time, over about 5 minutes.

Meanwhile, sift the flour and baking powder into a medium bowl and add the salt.

Add the egg yolk and vanilla to the still whisking meringue and whisk on medium speed for 20 seconds. Remove the bowl from the machine, sift in half the flour mixture and fold in gently with a spatula. Sift in the remaining flour and fold in with the spatula. Take a ladleful of the batter, mix it into the cooled melted butter, then return this to the batter and fold in gently. >

White chocolate, vanilla
and mascarpone cream
260 g (9¼ oz) whipping cream
1 vanilla bean, split lengthways
    and seeds scraped
finely grated zest of ½ orange
1 star anise, freshly grated
90 g (3¼ oz) white chocolate,
    melted
75 g (2¾ oz) mascarpone cheese

Chocolate soaking sauce
90 g (3¼ oz) unsweetened cocoa
    powder
270 g (9½ oz) caster (superfine)
    sugar
210 g (7½ oz) water
160 g (5¾ oz) pouring cream

To finish
250 g (9 oz) desiccated coconut
small handful of fresh strawberries,
    half of them hulled and some
    halved lengthways and/or sliced

Divide the batter evenly between your prepared tins and bake for 30 minutes, or until the cakes are a light golden brown on top and a skewer gently inserted into the centre comes out clean. Cool in the tins for 15 minutes, then release the clip and turn the cakes out onto a wire rack. Remove the baking paper and leave to cool completely.

For the white chocolate, vanilla and mascarpone cream, heat 100 ml (3½ fl oz) of the cream with the vanilla bean and seeds, orange zest and star anise in a small saucepan over medium heat. Bring to the boil, then remove from the heat and leave to infuse for 10 minutes. Return to the boil, then strain through a sieve onto the white chocolate. Leave to sit for 30 seconds before stirring well with a spatula to combine. Leave to cool for 20 minutes, then fold in the cold mascarpone and the remaining cream. Cover and refrigerate for at least 1 hour.

To make the chocolate soaking sauce, mix the cocoa powder with the sugar in a medium bowl and add the water, stirring to eliminate any lumps and to make a paste. Transfer to a medium heavy-based saucepan and add the cream, mixing well with a spatula. Bring to the boil over medium heat, stirring constantly with a heat-resistant spatula. Continue to cook for 1–2 minutes (to cook out the cocoa powder), stirring constantly. Strain through a sieve into a wide dish. Set aside.

To cover the sponges, pour half the desiccated coconut onto a wide plate or dish. Take a cooled sponge and dip it into the warm chocolate soaking sauce. Leave for a minute before gently flipping it to ensure the entire surface of the sponge is soaked and covered in the sauce. Lift the sponge out and drain off the excess before placing it in the coconut. Ensure an even covering of coconut all over. Place the sponge on a sheet of baking paper and repeat with the remaining sponge, replenishing the desiccated coconut as needed.

To finish the white chocolate, vanilla and mascarpone cream, transfer the chilled cream to a stand mixer with the whisk attachment and whip until thick and smooth. Do not overwhip or it may curdle. Spoon the cream into a piping bag fitted with a wide plain piping nozzle.

To assemble the lamington stack, put one sponge on a serving plate and put 1 tablespoon of jam in the centre. Use an angled palette knife to spread the jam evenly to within 1 cm (½ inch) of the edge of the sponge. Use more jam if needed, but don't put too much on or it will drip out (unless you like it that way). Pipe a ring of cream around the sponge 1 cm from the edge, then cover the top with the remaining cream. Place the second sponge on top of the cream and press down slightly. Top the cake with fresh strawberries and refrigerate for 30 minutes before serving.

Something *Savoury*

199 Spinach, leek and smoked cheddar cheese slab pie

203 Feta and dill biscuits with harissa honey butter

204 Little Picket potato bread with roasted garlic butter and parsley

206 Tomato, herb and quark tart

213 Fig-leaf sourdough tin loaf

215 Burnt fenugreek and sesame loaf

218 Jerusalem artichoke, chilli greens and goat's cheese focaccias

224 A1 pies, three ways (Za'atar manouche, Kafta manouche, Haloumi pies)

230 Pea and feta tart

Danielle Alvarez

Spinach, leek and smoked cheddar cheese slab pie (opposite)
Feta and dill biscuits with harissa honey butter (203)

Chef, recipe developer and cookbook author

Sydney, NSW
Gadigal Country

Danielle Alvarez distinctly recalls the formative moment she bit into a plum galette. It was while she was working in her native US in the celebrated kitchen of Alice Waters' Chez Panisse. 'It just felt like, how could so few ingredients be the most perfect bite you've ever had? And the most evocative of a moment in time? It was plum season and the plums were perfect, so that's what went on the galette. And it was always spectacular,' she says. It's this magical confluence she's been chasing in her baking ever since, using pastry as a canvas to show off the seasons.

Danielle is a chef who bakes – and who bakes exceptionally well. What she brings to the craft is an intuitive touch and flavour. In spades. Both qualities are gleaned as much from her training at top restaurants (or indeed her skill at taking a restaurant to the top, as she did when she moved to Australia to helm Fred's in Sydney) as from growing up in a large Cuban–American family, helping her mum and grandmother in the kitchen.

The galette, in a way, has been emblematic. 'My vibe tends to be more of a very simple, rustic sort of bake,' says Danielle. 'I always come to baking from a savoury cook's mentality, because that's who I am first and foremost. I like to add and taste and make things the way that I cook, as opposed to traditional baking, which says, "This is a recipe, don't deviate,"' she adds, before clarifying: 'I'm not here tasting bits of raw flour, but I try different flavour combinations that I know would work in another savoury dish, and nine times out of ten they also work in a baked dish.'

For Danielle, baking is to play, confidently. 'Baking is a lot about repetition, and technique is about repetition and understanding how things work,' she says. 'So when you understand the two sides of it, that's when the technical and that creative whimsy can come together.'

NOTES ON TEMPERATURE

'The temperature of your ingredients is super important. I know it took me years to really understand why it's so important for things like eggs and butter to be completely on temperature when you're making a cake. It's because it's an emulsion of ingredients, and when something is a little bit too cold or a little bit too warm, it's never going to combine perfectly, or it will split or it will break. It's not the end of the world. It'll still be good, but it's not as perfect as it can be. I always forget to leave eggs and butter out to get to room temperature, so here's what I do. With eggs, just put them in a cup of warm water and they'll come up to room temperature in a few minutes inside their shell. For butter, warm up a bowl in an oven or something, just so it's warm, and place it face down over your butter. The ambient heat will soften it really quickly.'

WORDS TO BAKE BY

'Butter, oil, a couple of eggs, flour, you know, a few little flavouring things here and there – with just these few ingredients you can make something amazing. At school, everyone would always bring store- or bakery-bought cupcakes for their birthdays, but my mum insisted on making them. I think she was coming from an economical standpoint, but they were always the ones that everyone loved the most. From then on, I could see that it actually isn't about how perfect something looks, it's about how delicious it is. And that's stayed with me through all of my cooking, but especially in baking. I'm not the kind of pastry chef who makes everything look really perfect. I'm just about: make it really, really delicious and people will love it.'

Spinach, leek and smoked cheddar cheese slab pie

SERVES 6–8
SPECIAL EQUIPMENT rolling pin, pastry brush, cheesecloth (optional)

But this can be a quick bake if you buy puff pastry.

This pie combines a few of my favourite things: my home-made flaky pastry, greens, and smoke in the way of smoked cheddar cheese. The pastry is simple to make and a signature recipe for me, but if you're intimidated by it, feel free to buy puff pastry instead. I've made this with both, and both ways are delicious. The important things to remember when making and baking pastry is that you want the ingredients for the pastry to be cold and remain cold while you make the dough, but when it's all assembled and ready to bake, you want your oven hot. The intense heat means the water trapped in the butter quickly melts, then steams, puffing up the flaky layers of dough. Once this happens, we turn the oven temperature down for a longer, slower bake to keep everything crispy. >

Pastry

- 340 g (12 oz) plain (all-purpose) flour, plus extra for dusting
- 1 teaspoon fine sea salt
- 1 tablespoon sugar
- 250 g (9 oz) chilled unsalted butter, diced
- 140–160 ml (4¾–5 fl oz) chilled water

Filling

- 1 tablespoon extra virgin olive oil
- 2 cups (200 g) thinly sliced leek (from about 1 large leek)
- 3 garlic cloves, very finely chopped
- pinch each of salt and freshly ground black pepper
- 280 g (10 oz) spinach leaves, chopped
- 50 g (1¾ oz) parmesan cheese, grated
- 1 egg, lightly beaten
- ⅛ teaspoon freshly grated nutmeg
- 150 g (5½ oz) smoked cheddar cheese, coarsely grated
- 1 tablespoon 'Everything bagel seasoning', or sesame seeds, flaky salt and black pepper (optional)

Egg wash

- 1 egg
- 1 teaspoon water

To serve (optional)

- Hot sauce

Start by making the pastry. Combine the flour, salt and sugar in a bowl and stir together. Add the diced butter and rub it through with your clean fingertips. You want some large chunks of butter and some finer mealier pieces; it should not be uniform.

Start by adding 140 ml (4¾ fl oz) of the cold water and stir to combine, then tip onto your clean work surface. Knead the dough together a few times. If it's not holding together, add a bit more cold water until it does. Press the dough into a rectangle, then cut the rectangle in half and stack the halves on top of each other. Press again and repeat this once more. Shape into a rectangle, wrap in baking paper and refrigerate for at least 1 hour or overnight.

Dust your work surface well with flour. Cut your dough in half and roll each half out to 2–3 mm (1/16–⅛ inch) thick. Cut both pieces into rectangles about 30 × 20 cm (12 × 8 inches). Place a sheet of baking paper between the rectangles and refrigerate until ready to bake. Wrap any trimmed-off dough in baking paper and freeze for another use.

To make the filling, heat the oil in a medium high-sided frying pan over medium heat, add the leek and garlic and season with the salt and pepper. Sauté for 3–4 minutes, until the leek is soft and tender but not browning. Stir in the spinach and cook for a minute until wilted. Transfer to a tray or bowl to cool completely.

When completely cooled, squeeze the mixture in your hands or through a piece of cheesecloth to extract as much water as possible. Taste and add more salt if needed. Add the parmesan, egg and nutmeg and stir to combine. Set aside.

Preheat the oven to 180°C/350°F fan-forced (200°C/400°F conventional).

Make the egg wash by lightly beating the egg with the water. Set aside.

To assemble, lay one sheet of your pastry on a sheet of baking paper, then place on a baking tray. Use a pastry brush to brush the edge of the pastry with the egg wash. Scatter half the smoked cheddar over the pastry, keeping it mostly clear of the egg wash. Scatter the spinach filling on top of the cheese, trying to spread it evenly. Scatter the remaining smoked cheddar over the spinach.

Top with your second sheet of pastry and press the edges together all the way around by pushing down with the tines of a fork.

Cut a small 'X' in the centre, then brush with the remaining egg wash. Sprinkle bagel seasoning over the top, if using.

Bake for 15 minutes, then reduce the heat to 160°C/325°F fan-forced (180°C/350°F conventional) and bake for a further 40–45 minutes, until the top is a deep golden brown. Carefully slip the pie off the tray and baking paper onto a wire rack to cool slightly.

To serve, cut into squares and serve warm, perhaps with hot sauce.

Something Savoury

Feta and dill biscuits with harissa honey butter

Danielle Alvarez
Profiled on page 198

MAKES 8
SPECIAL EQUIPMENT rolling pin, dough scraper, pastry brush (optional)

The key to delicate and light biscuits is keeping all the ingredients super cold until you bake them, and treating the dough delicately so as not to develop the gluten.

Feta and dill biscuits
300 g (10½ oz) plain (all-purpose) flour, plus extra for dusting
2 teaspoons baking powder
½ teaspoon fine sea salt
1 tablespoon sugar
1½ tablespoons chopped fresh dill sprigs
120 g (4¼ oz) butter, frozen
1 teaspoon white vinegar
170 ml chilled water
80 g (2¾ oz) sheep's milk feta cheese, crumbled
2 tablespoons pouring cream (optional)
freshly ground black pepper
sea salt flakes

Harissa honey butter
90 g (3¼ oz) butter, at room temperature
25 g (1 oz) honey
15 g (½ oz) harissa paste
pinch of sea salt

In America (where I'm from), what people call biscuits are similar in their ingredients and makeup to scones, but biscuits are typically served to accompany savoury foods, such as chicken or fried steak with gravy, or sausages for breakfast, while scones are usually served with jam and cream. I've tried to merge the savoury and the sweet in these biscuits, even if they are primarily savoury. The warming harissa heat comes through at the end of the bite and works perfectly with the sweet honey and butter and the salty feta for a truly surprising and utterly delicious combination. I think these biscuits are best served straight from the oven for breakfast alongside other delights, but you decide where they fit into your day.

Preheat your oven to 200°C/400°F fan-forced (220°C/425°F conventional) and line a baking tray with baking paper.

For the feta and dill biscuits, whisk together the flour, baking powder, salt, sugar and dill in a large bowl.

Coarsely grate the butter, keeping it as close to frozen as possible. If you feel it has softened, return the grated butter to the freezer to firm up again. Toss the frozen butter shavings with the dry ingredients.

Add the vinegar to the chilled water, pour onto the butter and flour mix and stir through using a spatula (the mixture will still be quite crumbly). Tip out onto a lightly floured work surface and knead the dough together a few times to just bring it together (when I say 'knead', I mean just press it together, rather than traditional bread kneading where you push and pull the dough with the heel of your hand). It should still be very shaggy and messy but mostly holding together.

Dust the top with more flour if needed, then use a rolling pin to roll out to a rectangle about 30 × 20 cm (12 × 8 inches). Sprinkle the feta on top of the dough, then cut the dough into three equal pieces. Stack those on top of each other and press those pieces together. Use a dough scraper to help push the sides in a bit so everything is flush.

Dust your rolling pin with flour and roll your dough stack to 2.5–3 cm (1–1¼ inches) tall. Use a dough scraper or knife to cut the dough into four squares, then cut each square diagonally to give two triangles.

Place the triangles on the baking tray. It's okay for them to be snug, but they shouldn't touch. If you have cream, use it to brush the tops. Sprinkle with black pepper and flaky sea salt.

Bake for 20–25 minutes, until the tops are golden brown and the biscuits feel light when you pick them up.

Make the harissa honey butter while the biscuits are baking. Stir together all the ingredients until smooth.

Serve your hot biscuits with the harissa honey butter and enjoy.

Little Picket potato bread with roasted garlic butter and parsley

Jo Barrett
Profiled on page 96

MAKES 20 buns
SPECIAL EQUIPMENT stand mixer with dough hook attachment, pastry brush, potato ricer

Dough
220 g (7¾ oz) potatoes
450 g (1 lb) plain (all-purpose) flour, plus extra for dusting
2 eggs
185 g (6½ oz) milk
25 g (1 oz) sugar
6 g (¼ oz) salt
115 g (4 oz) unsalted butter, softened
oil, for greasing

Ferment
60 g (2¼ oz) plain (all-purpose) flour
60 g (2¼ oz) water
7 g (¼ oz) dried yeast

At the restaurant I served these warm from the oven, doused in butter. They remind me of end-of-year basketball break-ups as a kid when someone would order shitty pizzas. I would bypass the pizza and go for the garlic bread wrapped in foil. It was oily as hell, but somehow still warm, fluffy and soft. I love texture in food, and it seems like I always have. This dough is enriched with butter and eggs, like a light brioche. The potato adds moisture, and its starch makes the fine fluffy texture. Rather than with garlic, you can flavour the butter however you desire – with 'nduja, herbs, olives or anchovies, say – and the bread will become the carrier for that flavour. So much so that it easily can be used for desserts too, like an ice-cream sandwich, served with custard. Even better, I sometimes fry the dough to make doughnuts and fill them with rice pudding.

For the dough, first peel and chop the potatoes into roughly 2 cm (¾ inch) cubes. Place in a small saucepan, cover with cold water and gently simmer over medium heat until tender and cooked through, 20–25 minutes. Drain and allow to cool for a moment before pressing through a potato ricer (or use a masher or fork). Measure out 200 g (7 oz) to use and set aside to cool.

For the ferment, mix all the ingredients in a small bowl to form a smooth paste. Cover and set aside until almost doubled in size, about 15 minutes.

Continue with the dough while the ferment is developing. Combine the flour, eggs, milk, sugar and salt in the bowl of a stand mixer with the dough hook attachment and mix on low speed to form a dough. Once the dough comes together, add the ferment. Mix for 2–3 minutes on medium speed, until completely combined and the dough feels elastic when stretched. Continue to mix on medium speed while gradually adding the butter until it is completely incorporated.

When the dough begins to come away from the side of the bowl and you can stretch a piece of it between your fingers so that it holds a 'window' of very thin dough without breaking, add the potato. Mix until evenly dispersed and smooth.

Lightly oil a large bowl, transfer the dough to the bowl, then cover with a clean tea towel (dish towel) and set aside at room temperature to rest for 1 hour. Lift and fold the outer edges of the dough over the centre to form a ball and knock out some gas. Rest for a further 30 minutes, then repeat the folding and degassing one more time.

Lightly spray two baking trays, then line them with baking paper and lightly spray the paper with oil. Lightly dust a work surface with flour and turn the degassed dough out onto it. Divide the dough into 20 portions of about 60 g (2¼ oz) each. Cup and rotate each piece anticlockwise with your hand to stretch the dough into a smooth, firm ball. The edge of your thumb and fingertips will shift the dough in a circle and you will feel the ball move and form against your palm. Place the shaped balls on your prepared baking trays. If you would like perfectly round rolls, leave a 10 cm (4 inch) gap between each ball. If you would like them to bake into each other to form pull-apart buns, place them 5 cm (2 inches) apart.

Egg wash
1 egg
1 tablespoon milk
pinch of salt

Garlic butter
200 g (7 oz) unsalted butter
2 garlic cloves, very thinly sliced
pinch of salt
1 tablespoon finely chopped curly parsley
1 tablespoon thinly snipped chives
freshly ground black pepper

Cover loosely with biodegradable plastic wrap or a beeswax cloth and set aside to prove at room temperature for 1–1½ hours, or until doubled in size. They will feel fluffy and springy when pressed gently.

Preheat the oven to 200°C/400°F fan-forced (220°C/425°F conventional).

Make the egg wash by mixing the egg, milk and salt until completely combined. Using a pastry brush, gently brush the tops of the dough with a light covering of egg wash.

Bake for 18–20 minutes or until golden brown. The buns should sound hollow when tapped.

Make the garlic butter while the buns are cooking. Heat the butter in a small saucepan over low heat, stirring as it begins to bubble. When it starts to turn golden brown, remove from the heat. Carefully stir in the garlic (it will make the butter foam) and the salt.

To serve, spoon the garlic butter generously over the buns to coat them, then sprinkle with the parsley, chives and pepper.

Tomato, herb and quark tart

Natasha Brownfield
Profiled on page 170

SERVES 12
SPECIAL EQUIPMENT 26 cm (10½ inch) diameter tart (flan) tin, stick blender (optional), rolling pin, pastry brush (optional), sugar thermometer, baking weights (e.g. dried legumes), pastry knife, kitchen scissors

Flaky pastry
250 g (9 oz) plain (all-purpose) flour
50 g (1¾ oz) whole spelt flour
1½ teaspoons fine salt
150 g (5½ oz) unsalted butter
90 g (3¼ oz) chilled water, plus extra as needed

You can bake the flaky pastry base a day or two in advance and store it at room temperature in an airtight container.

This is the first quiche I put on the menu when I opened my shop, a simple tart for peak summer breakfasts, lunches and dinners. When odd-shaped tomatoes are gleaming, I slice and lightly dress them with plenty of flaky salt, then nestle them on a bed of sharp and garlicky whipped quark. The quiche custard merely binds it all together – though a crack-free and leak-proof tart shell will be the main hurdle here (don't worry, there's troubleshooting advice in the recipe). I like to dress it with a fluffy grating of any sharp hard cheese, such as gruyère or pecorino, followed by a pillow of soft herbs, such as fine chives, dill sprigs and teeny basil leaves.

For the flaky pastry, combine the flours and salt in a large bowl that will fit in your freezer. Slice the butter into thin shards, add them to the bowl and set aside in the freezer for at least 30 minutes.

Using a pastry knife, chop the butter into the flour until the mixture has a sandy texture, with pea-sized butter chunks suspended throughout. I recommend setting it aside in the freezer again for a further 10 minutes.

Form a well in the centre of the flour mixture and add the cold water, gathering and pressing the ingredients together with clean hands until you can just form a rough dough. Be careful not to overwork the dough, or it will lose its flakiness.

If the dough feels slightly dry, sprinkle an additional tablespoon of chilled water over it and incorporate it by hand. Press the dough into a rough flattened disc, seal tightly in biodegradable plastic wrap, pressing out any cracks by hand, and refrigerate for 1 hour.

Lightly dust a work surface with extra flour and, using a rolling pin, roll out the pastry into a round about 30 cm (12 inches) in diameter and 2 mm (1/16 inch) thick. Carefully lift the pastry and drape it gently over a 26 cm (10½ inch) tart (flan) tin. Tuck the pastry snugly into the corner and use a pair of kitchen scissors to trim the edges, leaving an overhang of about 1 cm (½ inch). You can keep this stiffened upright edge to create more depth for filling. Refrigerate for about 15 minutes before blind baking.

Preheat the oven to 160°C/325°F fan-forced (180°C/350°F conventional).

Line the base with foil and fill with baking weights such as dried beans. Blind bake for about 40 minutes, then remove the foil and baking weights and bake for a further 15–20 minutes, until golden. I like to bake my pastry quite dark. (If any cracks have formed, you can seal them at this point by mixing an egg with 1 teaspoon of water, brushing it over the hole using a pastry brush and returning to the oven for a couple of minutes. Keep applying egg wash until the cracks are sealed.) Set aside to cool.

Reduce the oven temperature to 150°C/300°F fan-forced (170°C/350°F conventional).

Filling
250–300 g (9–10½ oz) quark
1 teaspoon sea salt flakes, plus extra to taste
3 garlic cloves, crushed
5–6 ripe tomatoes, sliced
freshly ground black pepper, to taste
handful of basil leaves
small handful of dill
small handful of chives, thinly snipped
gruyère or pecorino, to garnish

Quiche custard
225 g (8 oz) pouring cream
225 g (8 oz) egg (from about 5 eggs)
¾ teaspoon fine salt
pinch of freshly grated nutmeg
freshly ground black pepper, to taste

Meanwhile, begin preparing the filling. In a small bowl, mix the quark with the salt and two-thirds of the garlic and set aside.

Sprinkle the tomato slices with sea salt and freshly ground black pepper, plus the remaining garlic. I like to sprinkle the garlic with the salt to chill it out a touch, but you can make this as garlicky as you like.

For the quiche custard, use a hand whisk or stick blender to combine all the ingredients in a medium bowl.

To assemble the quiche, spread or pipe the garlicky quark over the base of the tart shell – it will act as a slight barrier between the watery tomatoes and the crisp pastry base. Set aside a few herb leaves to serve, then layer the remainder over the quark, followed by the seasoned tomato slices.

Fill the tart with the custard, allowing it to settle into the nooks before filling it all the way to the brim.

Bake for 45 minutes, until no custard rushes to the top when you poke it with a sharp knife, or a thermometer reads 70–80°C/160–175°F. Cool in the tin for 15 minutes, then carefully transfer to a wire rack to cool completely.

To serve, garnish the quiche with a grating of gruyère or pecorino and your reserved herbs. For perfect slices, cut with a sharp serrated knife. It's best eaten fresh, at room temperature for lunch or dinner.

Kimmy Gastmeier

Fig-leaf sourdough tin loaf (213)
Cherry pie (262)

Founder and head baker,
Cherry Moon General Store

Sydney, NSW
Gadigal Country

For Kimmy Gastmeier, baking has been a return to nature. 'I had one of those "aha moments" when I was working with sourdough,' she says. 'It was the living fermentation in my hands. It felt right and it felt purposeful.' The long journey to Cherry Moon, her wood-fired bakery and general store in Annandale, Sydney, began when she took a break from ten years in some of the city's top kitchens. She had honed her craft – but at a cost. 'I was really pushed to the limit with my health – and I don't regret a single moment I spent in any of those kitchens, but when you're in the grind, it's not our true nature,' she says. 'It was an incredible experience, but I just felt like I was backing everybody else's dream. I had this deep yearning, this desire to create something of my own.'

Kimmy uprooted herself and headed west to the Blue Mountains to hit pause, and set up as a sole trader, armed with a motorbike with a bag of flour on the back and a self-built mud-brick oven. 'What I really loved about being on my own journey was I had so much freedom. I was living by the skin of my teeth. I was living on the edge, when you don't know what an ingredient is going to do. I felt like I was just on a real, raw journey. It was very humbling to strip away the identity of being a chef,' she says. She got back to the roots of what it meant to cook, to be part of a community, and work with local sources of food, which would take her onwards over the years to the Northern Territory and back home to New Zealand, where she learned about native ingredients, food culture and preparations from the traditional custodians of the lands.

Today, as owner of Cherry Moon, Kimmy's purpose is to show care for the community and her team by bringing nourishing traditions back into urban life, one wood-fired loaf of sourdough pressed with a fig leaf, one oozing cherry pie, one crisp, seeded focaccia at a time. 'I feel like, when I look at my business, it was really built on when I stopped and I checked in with: "What are my values? What's my purpose? And what do I want to leave behind and what do I want to contribute?"' she says. Both the heart and hearth of the bakery is Apollonia, the wood-fired oven built in the revered Alan Scott style, complete with an upcycled oven door from late-nineteenth-century Ballarat (see opposite).

And though the challenges of small business ownership are real and various, Kimmy loops back to that purpose – it's people, nature and connection over tasks and the grind. 'Nature showed me so much when I stopped – and everyone's got that available to them. It's so hard to remember when we're up against everything,' she says. 'But as humans we are so capable, creative and connected.'

'There's that opportunity for people to get back into the old-school ways of cooking ... it's got a real earthiness to it, like that feeling when you're drinking tea out of a ceramic cup.'

WORDS TO BAKE BY

'I want people to come to Cherry Moon and walk away feeling inspired and reminded of nature. We're in the city and we're in this hustle-bustle grind, but our tasks are not the most important thing. It's caring for others, and for me it's showing that connection through food. If people come by and get the fig-leaf sourdough, maybe they can see that little bit of care that's gone in, that little reminder of nature – it's just a tiny little kiss from us to them. When I go into a store or if I'm out in nature, it's just the real simple little things that I remember – how someone took their time with you in the store, it's that care. I feel like the fig leaf on our bread (page 213) can offer that to people.'

NOTES ON WOOD-FIRED BAKING

'*The Bread Builders* is a book by Alan Scott and Daniel Wing about wood-fired ovens and baking. It was like my bible; I carried it around for years dreaming about building my own one day. Building the oven is one thing – it's got three layers of insulation – but then there's keeping it going. You light the fire directly on the oven floor – we're burning like 500°C (930°F) every day and about 60 kilos (130 pounds) of wood. It never stops, day in and day out, but it's a very romantic way of cooking because you're right on the edge. You've got to engage, you've got to be focused. It's a real fun wave to ride when you know what you're doing, and I love that we've created something like that in Sydney and that there's that opportunity for people to get back into the old-school ways of cooking. You can see it. You can taste it. I feel like it's got a real earthiness to it, like that feeling when you're drinking tea out of a ceramic cup.'

Fig-leaf sourdough tin loaf

Kimmy Gastmeier
Profiled on page 210

MAKES two loaves
SPECIAL EQUIPMENT two 18 × 38 cm (7 × 15 inch) bread tins about 11 cm (4¼ inches) deep, heavy-based, black steel or cast-iron baking tray (to imitate the fire bricks in a wood-fired oven), dough scraper, sugar thermometer

baker's flour, for dusting
2 fig leaves

To feed your starter (or see below)
75 g (2¾ oz) baker's flour
75 g (2¾ oz) water

Bread dough
675 g (1 lb 8 oz) water (at about 17°C/63°F in summer and 23°C/73°F in winter)
150 g (5½ oz) sourdough starter
750 g (1 lb 10 oz) khorosan flour, or white baker's flour
15 g (½ oz) Murray River pink salt

We're using a sourdough starter, which makes this a 3-day process. If you prefer using yeast (see below), this bread can be made in a day.

This recipe is working with 90 per cent hydration. Depending on weather and humidity, this may vary. For the yeast version, decrease the water to 85 per cent (i.e. 638 g/1 lb 6½ oz water, 750 g/1 lb 10 oz flour) and use 12.5 g (½ oz) fresh yeast or 6 g (¼ oz) dried yeast.

This loaf truly represents the essence of Cherry Moon, connecting nature and an everyday staple back into our lives and onto our table. The elements of the wood fire, natural fermentation and the fig leaf leave an earthy, heartfelt and floral–sweet scent. Our sourdough ferments over two days, which makes it more nourishing and easier to digest. Building a fire each day to create the heat for the next day's bake in our purpose-built wood-fired oven, Apollonia, is such a romantic way of cooking. We enjoy making the bread as much as we do eating it. We hope you do too – here's a recipe adapted for the home oven.

First feed your starter. Make sure you feed your starter 2 days before making this recipe. If you need to bring it back to its peak activity and strength, feed your starter twice a day, 3 days in advance, as you will need 150 g (5½ oz) for this recipe.

I feed 50 per cent flour and 50 per cent water (making sure it's double the starter base weight), then leave it out at room temperature until I see bubbles are starting to form. This will take about 1 hour. Then I put it in the fridge overnight. The next day it should have doubled in size. It should be full of bubbles, feel happy, soft and airy but have a good strength to touch. Take it out of the fridge about 30 minutes before using it (or earlier in cooler seasons).

To start making the bread dough, weigh the water into a medium–large bowl. Add the starter – if it's healthy it will float (or if using yeast instead, add it at this point; see the note below).

Add the flour and mix by hand until all the ingredients are combined. It will feel wet and sticky, but with every 30-minute rest it will feel more and more like dough. (It helps to have wet hands when handling the dough, so during this process, keep a jug of water handy and pop your dough scraper inside.) This stage is only to bring all the ingredients together (minus the salt) and not about the gluten development. Let the dough rest (this stage is called 'autolyse') for 30 minutes. Keep a jug of water handy with a dough scraper in it. I like to work the dough with a wet hand to avoid it sticking to me.

After 30 minutes, mix in the salt with a wet hand and make sure it gets evenly distributed through the dough. I mix by pulling the outside dough into the middle of the bowl and keep working my way around. It will start to feel tight, but don't let it tear. Rest for another 30 minutes.

Work the dough again in the same way. Repeat this step at 30-minute intervals twice more (four folds in total since adding the salt). I always do a window test (when you can stretch a piece of dough between your fingers and it holds a semi-transparent 'window' of very thin dough without breaking) to check the gluten development.

Transfer to a large container greased with oil so the dough doesn't stick and is easy to tip out after its bulk prove. Leave in the container, covered with the greased lid, on the bench for 2 hours so the dough can build up air and rise. It's optimal for the dough to be at 25°C/77°F at this stage. >

To pre-shape the dough, lightly dust a work surface with baker's flour and turn the dough out onto it. Cut the dough in half, shape into two balls and dust each lightly with flour. Leave for 15–20 minutes to rest.

Prepare two 18 × 38 cm (7 × 15 inch) bread tins while you're waiting. I spray my tins with oil and pop a fresh fig leaf on the bottom. Alternatively, you can place your fig leaf on top of the dough after shaping it in the next step, then flip it all into the tin together.

Once the balls of dough look relaxed, flip them over onto a lightly dusted surface. Have a go at shaping the dough into logs that will fit perfectly into your bread tins. It will be sticky. To do this, fold the top third of the dough into the middle, roll the dough into itself, creating tension on the bench so it's tight, then place the shaped dough in the prepared tin.

If you went with the sourdough option, put the tins straight in the fridge with a tea towel (dish towel) on top overnight. If using yeast and you're keen to bake the same day, leave the bread tins on the bench for 1 hour, or until the dough has risen to the top of the tin, before baking.

Preheat the oven for 20 minutes at 240°C/475°F conventional (no fan) with a heavy-based, black steel or cast-iron baking tray inside (you'll place your tins on top) and your small ovenproof dish at the bottom of the oven (you'll pour boiling water or ice cubes in to create steam when baking).

Boil a cup of water (or have ice cubes ready). If you are keen to score your bread, score a design now, just before you put the loaves in the oven. Pop the tins on the heavy tray and carefully pour the boiling water or ice cubes into the hot dish to create steam. Immediately and gently close the oven to avoid losing heat. Bake for 15 minutes, then drop the temperature to 220°C/425°F for 15 minutes. Depending on the colour you are after, drop the oven to 170–180°C/350°F and bake for about 10 more minutes.

Carefully tip the loaves onto a wire rack to cool. May the fragrance of the freshly baked fig-leaf bread fill your home with inspiration and nourishment!

I encourage you to follow your intuition. You are going to learn from every single loaf of bread you make.

Burnt fenugreek and sesame loaf

Dougal Muffet
Profiled on page 132

MAKES one 700 g (1 lb 9 oz) loaf
SPECIAL EQUIPMENT cast-iron casserole dish (e.g. Le Creuset), blender or mortar and pestle, proving basket or any container that will hold your unproved loaf snugly

4 g (⅛ oz) fenugreek seeds
290 g (10¼ oz) baker's flour
50 g (1¾ oz) stoneground whole-wheat flour
60 g (2¼ oz) sourdough starter
245 g (8¾ oz) warm water (ideally 26°C/79°F)
8 g (¼ oz) salt
3 g (⅛ oz) malted barley
55 g (2 oz) sesame seeds, toasted, plus extra for coating

This loaf came about by accident in a way. A chef walked past with a pan of 'burnt' fenugreek that was destined for the bin. Turns out the savoury aromas coming from the slightly torched seeds was the little addition I was looking for to elevate a loaf we were working on.

We add malted barley to this loaf. If you can track it down, I highly recommend it (try home-brew shops). Turn it into a flour using a blender, spice grinder or mortar and pestle. A little goes a long way, speeding up an important enzymatic reaction in the loaf and greatly improving the flavour and the crust colour. If you can't track any down, the loaf will still work without.

I recommend making more of this bread than you need, as it's truly best enjoyed once it stales and you reheat it in a chargrill pan. The savouriness of the sesame and fenugreek come alive.

Set a ripe starter overnight by following your usual method or mixing 100 g (3½ oz) baker's flour and 100 g (3½ oz) water with 10 g (¼ oz) ripe starter and leaving in a warmish spot overnight.

Toast the fenugreek seeds on a dry baking tray in a 175°C/350°F fan-forced (195°C/375°F conventional) oven or in a dry frying pan over medium–high heat until dark and fragrant, about 8 minutes. Fenugreek is inherently bitter, so pushing the colour on the seeds isn't an issue. The magic really only happens once you go past dark tan. Cool completely, then grind in a blender or using a mortar and pestle.

Combine all the ingredients in a large bowl and mix together by hand until you have a shaggy mess. Leave to rest for 20 minutes.

Turn out onto a clean work surface. With slightly damp clean hands, slap and fold the dough onto itself a few times. To do this, loosen the dough from the bowl, lift it out and slap one side down on the work surface, then fold the dough after it. (If you are unfamiliar with this very useful technique, I recommend checking it out on YouTube.) Do this five or six times, until the dough starts to look less wild.

Transfer to a bowl, cover with a clean tea towel (dish towel) and leave at room temperature for 40 minutes, then repeat the slap and fold process and leave for another 2 hours. Be mindful not to overdo this technique – you can stress the dough if you do it too frequently or too vigorously.

Now shape the dough into a taut boule. I like to use wet hands for this rather than flour. Gently tip the dough out onto the work surface and, in an anticlockwise motion with a small amount of downward pressure, bring the dough in and under itself until it forms a tight ball. Make sure there is no flour or water on the bench – you want the friction of the dough sticking to the bench and the movement of your hands to be the two opposing forces that develop the tension in the dough.

Return the dough to the bowl, cover with the tea towel and leave to rest at room temperature for 30 minutes. >

Have a damp tea towel ready and next to it plenty of extra sesame seeds in a container large enough to roll your loaf in. The purpose of the damp tea towel is to lightly moisten the loaf so that the sesame seeds will stick to it. Line a proofing basket or any container that will hold your loaf snugly with a clean, dry tea towel.

Shape your dough into a torpedo by lightly flattening it, rolling it up, then tapering off the edges with your palms. Roll the loaf onto your damp cloth, then pick it up in the towel and dredge it through sesame seeds.

Gently place your seeded loaf in the prepared proofing basket and refrigerate overnight.

Preheat your oven to 250°C/500°F fan-forced (or as close to this as your oven will go) and place a cast-iron casserole dish inside. During this time, check your bread. If it feels firm to the touch, leave it out while your oven is preheating. If it feels gassy and soft to the touch, leave it in the fridge until your oven is preheated.

Cut a generous piece of baking paper wide enough for you to lower the proved loaf into the hot cast-iron dish. (This is a delicate operation as the pot is extremely hot, so give yourself enough paper to do it comfortably.) Before lowering, use a serrated knife to score the loaf at a 45-degree angle straight down the middle. Scoring is a true skill in itself and something to develop over time, but a cut about 5 mm (¼ inch) deep will allow the loaf to expand through this weakened point.

Lower the loaf in, put on the lid and bake for 20 minutes. Carefully remove the lid, reduce the temperature to 230°C/450°F fan-forced (250°C/500°F conventional, if possible) and bake for a further 15–20 minutes. This loaf must be baked dark, so don't be timid. The flavours and aromas change right at the end of the bake with this one, and it's chalk and cheese between when it's pushed dark and a lighter-baked loaf.

Cool completely on a wire rack before slicing.

Jerusalem artichoke, chilli greens and goat's cheese focaccias

Giorgia McAllister Forte
Profiled on page 68

MAKES two (155 g/5½ oz) focaccias
SPECIAL EQUIPMENT stand mixer with dough hook attachment, rolling pin, pastry brush, mandoline

Focaccia dough
0.6 g (scant ¼ teaspoon) dried yeast or 1.5 g fresh yeast
105 g (3¾ oz) lukewarm water
170 g (6 oz) 00 flour, plus extra for dusting
16 g (½ oz) honey
15 g (½ oz) extra virgin olive oil
3 g (⅛ oz) fine salt
fresh rosemary leaves and sea salt, to top

Jerusalem artichoke, chilli greens and goat's cheese filling
1 tablespoon rice bran oil
1 brown onion, thinly sliced
sea salt, as needed
20 g (¾ oz) extra virgin olive oil, plus extra for drizzling
100 g (3½ oz) lemon juice
3 garlic cloves
1 bird's eye chilli
125 g (4½ oz) tuscan kale (cavolo nero)
80 g (2¾ oz) jerusalem artichoke
75 g (2¾ oz) chèvre cheese

These delicious focaccias are great as a side dish to the main event, or as a whole meal in themselves alongside a salad. The filling can be whatever you have to hand (see note opposite); ours vary from smoky eggplant (aubergine), confit garlic and ricotta salata in late summer to these ever-pleasing lemony chilli greens in winter.

First make the focaccia dough. If using dried yeast, stir it into the water, then leave it to sit for 5 minutes to activate. If using fresh yeast, it doesn't need to be activated and can be crumbled directly into the mixing bowl with the other ingredients.

Combine the remaining ingredients except the toppings in a stand mixer with the dough hook attachment and mix for 15–18 minutes on medium–high, until a smooth dough forms and pulls away from the side into one ball.

Lightly oil a bowl and transfer the dough to it. Cover loosely with biodegradable plastic wrap and leave in a warm place until doubled in size, about 1 hour.

Meanwhile, make the jerusalem artichoke, chilli greens and goat's cheese filling. Heat a small frying pan over medium heat and add the rice bran oil. Add the onion and a generous sprinkle of sea salt to help draw out the water in the onion. Cook gently, stirring regularly, until the onion begins to brown. Continue cooking, adding a touch more oil as needed and checking the seasoning as you go, until the onion is deep brown and jammy.

While the onion is cooking, combine the olive oil, lemon juice and a couple of pinches of sea salt in a large bowl.

Crush, grate or finely chop the garlic and thinly slice the chilli (remove the seeds if you prefer less heat). Stir both into the oil and lemon juice. Remove the stalks from the tuscan kale, then tear or roughly chop the leaves. Add to the oil and lemon juice. Thinly slice the artichoke – a mandoline is perfect for this – and add to the oil as well.

Using clean hands, toss everything together, rubbing the oil thoroughly into the kale and artichoke, before setting aside to marinate for 20 minutes.

Meanwhile, remove the onions from the heat and set aside to cool. Stir the onion into the marinated greens.

To assemble, knock back the focaccia dough by punching to deflate, then divide into two balls of about 155 g (5½ oz) each.

Dust a work surface lightly with flour. Using a rolling pin, roll each ball into a large, flat round. Place a large handful of the marinated greens in the centre of each dough round and dot chèvre over the top. Pull in the edges of the dough to meet in the middle, working your way around the circle of dough, then pinching the edges together to seal. Place seam-side down on a baking tray lined with baking paper and brush with olive oil using a pastry brush.

Poke a small steam hole in the centre of each focaccia, cover loosely with biodegradable plastic wrap, and leave in a warm place for 60–90 minutes, until doubled in size.

Preheat the oven to 200°C/400°F fan-forced (220°C/425°F conventional).

Gently dimple the tops of the dough with your fingertips, then drizzle with plenty of olive oil and sprinkle generously with rosemary and sea salt.

Bake for 20–25 minutes, until golden.

Drizzle once more with olive oil once baked. The focaccia is best served warm from the oven, but it makes an excellent picnic food if served cold.

You can fill these focaccias with anything you like depending on what's in season. The greens used here are interchangeable with any you have to hand. If you want a meat hit, sobrassada or 'nduja is a great choice, or sausages removed from their casing, torn and pan-fried, then added to the rest of the filling. We've also made these focaccias with caramelised onions, aleppo pepper and fried eggplant (aubergine) – and they were delicious.

Haikal Raji

A1 pies, three ways (Za'atar manouche, Kafta manouche, Haloumi pies) (224)

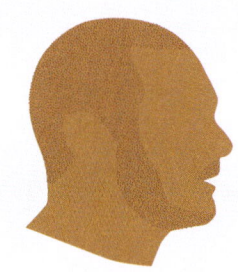

Co-owner, A1 Bakery

Melbourne, Vic
Wurundjeri Country

For decades, Melburnians have met up in A1 Bakery's hall-sized space for Lebanese pizzas and pies – from tangy sumac-forward spinach triangles to flatbreads spread with spiced lamb. Or they've dropped by to pick up a bread or sat out the front for coffee, sweets and people watching. But the most famous of the Brunswick institution's callings is the haloumi pie – a large crescent filled with shredded haloumi cheese, as creamy as it is salty, inside pillowy, ever-so-sweet dough (see page 224). When asked about the enduring appeal, Haikal Raji, who runs the business with his two brothers, twins Daniel and Anthony, says, 'I think it's just the texture – it's soft and creamy at the same time. And it's very light to eat. I think people get addicted to that.'

Haikal's dad, Elias, opened the bakery in 1992 with his brother-in-law, not long after migrating to Australia from Lebanon. At the time there were only ten pizzas on the menu – the focus was on groceries, giving the community access to hard-to-find Lebanese ingredients – but the demand grew. Haikal and his siblings grew up here: watching the bakers work (some of them are still there today), picking up baking tricks along the way, and helping out by cleaning tables and stacking shelves after school. 'I see adults, who I used to see as little kids when they came in with their parents, because I've been here for that long. I forget how old I am sometimes until I see them walking in with their own families,' says Haikal. 'There are still faces that have been coming here for over twenty years. It's amazing like that – they're still in the area. And then there are some faces you see every day, and then when you don't see them for a couple of days, you start wondering where they are.'

These days, A1 is busier than ever – even Elias is shocked when he comes back in. 'Dad can't stand seeing people waiting, but it's so much busier now. On Saturdays and Sundays we do dine-in lines. Dad will come and say, "Why are people waiting there?" Even though we've been doing this for ages, for him, it's still – "Nah, that's not the way it's done,"' Haikal says, laughing. But even on its busiest days, when you're in the thick of the crowd listening for your order to be shouted out, while Haikal and the twins zip around and chat to regulars, it still feels like space can somehow be made. Haikal says that's what the intention always was: 'We're pretty generous in nature here, that's how Dad's always been.'

> 'The texture of the pizzas is so important, and it's related to how fresh they are … it's best to eat them straight away.'

It's why he's happy not to change what works so well. 'When we renovate, we don't go full, brand-new shopfront. I think people tend to get uncomfortable when everything's too nice. There are always kids running around. If you break a glass here, it's not the biggest deal. I think it just makes it feel more comfortable for everyone,' he says. Haikal makes a good point. It's not just food, but the places we share it in that make us feel at home. Brunswick, like so many inner-city suburbs, has seen gentrification push communities out and, with it, bakeries and restaurants by the dozen. But not A1. 'It's cool, Brunswick's come a long way – but we want to try to keep this little pocket as authentic as possible. Just so people can come back. I remember coming in when I was little and I feel like it's still the same.'

NOTES ON TEXTURE

'The texture of the pizzas is so important, and it's related to how fresh they are. We start baking at 6 am. When you're baking all day, you don't need to start too early. During the day, we constantly bake so everything's fresh out of the oven. If they sit for a while, you don't get that same texture, so we keep everything coming out. It's the same when you're making the pizzas at home, it's best to eat them straight away.'

A1 pies, three ways

Haikal Raji
Profiled on page 222

MAKES 8 manouche or 10 haloumi pies
SPECIAL EQUIPMENT stand mixer with dough hook attachment, rolling pin, pastry brush

A1 dough
1 kg (2 lb 4 oz) 00 flour, plus extra for dusting
1 tablespoon sugar
1½ teaspoons fine salt
2 tablespoons dried yeast
½ teaspoon freshly grated nutmeg
2 tablespoons honey
550–650 ml (19–22½ fl oz) lukewarm water
150 ml (5 fl oz) vegetable oil

Za'atar manouche
1 tablespoon sesame seeds, toasted
1 tablespoon sumac
2 tablespoons Middle Eastern oregano
½ cup (125 ml) vegetable oil

This is a simple version of our classic A1 dough, which you can use to make different kinds of savoury Lebanese pastries. The haloumi pie and za'atar manouche are crowd favourites at A1, but we've added a home-style kafta mix for you here. Once you've nailed the dough, the rest is easy – no matter which pie (or pies) you choose to make. The ingredients for each variation make enough for one quantity of A1 dough, so make more dough or less of each of the fillings if you want to have a mix of different kinds.

For the dough, combine all the dry ingredients in a stand mixer with the dough hook attachment and mix on low speed. Mix the honey with ½ cup (125 ml) of the warm water and stir to dissolve. Add the honey mixture and oil to the dry ingredients and mix to combine. With the motor on low speed, gradually add enough of the remaining warm water to form a smooth, soft dough. (Alternatively, you can do this by hand.) Shape the dough into a loose ball, place back in the bowl, then cover with a clean tea towel (dish towel) and leave in a warm place for 20 minutes or until doubled in size.

For za'atar manouche, combine all the ingredients in a small bowl.

For kafta manouche, combine all the kafta ingredients into a uniform mixture in a small bowl.

For all variations, turn the dough out onto a work surface lightly dusted with flour and cut into eight equal portions for manouche or 10 equal portions for haloumi pies. Shape the portions into balls, place on a lightly floured tray, cover with a cloth and leave for another 15–20 minutes (freezer bags and a clean tablecloth are great for covering the dough at this point).

Preheat the oven to 250°C/500°F fan-forced (or as close to this as your oven will go) for the manouche, or 240°C/475°F fan-forced for the haloumi pies.

Kafta manouche

- 1 kg (2 lb 4 oz) finely minced (ground) lamb
- 100 g (3½ oz) parsley, finely chopped
- 100 g (3½ oz) onion (about ½ onion), finely chopped
- 1½ teaspoons Lebanese seven spice
- 1½ teaspoons ground cinnamon
- 1 teaspoon sweet paprika
- 2 teaspoons salt
- ½ teaspoon ground nutmeg
- ½ teaspoon ground black pepper

Haloumi pies

- 900 g (2 lb) haloumi cheese, grated
- vegetable oil, for brushing

For the kafta mix, you want the lamb to be really finely minced (ground) and on the leaner side (though still with enough fat to give it flavour), as it cooks best on top of the dough this way.

Any leftover kafta mix can be rolled into kafta and fried in a pan or barbecued. You can also simply spread it on pita bread and bake at 200°C/400°F fan-forced until crisp.

We use really creamy haloumi in brine (Mama Lucia or Cottage Cheese Farm), which tends to be slightly yellower.

For manouche, roll out each dough portion on a lightly floured surface into a 25 cm (10 inch) round. Cooking in batches, place on a baking tray lined with baking paper. Either cover with the za'atar mixture, leaving a 2 cm (¾ inch) border so it doesn't spill over in the oven or, using your hands, pat on a thin, even layer of the kafta mixture (about 3 mm/⅛ inch), again leaving a 2 cm border. Cook the za'atar for 8–10 minutes and the kafta for 10–15 minutes, or to your liking.

For haloumi pies, roll out each dough portion on a lightly floured surface into a 20 cm (8 inch) round about 5 mm (¼ inch) thick. Place 70–80 g (2½–2¾ oz) of shredded haloumi on one side of each round, then fold the dough over, to enclose the filling, making a half-moon shape. Using lightly floured fingers, pinch the two sides together to seal the pies well. Place the pies on baking trays lined with baking paper, then cover and leave for another 10 minutes.

Bake for 8–12 minutes or until golden. Remove from the oven, brush lightly with oil using a pastry brush and cool slightly before serving.

Gareth Whitton

Pea and feta tart (230)

White chocolate and rhubarb pudding with lemon myrtle (276)

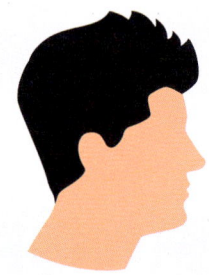

Founder and head pastry chef, Tarts Anon

Melbourne, Vic
Wurundjeri Country

Gareth Whitton attributes at least some of his baking success to a particular trait. 'I've always been super stubborn,' he says. 'Once I'm in, it's a one-way street. I feel really comfortable committing to something.' And what he's really committed to is tarts. A Tarts Anon creation speaks for itself, cut so perfectly it could have been done by laser beam (not quite – try three different knives), and stratified into elements that would make a geologist jealous – layers of cakes, custards, pralines, compotes, jams and chocolate appear in different combinations inside their crisp, darkly baked crusts. 'I guess if I feel like something is remotely achievable, I'll stick it through to the end for that satisfaction. I'm not necessarily a high achiever in that sense, but I just think that if something's worth doing it's worth doing properly,' he says, before reaching for a kinder word to describe this quality in himself: 'I think a bit of tenacity is very much part of my personality.'

This insight comes up in conversation as he reflects on a candy-cane-themed tart his business and life partner, Catherine Way, convinced him to develop – his reticence gave way to a full-blown reconnaissance mission into Candyland. But you can easily apply this tenacity to his wider achievements – be it honing his craft under the likes of Heston Blumenthal, turning a lockdown project making exquisite tarts in a humble microwave oven into a burgeoning Cremorne-based business, or winning the title of 'Dessert Master' on the TV show of the same name. Gareth goes down a rabbit hole every time he makes a tart – usually, it's one that burrows back into history. 'Food's food, but we're in such a privileged position as chefs and hospitality people to be able to use storytelling to enhance an experience. It's that special thing I look forward to when I go out to eat at a restaurant,' he says. 'I care about what makes the food great. And that comes down, usually, to why things of that same nature have been appreciated for the longest time.'

His approach is to bring classics into today with modern techniques and resources – but to keep their identity intact ('Bottom line, it's got to be delicious'). His famous Black Forest tart is a good example: baked chocolate mousse sandwiched between two cherry layers, with a paper-thin chocolate top held up by a dainty structural network of piped dots of aerated kirsch and white chocolate (Gareth confesses he convinced a steel fabricator to make a bespoke cutter for the shop to help cut it). In many ways the Black Forest tart sums up the blueprint for a Tarts Anon tart – an elevated, reconfigured classic, that, for all its form, will still taste like Black Forest when you bite into it – just the best you've ever had.

For Gareth and Cat, the joy is in creating something that's refined and selling it by the slice in a paper box, ready to be whisked away to a park with friends, plated up for a fancy dessert, or eaten with all the elegance of a slice of pizza. 'We want everything to be about the quality of what we're trying to present. We want to do away with the tablecloths, with the white gloves, with the contrived service. It's about intimate, personal reactions with our customers.'

'Never underestimate the value of a stick blender. It's not just a means of puréeing; what it's able to do in term of emulsification is terrific.'

NOTES ON STICK BLENDERS

'Never underestimate the value of a stick blender. It's not just a means of puréeing; what it's able to do in terms of emulsification is terrific. For all our baked custards, we stick-blend the custard mix before it goes in. If you whisk it together, it'll look like a nice custard mix, but if you stick blend it, you'll quickly see – ah, this is much better.'

WORDS TO BAKE BY

'A mentor of mine said to me: "What you need to understand is that the cooking that we're doing here, of course it's about precision and being accurate with your measurements, but that's only the case because the hard part's been done – and that's understanding. You need to learn to understand the ingredients, the process, the temperatures, the equipment, and then form an intimate relationship with those concepts – those parts are then what give you the tools to create the precision. Science in cooking isn't all about whiz-bang explosions and nitrogen and that sort of crap, it's just understanding reactions, why food's doing what it's doing. We're talking gluten development, the Maillard reaction, the caramelisation of sugars. And then, once you understand, you know just how great things can be."'

Pea and feta tart

Gareth Whitton
Profiled on page 228

SERVES 10

SPECIAL EQUIPMENT 25 cm (10 inch) diameter loose-based fluted tart (flan) tin about 3.5 cm (3½ inches) deep (or any fluted tart tin), stand mixer with paddle and whisk attachments or food processor, blender, rolling pin, sugar thermometer, baking weights (e.g. rice or dried lentils)

I've always liked to cook thematic food. I'm not sure whether it's the time that I spent with Dinner by Heston, where all the food was in one way or another conceptual. Obviously, flavour, texture, cohesion and eatability were always paramount, but to be able to tell a story or give a bit of emotional connection to a dish is such a powerful tool.

This tart is perhaps one example where that isn't the case. Sure, many things appear in this recipe that might seem to tie in to a familiar format, and the construction is somewhat unique, but these flavour profiles aren't new things. Bright, fresh and vibrant spring vegetable dishes were the inspiration for this tart, with leeks, peas and zucchini (courgettes) as the stars. Throw in an acidic and creamy cheese and fresh lemon, and it's about as springtime as you can get. It wasn't until we went through the tasting process that we noticed the sweet dill pickles against the more umami notes of the parmesan were strangely reminiscent of a Big Mac. This wasn't originally part of the brief, but it was definitely enough to make it worthy of doing several rounds on the Tarts Anon menu.

Pickled zucchini

1 large zucchini (courgette), cut into 1.5 cm (⅝ inch) dice
2 dill sprigs
50 g (1¾ oz) sugar
150 g (5½ oz) water
100 g (3½ oz) white wine vinegar
5 g (⅛ oz) salt

Shortcrust pastry

100 g (3½ oz) chilled unsalted butter, diced
200 g (7 oz) plain (all-purpose) flour
3 g (⅛ oz) salt
50 g (1¾ oz) cold water

First prepare the pickled zucchini. This can be done well ahead of time, and it will hold up for a while after, too. Put the zucchini in a clean jar or airtight container with the dill sprigs, then bring the remaining ingredients to the boil in a small saucepan over medium heat. Pour over the zucchini, then seal the jar well, and cool completely. Refrigerate for at least 6 hours.

To make the shortcrust pastry, combine the butter, flour and salt in a stand mixer with the paddle attachment or a food processor (or do this part by rubbing the ingredients together with clean fingers). Work the ingredients together until the mixture resembles fine breadcrumbs and no lumps of butter remain. Be sure not to overwork at this stage – we're trying to get the butter to coat the flour to prevent any gluten structure forming, and this will only happen if the butter is cold and not melted.

Add the cold water, a little at a time, until the mixture is firm but malleable (if using a food processor, it's best to finish off by hand – there's a very small window when the water is incorporated but the dough won't be overworked). Work the dough into a round puck shape and refrigerate for at least 30 minutes. This will help the flour hydrate properly and will result in a more pliant dough.

Using a rolling pin, roll the pastry out between two sheets of baking paper into a circle roughly 35 cm (14 inches) in diameter and about 3 mm (⅛ inch) thick. Refrigerate the pastry between the baking paper sheets for about 20 minutes to firm up.

Preheat the oven to 180°C/350°F fan-forced (200°C/400°F conventional). Have ready a 25 cm (10 inch) diameter loose-based fluted tart (flan) tin about 3.5 cm (3½ inches) deep (or any fluted tart tin) – there is no need to grease or line it.

Remove both sheets of baking paper, and loosely wrap the pastry around a rolling pin, then drape it over the tart tin. Gently lift the edges of the pastry and, using clean fingers, press into the corners of the tin. It is important to have clearly defined corners at this stage, as that will prevent the sides slipping and shrinking in the oven. Press into the sides of the tin and trim off the excess with a sharp knife, retaining the trimmings, then freeze the pastry shell for about 15 minutes.

Line the inside of the pastry shell with two sheets of foil large enough to go above the rim and completely cover the pastry, pressing them into the corners. Fill to the brim with the baking weights (such as 2 kg/2 lb 4 oz uncooked rice, dried lentils or similar). Bake for 30–35 minutes, until the edges of the pastry are nicely mid-golden. Remove from the oven, then remove the rice and foil when cool enough to touch.

Reduce the oven temperature to 165°C/325°F fan-forced (185°C/375°F conventional). >

Cake

3 g (⅛ oz) salt, plus extra for blanching leek
iced water, for refreshing leek
150 g (5½ oz) leek, cut into 2 mm (1/16 inch) slices
75 g (2¾ oz) pickled zucchini (see 231)
120 g (4¼ oz) fresh peas, blanched, or frozen peas
100 g (3½ oz) butter
75 g (2¾ oz) almond meal
3 g (⅛ oz) baking powder
125 g (4½ oz) egg (from about 3 eggs)
130 g (4½ oz) Bulgarian or Danish feta, cut into 1.5 cm (⅝ inch) dice

Pea custard

25 g (1 oz) unsalted butter
100 g (3½ oz) shallots, thinly sliced
180 g (6¼ oz) thawed frozen peas
100 g (3½ oz) pouring cream
75 g (2¾ oz) cream cheese
20 g (¾ oz) caster (superfine) sugar
6 g (¼ oz) salt
100 g (3½ oz) egg yolk (from about 5 eggs)

To serve

quality parmesan cheese
dill sprigs
zest of 1 lemon

To make the cake, bring a medium saucepan of water to the boil over medium heat and season with plenty of extra salt (about 25 g/1 oz per 4 cups/1 litre of water). Prepare a medium bowl of iced water. Blanch the leek in the boiling water for 15 seconds, then remove from the water, immediately refresh in the iced water, then squeeze the water out. You should have about 100 g (3½ oz) of leek.

Strain the pickled zucchini, removing the dill, then combine in a large bowl with the peas and the blanched leek.

Melt the butter in a small saucepan over medium heat. Heat until the milk solids start to colour and the butter begins to foam. Remove from the heat and keep at about 100°C/210°F.

Combine the almond meal, baking powder and salt in a medium bowl and stir together. In a stand mixer with the whisk attachment or whisking by hand, beat the egg on low speed.

With the mixer now running on medium speed, or hand-whisking constantly, slowly pour in the butter. Ensure that the mixture is well emulsified, as this will ensure that the butter doesn't bleed out later and give the cake a greasy texture. Finally, whisk in the dry ingredients, ensuring that there are no lumps. Stir the leek, peas and pickled zucchini into the cake batter, ensuring they are distributed throughout.

Pour the batter into the tart crust. Scatter the feta evenly over the top, then press each piece into the batter so that the top of the batter is flat.

Bake for about 18 minutes, or until the crust is an even golden brown and the centre of the tart is springy but not too firm. Remove from the oven, then leave to cool in the tin. Using the back of a spoon, press down firmly on areas where the cake has risen unevenly so that the surface is flat.

To make the pea custard, melt the butter in a small saucepan over medium heat until foaming. Add the shallots and cook until soft and translucent. Add the peas and stir quickly to ensure they keep their vibrant green. Once warmed through, add the cream, cream cheese, sugar and salt, and bring to the boil.

Pour the mixture into a blender and blitz to a smooth and glossy purée. With the blender still running, add the egg yolk and mix through. Strain through a fine-mesh sieve into a large jug. Pour over the cake layer, and bake for 15 minutes, or until set. Cool in the tin.

To serve, grate a liberal coating of parmesan cheese on top and garnish with a scattering of picked dill sprigs and a light grating of lemon zest. Cut into 10 pieces using a hot, sharp knife.

Time for *Dessert*

239 Lemon tart

243 Negroni chocolate tart

246 Peaches and cream meringue tower

250 Chocolate and rye tart with olive oil mascarpone cream

255 Amaro crème caramel with salted, caramelised cacao

257 Pandan, coconut and mango chiffon roll

262 Cherry pie

267 Fig, chocolate and sweet dukkah sundaes

268 Huon apple crumble

270 Basque cheesecake

273 Unbaked strawberry cheesecake

276 White chocolate and rhubarb pudding with lemon myrtle

Audrey Allard

Lemon tart (239)

Founder and head pastry chef, Holy Sugar

Melbourne, Vic
Wurundjeri Country

If baking is Audrey Allard's medium, golden is her palette. Her work – be it the glazed chocolate top of a deliciously wobbly tiramisu cake, a pool of passionfruit in a boat of torched meringue, or the glassy top of a brûléed custard tart – has a way of catching the light. 'There are more caramel colours in my baking. It's a strange way to describe pastry, but I personally feel it's on the earthier side.'

Audrey's penchant for pushing flavour means often replacing refined sugar with darker sugars in custards and stirring brown butter into sponges. 'I like to call it rustic but with attention to detail,' she says. 'I keep it quite raw in terms of the process, the ingredients. I don't use food colourings or glazes and rarely use gelatine, but there's always the detail that ties it together.' This is true of the Holy Sugar shop in Northcote, too – a homely spot anchored by the warmth of its walls, stripped back to the patina of its undercoat, a long farm-style table that takes pride of place, and a lemon-yellow sideboard filled with ornamental crockery (some of it her great-grand-mother's) and vintage souvenir teaspoons. Above it, there's a mosaic of lemons she made herself.

When Audrey finished high school, it was a toss-up between studying visual arts or baking. 'I just decided I would do an apprenticeship in pastry and implement my art in my food. And so I got a job in a patisserie and haven't stopped since,' she says. There are no regrets. 'I feel like in my case, I'm being fulfilled in the artistic area that I need.' It's not hard to see – Audrey goes on to describe the satisfying process of smearing waves of movement into silky Italian meringue or embellishing cut slices so they arrive with all the flair of a plated dessert.

Like all creative endeavours, it took time for her to hone her touch. And in a world of polished origin stories, Audrey is determined to acknowledge the growth and grit it takes to refine your craft. She's pointedly kept all her photos from her first-year apprenticeship up until now on Holy Sugar's Instagram account. 'People have said to me, "Why didn't you archive all those photos and have a more professional, clean slate for the shop?" But I want people to know my journey and what I've done and how far I've come in those nine years,' she says. 'It's part of the story. And my ego is not too hectic to hide it from people. I didn't just get given a shop and all of a sudden I'm making cakes and it's all happening. It was a process.'

NOTES ON LEMON ZEST

'I love lemon. I put lemon zest in almost everything. Our Basque has lemon zest in it and our sponges have lemon zest in them. Custards, lemon zest. I feel like sometimes people don't even know it's in there. I feel like it'll just elevate the flavour to a point that you can't quite put your finger on and it just tastes really good. For my caramel brûlée custard tart, I basically grab the sugar and I make it into a dark caramel. I add the cream to that, whisk in the eggs and add a pinch of lemon zest and a bit of vanilla bean. It just makes the nicest custard after it's baked in the oven. I really don't think anyone would ever know that there's lemon zest in there, but it just tastes so nice together.'

WORDS TO BAKE BY

'I feel like baking is like your handwriting in a way. People can try to copy your handwriting, but it's never going to be the same. I think that's a great thing. People always ask me, "Are you ever worried about competition?" And my answer is always no. Everyone is so different, we all have such different ideas – which means everyone brings different things. And also there's that great idea that the audience for your particular work will come to you.'

Lemon tart

SERVES 10

SPECIAL EQUIPMENT 25 cm (10 inch) diameter tart (flan) tin, stand mixer with paddle and whisk attachments, rolling pin, pastry brush, sugar thermometer, baking weights (such as 200 g/7 oz rice)

Tart base (see note, page 240)
450 g (1 lb) baker's flour, plus extra for dusting
225 g (8 oz) chilled butter, diced
180 g (6¼ oz) caster (superfine) sugar
2 egg yolks
1 egg
1 teaspoon lemon zest

Egg wash
36 g (1¼ oz) egg yolk (from about 2 eggs), lightly whisked

Lemon filling (see note, page 240)
400 g (14 oz) egg yolk (from about 20 eggs)
300 g (10½ oz) caster (superfine) sugar
160 g (5¾ oz) whipping cream
80 g (2¾ oz) milk
350 g (12 oz) freshly squeezed, strained lemon juice

Yes, this lemon tart has a high yolk ratio — it makes it super luscious, silky, crack-proof and creamy. It portions perfectly with a wet, sharp knife and allows you to brûlée the top without it splitting. I usually save the whites for an angel food cake or Italian meringue — refrigerate and use within 4 days, or freeze to use later.

I think it's very important to have a go-to recipe for the perfect baked lemon tart. Luckily, I've spent years tweaking this one for you. The yolk to egg ratio in the base is important; not only does it prevent the pastry shrinking, but it also ensures the blind-baking foil doesn't stick. The high yolk content of the filling is vital for achieving a creamy baked custard that doesn't crack. I'm so thrilled to be able to share this recipe with you, and I hope you think of me the next time you have an urge to make a lemon tart.

Line the base of your 25 cm (10 inch) diameter tart (flan) tin with baking paper.

Start by making the tart base. Using a stand mixer with the paddle attachment, combine your flour and butter on medium speed for about 3 minutes, until the texture resembles sand. Transfer to another bowl and set aside.

Combine your caster sugar, egg yolks, egg and lemon zest in your stand mixer with the whisk attachment and whisk for about 3 minutes on high speed, until pale and fluffy. Switch back to the paddle attachment and add the flour mixture. Mix on low speed for another 3 minutes, until a smooth dough forms.

This tart dough doesn't need to rest before rolling out, but it is important to be in a cool environment. If you're making this dough in summer, I recommend chilling it for 30 minutes before rolling it out.

Lightly dust your bench with flour. Divide your dough in half (see the note on page 240) and roll it out into a disc about 35 cm (14 inches) in diameter and 4 mm (⅛ inch) thick. Place your tin right side up over the circle and cut around about 4 cm (1½ inches) from the tin. Remove your excess dough, roll your circle onto your rolling pin and drape it over your tart tin.

Gently manoeuvre your pastry to nestle into the corner of your tin, then use your fingers to press the dough in, removing all air pockets. Run a knife around the top of your tin to trim off the excess pastry and set aside to rest in the freezer for 1 hour.

After 30 minutes, preheat your oven to 165°C/325°F fan-forced (185°C/375°F conventional).

For the lemon filling, combine your yolks in a medium bowl. Add your caster sugar and whisk by hand for 1 minute, until combined but not fluffy, working quickly so that your yolks don't harden. Add your cream and milk, whisk for 30 seconds until combined, then add your lemon juice and whisk for another 30 seconds, making sure you combine all the ingredients without creating too much foam. Also make sure you add these ingredients in the order given, to prevent the mixture splitting. Pour your filling into a medium saucepan and set aside. >

Prepare your tart base for blind-baking by lining your frozen tart shell with foil, squeezing it around the edges. Pour your baking weights into the base. Turn your oven down to 160°C/325°F fan-forced (180°C/350°F conventional) and bake for 17 minutes. Remove from the oven and leave the foil on for 10 minutes to help prevent shrinkage. Remove the foil and return the tart shell to the oven. Turn your oven down to 155°C/300°F fan-forced (175°C/350°F conventional). After the 10 minutes' resting time, remove the rice and foil, then return the pastry to the oven for a further 10 minutes or until your shell is an even deep golden brown.

Meanwhile, continue with the filling. Place the saucepan containing your lemon mixture over medium–low heat and, whisking gently (without creating air bubbles), keep your mixture moving while bringing your lemon custard up to 60°C/140°F. Remove from the heat and set aside.

Once your tart is golden, remove from the oven and brush the inside all over with your egg wash using a pastry brush. This will waterproof your tart and keep it crisp during and after baking. The heat from the hot tart base will cook the yolk to seal it (it's all about timing).

Reduce the oven temperature to 150°C/300°F fan-forced (170°C/350°F conventional).

To assemble the tart, transfer your warm lemon mixture to a large jug, skimming off any foam or bubbles. Return your tart shell to your oven and slowly pour in your lemon filling. Fill it to the brim. Be careful with your oven fan; if it's too strong, it will blow your filling out and spill it). Shield your tart from the fan with a baking tray or turn your fan down if you can. Bake for 15 minutes or until there is still an 'unset' wobble in the middle. Turn off the oven and leave the tart in there with the door closed for a further 5 minutes. There should still be a tiny wobble of unset lemon mix. Leave the tart to cool in the oven with the door ajar for another 10–15 minutes. After this, refrigerate the tart for at least 30 minutes before removing from the tin and cutting into portions to serve.

This recipe makes two tart shells. I recommend preparing two if you have two tins and the space to freeze one for future baking. It will keep in the freezer for up to 3 months. If you just have the one tin, wrap the excess dough in plastic wrap and prepare a tart shell once your tin becomes available. Your future self will thank you! If you would like to make a passionfruit tart, use half passionfruit juice and half lemon juice.

Audrey Allard

Negroni chocolate tart

Rosemary Andrews
Profiled on page 158

SERVES 8
SPECIAL EQUIPMENT 23 cm (9 inch) diameter tart (flan) tin, stand mixer with paddle attachment, sugar thermometer, baking weights (e.g. rice)

Chocolate pastry
100 g (3½ oz) plain (all-purpose) flour, plus extra for dusting
70 g (2½ oz) cake flour
62 g (2¼ oz) icing (confectioners') sugar
pinch of sea salt
155 g (5½ oz) unsalted butter
50 g (1¾ oz) egg (from about 1 egg)
25 g (1 oz) unsweetened cocoa powder
20 g (¾ oz) almond meal

Chocolate filling
200 g (7 oz) unsalted butter
200 g (7 oz) dark chocolate, 70%
pinch of sea salt
360 g (12¾ oz) egg (from about 8 eggs)
240 g (8½ oz) caster (superfine) sugar
24 g (¾ oz) unsweetened cocoa powder, plus extra for dusting (optional)

To assemble and serve
140 g (5 oz) Four Pillars Breakfast Negroni marmalade
crème fraîche or chocolate sauce, to serve

I can assure you, if you love chocolate and orange, then this is your jam. This delicious and divinely rich chocolate tart made with Four Pillars Breakfast Negroni marmalade (order online or find at a local grocer in an Australian city) is perfect as an afternoon pick-me-up with an espresso or as a dessert to be shared with loved ones. It's an easy-to-follow recipe, and the results will wow your guests and make an ultimate special moment to share.

For the chocolate pastry, combine the flours, icing sugar, salt and butter in a stand mixer with the paddle attachment and beat on low speed for 4–5 minutes or until the mixture is sandy, with no large lumps of butter.

Add the egg, cocoa powder and almond meal, mixing until just combined. Press into a flattened disc, seal in biodegradable plastic wrap and refrigerate for at least 2 hours, or overnight is best.

Generously grease a 23 cm (9 inch) diameter tart (flan) tart tin with canola oil spray. Lightly dust a work surface with flour and roll out your dough into a round about 28 cm (11¼ inches) in diameter. Fit the pastry into the prepared tin, trimming off any overhang and setting aside the offcuts. Work while the dough is still cold and try to be quick, as the pastry is not easy to work with once it is pliable or in an uncontrolled temperature environment. Freeze the pastry-lined tin for 15 minutes, as this helps to prevent the pastry from shrinking.

Preheat the oven to 155°C/300°F fan-forced (175°C/350°F conventional). Line your tart shell with baking paper and fill to the top with rice or other baking weights. Bake for 25–30 minutes, until the visible edges are lightly golden. Reduce the oven to 150°C/300°F fan-forced (170°C/350°F conventional). Remove the baking paper and rice and fix any holes with your pastry offcuts. Bake for a further 15–20 minutes, until lightly golden. Set aside to cool.

To make the chocolate filling, combine the butter, chocolate and salt in a small saucepan over low heat until melted. Set aside cool to 50°C/120°F.

Preheat the oven to 110°C/225°F fan-forced (130°C/250°F conventional).

In a medium bowl, whisk together the egg and caster sugar until the sugar dissolves. Whisk in the melted chocolate and butter, then sift in the cocoa powder and whisk until smooth.

To assemble the tart, spread the negroni marmalade over the cooled tart base, then pour in the filling to the top, being careful not to overfill.

Bake for 40–45 minutes, until the filling is cooked – there should still be a slight wobble in the centre. Leave to cool.

Refrigerate for at least 6 hours or overnight. Slice into eight pieces and leave at room temperature for 4 hours before consuming. This cooling and rewarming ensures the ganache sets, then turns lovely and gooey. The tart is best eaten at room temperature, as this changes both the texture and the flavour of the chocolate on the palate.

Dust with extra cocoa powder, if liked, and serve with crème fraîche or any chocolate sauce for a luscious moment.

Anneliese Brancatisano

Peaches and cream meringue tower (246)
Chocolate and rye tart with olive oil mascarpone cream (250)

Pastry chef,
Peaches la Crème

Melbourne, Vic
Wurundjeri Country

Growing up, Anneliese was the mandatory cake baker for everyone's celebrations. That hasn't changed since she became a professional pastry chef – it's just that her pool of fans is larger than ever. Anneliese's baking is all woozy nostalgia and the invitation to indulge. It draws as much from memories of after-school jam-and-cream-filled doughnuts as it does from her German–Italian background, which you might spot in her grandly piped tortes or olive-oil-spiked chocolate mousses with fennel seed biscotti. 'For me it's about what's simple, what's a bit exciting, but not out of reach,' she says. 'Sweet cream is the best thing in the world, but you add a bit of salt to it, it's not just cream any more. And I think that's exciting, because it invokes that question of: "What am I eating right now?"'

As a teenager, Anneliese found an all-important calling while baking for a local cafe in the Macedon Ranges, Victoria. 'It was the first time in my life where I felt like there was a spot for me, where it felt like people around me were saying, "Wow, you're actually doing a good thing,"' she says. 'It was a confusing time – I thought I was really erratic and that I couldn't do anything properly. But then I found I could make all these amazing cakes.'

Thankfully, it's become clearer over the years. And the insight she's gained from her experience in cafes and restaurants in Melbourne – as well as running her independent business – is equally useful to anyone baking at home. Or perhaps any one of us in this world.

'In my head, I used to think: "If I don't get it right the first time – even if it's a recipe I've never made before, a technique I've never done before – then I'm a failure." And ever since, I realised that it was my mindset that was causing me so much stress,' she says. 'I'd focus it all on me and think that the reason it didn't work was because I was so bad at my job. That's not how you get a good outcome. You get a good outcome from being set up properly. And from being supported and prepared.'

She's grateful for the mentors and bosses who held that all-important metaphorical mirror up to her talents. And the growing audience for the cakes she was churning out on the side as 'Peaches la Crème', the chance to head up the pastry section at Melbourne restaurant Theodore's, and being celebrated as one of Melbourne Food and Wine's 30 under 30 – all helped her to see a future that could be hers. 'It pushed me to really want to be a professional. To consider my own vision and find refinement in my own way, my style,' she says. 'I realised you don't have to be good at everything. You don't have to be the one who's the best at everything. You can just be in your niche. And that's the beauty of it.' Her advice? Enjoy what you can offer. 'Just because it's not, say, what's on trend or as technical as someone else's work, it doesn't mean it doesn't have a really big place.' And always remember to celebrate your successes: 'You can stuff something up and still be the person who made the croquembouche last night.'

'Life can feel very routine, it gets glum, it's stressful. And then there's home-made crème caramel.'

NOTES ON REFRIGERATION

'I think people get so scared of baking because they start reading the recipe and think, I don't have three hours. Remember that the freezer is your best friend. Freeze your icing, your Swiss meringue buttercreams, defrost them in the microwave and then whip them again. You don't have to make everything from scratch on the day. I always keep some choux pastry in the freezer – just pipe it and freeze it. You can take them out and bake them from frozen, and the moisture from the freezer creates steam, which will help them puff up even more.'

WORDS TO BAKE BY

'Life can feel very routine, it gets glum, it's stressful. And then there's home-made crème caramel. The look in my boyfriend's eye when I'm plating one up at 9.30 pm on a school night is priceless. The fact that I can bring something that used to blow my mind into my home so easily – I think it'd be a shame to waste it. As much as I love doing it for work, I know I'm in a bad place when I'm not cooking at home. That's when I know something has to change. Because if I can't have this pleasure and creativity at home, for me, there's no point in doing it.'

Peaches and cream meringue tower

Anneliese Brancatisano
Profiled on page 244

SERVES 8–10
SPECIAL EQUIPMENT 30 × 40 cm (12 × 16 inch) baking tray, stand mixer with whisk attachment, stick blender, sugar thermometer

Heat-and-whip meringues
210 g (7½ oz) egg white (from about 7 eggs)
300 g (10½ oz) caster (superfine) sugar
125 g (4½ oz) brown sugar
10 g (¼ oz) vanilla bean paste
2 g (¹⁄₁₆ oz) fine sea salt

Crème anglaise
375 g (13 oz) whipping cream
375 g (13 oz) milk
15 g (½ oz) vanilla bean paste
180 g (6¼ oz) egg yolk (from about 9 eggs)
200 g (7 oz) caster (superfine) sugar
fine sea salt, to taste

This recipe is devoted to Natalie Paull, not only because it uses her incredible meringue recipe (which she generously shared with me to include in this creation), but because I will always remember the starstruck feeling I experienced when I first visited Natalie's North Melbourne cake shop Beatrix Bakes. I could not believe that she was still handing out the boxes of sweets herself to people patiently waiting on the street. From that day on, I knew I wanted to be like Nat in my endeavours, if I ever became a baker, let alone a notable one. The meringue tower is possibly the simplest yet grandest dessert to create for a dinner party or celebration or, if you're anything like me, a moreish late-night dessert – but I do recommend halving the recipe for this purpose!

Preheat the oven to 170°C/350°F fan-forced (190°C/375°F conventional). Spray a 30 × 40 cm (12 × 16 inch) baking tray with oil and line it with baking paper.

For the heat-and-whip meringues, make a bain-marie by choosing a saucepan that you can nestle your stand mixer bowl on top of but that leaves a clearance at the bottom of at least 8 cm (3¼ inches). Fill the pan with 5 cm (2 inches) of water and bring to a gentle simmer.

Combine the egg white and caster sugar in the stand mixer bowl, place over the simmering water and whisk gently, just enough to keep the mixture moving as it warms up – you don't want to add air at this point. It should take 5–8 minutes to bring the mixture up to 70°C/160°F.

Remove the bowl from the pan and fit it to the stand mixer. Using the whisk attachment, whip on medium–high speed for 2 minutes, until it looks like glossy-white whipped cream. Stop the mixer and add the brown sugar, vanilla and salt. Continue to whip for a further 2–5 minutes, until the mix is marshmallowy thick and a pale, malty brown.

Remove the bowl from the mixer and scrape the meringue off the whisk. Using your clean hand or a spoon (I like to spray this with oil to make for an easy release), scoop up about ½ cup of meringue, then push it off your hand or spoon and onto the prepared baking tray. Repeat with the remaining meringue, leaving about 3 cm (1¼ inches) between each dollop. Place the tray in the oven, then immediately reduce the oven temperature to 90°C/200°F fan-forced (110°C/225°F conventional). Bake for 1 hour. Once done, leave in the oven to cool, with the door ajar, for 1 hour or preferably overnight.

For the crème anglaise, combine the cream, milk and vanilla in a large heavy-based saucepan over medium heat and bring to a hard simmer, watching that it doesn't boil over. While it comes to a simmer, using a hand whisk, whisk your egg yolk with the caster sugar in a large separate bowl until slightly pale and thoroughly combined.

Salted vanilla cream

500 g (1 lb 2 oz) whipping cream
200 g (7 oz) caster (superfine) sugar
50 g (1¾ oz) sour cream
5 g (⅛ oz) vanilla bean paste
fine sea salt, to taste

Fruit and nuts

200 g (7 oz) raw pistachio nut kernels
50 g (1¾ oz) caster (superfine) sugar
700 g (1 lb 9 oz) tinned peaches in syrup, drained

You can use very ripe fresh peaches, but I think tinned peaches are supreme here.

This is a versatile year-round recipe that you can adapt to the seasons. Try out combinations such as cherry, lime and salted almond; rhubarb and pistachio; chocolate crème anglaise with poached pear and toasted hazelnuts; or watermelon and fresh mint.

Pour a quarter of the hot milk mixture into the yolk and whisk quickly to temper the egg mixture. Pour the rest of the hot milk mixture in, and continue whisking until all combined. Strain the mixture back into the saucepan, and whisk over medium heat until it reaches 75–80°C/160–175°F and starts to thicken. Take off the heat, strain again, into a bowl, and add salt to taste. (If your custard splits, simply place your bowl over another bowl filled with iced water and use a stick blender to emulsify back together. Cover with biodegradable plastic wrap, with the wrap touching the surface of your custard so it doesn't form a skin. Cool to room temperature, then refrigerate until ready to use.

For the salted vanilla cream, combine all the ingredients in a stand mixer with the whisk attachment and beat on medium–high speed until the mixture forms medium–firm peaks. Be careful not to overwhip. If you're worried, you can beat to soft peaks in the stand mixer, then finish off with a hand whisk.

For the fruit and nuts, put the pistachios in a small saucepan with the caster sugar, and stir or toss constantly over low heat until the sugar starts melting and the pistachios are lightly toasted. Keep it low and slow, as the sugar can burn, but don't worry if your sugar starts to harden on some pistachios – it gives them a nice crunch. Just stir or toss constantly until they are all coated. Transfer to a baking tray lined with baking paper to cool completely.

Roughly chop the cooled pistachios.

To assemble the tower, have all your elements ready. Grab your favourite plate. Place some salted vanilla cream on the plate, then place your first four meringues side by side on top – you can do this a little quirkily and have them overlap each other a little. Add some salted vanilla cream on top of each meringue, then start stacking the rest of the meringues to form a mountain shape, with salted vanilla cream between each meringue layer like glue. Once the meringues are stacked and stable, arrange the peaches over them, along with any leftover cream. Whisk your crème anglaise well, then pour it all over the meringue tower. Scatter the candied pistachios over the top and serve immediately.

Chocolate and rye tart with olive oil mascarpone cream

Anneliese Brancatisano
Profiled on page 244

SERVES 12–15
SPECIAL EQUIPMENT 20 cm (8 inch) diameter loose-based tart (flan) tin, stand mixer with whisk attachment, baking weights (e.g. rice or dried legumes), angled palette knife

Rye pastry
200 g (7 oz) plain (all-purpose) flour, plus extra for dusting
50 g (1¾ oz) rye flour
80 g (2¾ oz) caster (superfine) sugar
2 g (1/16 oz) fine salt
160 g (5¾ oz) chilled butter, diced
60 g (2¼ oz) pouring cream
1 egg yolk

Chocolate filling
230 g (8 oz) dark chocolate, roughly chopped
260 g (9¼ oz) pouring cream
50 g (1¾ oz) caster (superfine) sugar
3 g (⅛ oz) fine salt
2 eggs
4 g (⅛ oz) vanilla bean paste

For someone who isn't chocolate crazy, I love this tart. I created it keeping in mind the richness and boldness of a classic chocolate tart but wanting to balance it with the cream topping. The fruitiness of the olive oil and salt complements the dark chocolate and pairs perfectly with the biscuity rye base. The look of the tart is heavily inspired by US artist Wayne Thiebaud – his paintings are a never-ending inspiration for me when it comes to baking. Heavy nostalgia is what I'm after – and excitement.

For the rye pastry, combine the flours, sugar and salt in a medium bowl. With your clean hands, rub in the butter until the flour is coated and the mixture resembles coarse almond meal.

In a separate bowl, combine the cream and egg yolk, then add to the flour mixture and mix through. Make sure not to overwork the dough – stop as soon as it is hydrated enough to come together and form a disc. Wrap in biodegradable plastic wrap and refrigerate for 15 minutes. Lightly dust your surface with the extra plain flour, then roll out your pastry into a round about 4 mm (⅛ inch) thick. Place the pastry in a round 20 cm (8 inch) loose-based tart (flan) tin, trimming away any excess. Cover the top and sides with foil, shaping the foil to the inside of the base, and freeze for 40 minutes. After 25 minutes, preheat your oven to 180°C/350°F fan-forced (200°C/400°F conventional).

With the foil still on, fill the base with baking weights (such as rice or dried legumes). Bake for 30 minutes. Remove the foil and weights, and bake for a further 15 minutes. Cool completely in the tin.

Start your chocolate filling once the tart shell has cooled (or see the note opposite). Preheat your oven to 175°C/350°F fan-forced (195°C/375°F conventional).

Put the chocolate in a medium bowl and set aside.

Heat the cream in a small saucepan over medium heat. Just before it reaches the boil, remove from the heat and pour it over your chocolate. Let it sit for 2 minutes, then whisk to combine. Add the sugar and salt and whisk again. Lightly whisk the eggs and vanilla in a separate small bowl, then add to the chocolate mixture and whisk to combine.

To assemble the tart, place your tart shell (still in the tin) on a baking tray, and pour in your chocolate mixture. Bake on the middle shelf of the oven for 16–18 minutes – you still want a slight wobble in the centre.

Set aside to cool completely.

I like to use a mix of dark chocolate: half Ecuadorian, half Dominican Republic, both from local chocolatiers Hunted + Gathered (see page 281).

Olive oil mascarpone cream

250 g (9 oz) mascarpone cheese

15 g (½ oz) quality extra virgin olive oil

250 g (9 oz) pouring cream

100 g (3½ oz) caster (superfine) sugar

2 g (¹⁄₁₆ oz) fine salt

To decorate (optional)

5–6 maraschino cherries, halved and stones removed

Meanwhile, make the olive oil mascarpone cream. Using a hand whisk, whisk the mascarpone in a small bowl just to loosen it, then add the olive oil in a thin stream, whisking constantly to combine.

In a stand mixer with the whisk attachment, whisk the cream and sugar on medium–high speed until soft peaks form. Once the cream has reached soft peaks, add your mascarpone mixture with your salt and mix on medium speed until medium–stiff peaks form, taking care not to overwhip. If you're worried, you can complete this step using a hand whisk.

Refrigerate the cream mixture while your tart cools down.

To assemble your tart, top the chocolate filling with the mascarpone cream and smooth it out using an angled palette knife or spatula. You can pipe it if you like, but the simplicity of the layered cream and chocolate is a beautiful sight once cut.

Refrigerate the tart for at least 30 minutes before cutting. Dip a sharp straight-edged knife in a cup of boiling water before cutting each slice, wiping the knife with a wet cloth after each cut.

You can also make your base the night before and the chocolate filling the next day. Just make sure to store the base, still in its tin, at room temperature in an airtight container or wrapped in foil or biodegradable plastic wrap.

Amaro crème caramel with salted, caramelised cacao

Charlie Duffy
Profiled on page 44

SERVES 6
SPECIAL EQUIPMENT 20 × 5 cm (8 × 2 inch) diameter non-stick baking dish, deep roasting dish or tin, rolling pin

Amaro caramel
80 g (2¾ oz) amaro liqueur
160 g (5¾ oz) caster (superfine) sugar
40 g (1½ oz) water

Custard
460 g (1 lb) milk
140 g (5 oz) whipping cream
1 vanilla bean, split lengthways and seeds scraped
200 g (7 oz) egg (from about 4 eggs)
50 g (1¾ oz) egg yolk (from about 3 eggs)
75 g (2¾ oz) caster (superfine) sugar
50 g (1¾ oz) brown sugar

The custard is best when it contains no air bubbles. For an even denser, creamier texture, use a stick blender to mix the eggs and sugar, then blend in the warm cream and milk. Be sure to have the head of the stick blender fully immersed in the mix to prevent aeration.

This simple and textural dessert will happily sit in your fridge until it's time to eat. The key to this dish is getting the caramelised sugar and cooked egg custard just right – so be sure not to under- or over-caramelise the sugar, and ensure the custard is cooked just enough that it sets. I love the herbaceousness of the amaro caramel, and the salty caramelised cacao helps temper the tannins. Feel free to splash on some extra amaro when serving – for this recipe, I like to use the Native Australian Amaro by Autonomy Distillers, which is based locally to me in the Melbourne suburb of Spotswood.

Preheat the oven to 140°C/275°F fan-forced (160°C/325°F conventional) and boil a full kettle of water.

For the amaro caramel, gently warm the amaro in a small saucepan over medium heat. This will help prevent the sugar from shocking and spitting at you when you add it to the caramel. Combine the caster sugar and water in a separate small saucepan and gently mix with a spoon to wet all the sugar. Place the saucepan over high heat and, without stirring (or the sugar will crystallise), gently bring to a dark amber caramel, removing the saucepan from the heat just as the sugar begins to darken, and letting the residual heat finish the caramel. This will allow you a bit more time to judge and obtain a perfect dark amber caramel. Once the caramel is coloured to perfection, gradually add the warmed amaro.

Return the saucepan to high heat and boil for exactly 2 minutes. Pour the amaro caramel into a round 20 × 5 cm (8 × 2 inch) non-stick baking dish, swirling the dish to coat the side. Leave to cool completely.

Meanwhile, to make the custard, combine the milk, cream and vanilla bean and seeds in a saucepan over medium heat and heat to just below a simmer. In a mixing bowl, combine the egg, egg yolk, caster sugar and brown sugar. Stir gently with a whisk until the eggs and sugar are combined. Slowly pour the warm milk and cream mixture into the egg mixture and stir to combine. Leave to cool and infuse slightly at room temperature.

Place the caramel-coated baking dish in a deep roasting dish or tin large enough to hold it. Strain the custard mixture through a fine-mesh sieve directly into the baking dish. Pour the hot water into the roasting dish so that it comes halfway up the side of the round dish. Cover the whole roasting dish with foil, then carefully place in the oven and bake for 35–45 minutes. You're looking for a slight ripple and wobble in the custard when it is ready.

Remove the roasting dish and crème caramel from the oven and leave to cool for 10 minutes or until the crème caramel dish is cool enough to handle. At that point, remove from the roasting dish and leave to cool at room temperature for 1 hour. Refrigerate for at least 4 hours or even overnight. >

Salted caramelised cacao
30 g (1 oz) water
50 g (1¾ oz) caster (superfine) sugar
50 g (1¾ oz) cacao nibs
1 g (1/32 oz) sea salt
10 g (¼ oz) unsalted butter

Try to source cacao nibs from a cacao-roasting business near you if possible. The difference between freshly roasted cacao nibs and cacao from the shelf is remarkable. Even if they don't sell them as a product, ask nicely and I'm sure they will help.

To make the salted caramelised cacao, combine the water and caster sugar in a small saucepan over high heat and boil, without stirring (or the sugar will crystallise), until the syrup starts to turn very light golden. Add the cacao nibs and salt and continue cooking over high heat until the sugar starts to fully caramelise, turning golden amber. Remove from the heat and add the butter. Mix until the butter is melted and combined, then immediately pour onto a silicone baking mat or baking paper. Once cooled completely, crush with a rolling pin to form a coarse crumble texture.

To serve, run a small knife around the edge of the crème caramel and invert onto a flat plate. Scatter the salted caramelised cacao over the top and serve.

Pandan, coconut and mango chiffon roll

Patchanida Chimkire
Profiled on page 174

SERVES 5
SPECIAL EQUIPMENT 25 × 38 × 2.5 cm (10 × 15 × 1 in) rectangular baking tray, two large wire racks, stand mixer with whisk attachment, blender or food processor, sugar thermometer (optional), angled palette knife, cheesecloth, piping bag and saint honoré nozzle (optional)

Mango curd
about 325 g (11½ oz) mango (from about 1 large mango)
70 g (2½ oz) egg yolk (from about 4 eggs)
50 g (1¾ oz) caster (superfine) sugar
1 g (1/32 oz) salt
50 g (1¾ oz) lemon juice (from 1 large lemon)
zest of 1 lemon
85 g (3 oz) chilled butter, diced

Whipped toasted coconut cream
140 g (5 oz) flaked coconut
700 g (1 lb 9 oz) whipping cream
1 3 g (1/8 oz) fine sea salt
40 g (5 oz) coconut cream
70 g (2¼ oz) icing (confectioners') sugar, sifted, plus extra to finish
1½ ripe mangoes, peeled and cut into 1 cm (½ inch) dice

This cake is reminiscent of my childhood in Thailand. It's made up of memories of sun-soaked summers and the perfume of perfectly ripened mangoes wafting through my grandparents' garden. Add pandan – a grassy plant with sweet floral notes and a vibrant green hue – and a slightly salted coconut cream, and I can move towards that dream, bite by bite, all rolled up in a cloud-like chiffon cake. Although this is easy to make, the key to perfection lies in preparation and timing: having all your ingredients and equipment ready allows for seamless continuity. Once you've started the chiffon, there's no turning back. Baking your chiffon at a high temperature ensures a swift rise for that perfectly light and airy texture.

For the mango curd, first purée the mango in a blender or food processor until smooth. Weigh out 120 g (4¼ oz) to use and set aside.

In a heatproof bowl that fits into a saucepan with clearance beneath, whisk together the egg yolk, caster sugar and salt until well combined. Make a bain-marie by bringing water to a simmer in the saucepan and placing the bowl on top, ensuring it doesn't touch the water. Whisking continuously, gradually add the mango purée, lemon juice and lemon zest to the egg mixture. Once the mixture has thickened to a custard-like consistency and coats the back of a spoon or has reached 75°C/165°F (this may take 10–15 minutes), remove the bowl from the heat. Add the butter, stirring until the butter is completely melted and the curd is smooth.

Strain the mango curd through a fine-mesh sieve into a clean bowl. Cool at room temperature, then cover with biodegradable plastic wrap, with the wrap directly touching the surface of the curd to prevent a skin forming. Refrigerate for at least 1–2 hours to cool completely before using. The curd will continue to thicken as it cools.

For the whipped toasted coconut cream, gently toast the flaked coconut by spreading on a dry baking tray and toasting in an 180°C/350°F fan-forced (200°C/400°F conventional) oven for 8–10 minutes or toasting in a small dry frying pan over medium heat until light golden. Stir every 2–3 minutes to make sure it doesn't burn. Once you've achieved that lovely light golden colour, remove from the heat and set aside to cool completely. (This step is the key to unlocking that nutty coconut flavour, so give it the attention it deserves for the best results.) Set aside half of the coconut in an airtight container to use as a garnish later.

In a small saucepan over medium–low heat, heat the cream, toasted coconut and salt until just hot. Pour into a small airtight container and leave to steep in the fridge for at least 3 hours or overnight. >

You can prepare the mango curd ahead. The whipped toasted coconut cream is best made just before using.

Pandan juice

30 g (1 oz) fresh pandan leaves, thinly sliced
120 g (4¼ oz) cold water

Buy tinned pandan juice in Asian supermarkets.
I prefer to avoid using pandan essence, as the flavour can be overly artificial.

Pandan chiffon

120 g (4¼ oz) cake flour (or 100 g/ 3½ oz plain/all-purpose flour mixed with 20 g/¾ oz cornflour/ cornstarch)
½ teaspoon baking powder
¼ teaspoon salt
2 teaspoons full-fat powdered milk
180 g (6¼ oz) chilled egg white (from about 6 eggs)
100 g (3½ oz) caster (superfine) sugar, plus extra for sprinkling
½ teaspoon cream of tartar
120 g (4¼ oz) egg yolk (from about 6 eggs), at room temperature
100 g (3½ oz) pandan juice (see above)
80 g (2¾ oz) vegetable oil
4 drops of green food colouring

For the pandan juice, blend the sliced pandan leaves and water in a blender on high speed until the liquid turns a vibrant green. Strain through a piece of cheesecloth. Set aside 100 g (3½ oz) of pandan juice to use in the chiffon cake.

Preheat the oven to 180°C/350°F fan-forced (200°C/400°F conventional). Line a 25 × 38 × 2.5 cm (10 × 15 × 1 inch) rectangular baking tray with baking paper.

For the pandan chiffon, sift the flour, baking powder, salt and milk powder into a small bowl.

Combine the egg white, 100 g (3½ oz) of the caster sugar and the cream of tartar in your clean stand mixer bowl. Whisk gently by hand until the sugar dissolves completely – you want to avoid incorporating air at this stage. (This method is great for making sure there are no sugar granules left behind in your meringue.)

In a separate medium mixing bowl, slightly break up the egg yolk with a hand whisk, then add the remaining sugar. Whisk until the sugar is fully dissolved, and the mixture turns slightly pale yellow. Add the pandan juice, oil and green food colouring to the yolk mixture, mixing well.

Fit your stand mixer bowl with the egg white mixture to the stand mixer with the whisk attachment. Whisk on high speed until stiff peaks form, about 7 minutes (whipping egg whites when they are cold rather than at room temperature can take longer, but results in a much more stable meringue). To check if the meringue has reached stiff peaks, stop the mixer and lift the whisk. If the peaks stand upright and don't bend or flop over, the meringue is ready. Be careful not to overbeat.

Sift the flour mixture into the egg yolk and pandan mixture one-third at a time, using a silicone spatula to fold in after each addition and ensuring there are no lumps. (It's important to add the dry ingredients to the egg yolk and pandan mixture only at this point. If the baking powder sits in the liquid for too long it will activate too soon and the chiffon won't rise properly. The same applies if your meringue sits for too long.)

Gently fold half of the meringue into the batter, then add the remaining meringue and fold carefully until well incorporated.

Pour the batter into the prepared tray and smooth the top with an angled palette knife. Tap the tray on the work surface three times to eliminate any large air bubbles. Bake for 12 minutes or until the top turns golden brown.

Lightly spray two large wire racks with oil to prevent sticking. Place the cooked chiffon, in the tin, on the first rack and cool for 5 minutes.

Use a small knife to release the cake from the sides of the tray. Place the second cooling rack on top and flip the tin by holding it between the two cooling racks. Gently remove the baking tray and paper, then leave the cake to cool for a further 5 minutes. The lovely green side of the cake should now be facing up and the browned side down.

To assemble

1½ ripe mangoes, peeled and cut into 1 cm (½ inch) dice

Sprinkle a small amount of extra caster sugar over the cake, cover with a tea towel (dish towel) slightly larger than the cake, and place the other wire rack on top of the towel. Flip the cake between the racks again, so that the brown side is now facing up and the tea towel is under the cake.

Slowly peel the top wire rack from the cake. Using a small knife, scrape off that golden crust (to help the mango curd soak into the cake and make sure the cream sticks on just right).

With the cake still warm, use the tea towel under the cake to roll the cake up into a log, starting from a short edge. The tea towel will be rolled into the cake and will prevent it from sticking together. Let the cake cool completely before filling.

To finish the whipped toasted coconut cream, refrigerate your stand mixer bowl for at least 30 minutes. Strain the coconut-infused cream, discarding the coconut, then combine with the coconut cream and icing sugar in the chilled bowl. Whisk using the stand mixer with the whisk attachment on medium–high speed until stiff peaks form. Measure out 600 g (1 lb 5 oz) and refrigerate the remainder in an airtight container to use as a garnish later.

To assemble the roll, begin by carefully unrolling the cake while keeping the tea towel beneath it for support. Position the short edge that will be on the inside of the roll facing towards you and have the outer edge pointing in the opposite direction.

Using an angled palette knife, evenly spread 4 tablespoons of mango curd thinly over the cake. Next, add 500 g (1 lb 2 oz) of the toasted coconut cream, using the angled palette knife to create a smooth, creamy layer over the entire surface of the cake. Scatter the fresh mango evenly on top.

With a gentle touch, start rolling the cake back up. Hold on to the tea towel to guide the rolling and prevent the cake from breaking. Ensure the roll is sitting on its seam, then cover with biodegradable plastic wrap and refrigerate overnight.

When ready to serve, trim each end off the roll to neaten. Remove the reserved whipped toasted coconut cream from the fridge and use a hand whisk to whip lightly, as it may have deflated slightly overnight. Spoon the cream into a piping bag fitted with a saint honoré (or your preferred) piping nozzle. Pipe a swirl of coconut cream along the top of the roll and garnish with the reserved toasted coconut. Dust with extra icing sugar, then cut into five slices about 4 cm (1½ inches) thick using a hot knife.

This part is important – if you don't refrigerate the roll overnight, it won't set.

Patchanida Chimkire

Cherry pie

Kimmy Gastmeier
Profiled on page 210

SERVES 6–8

SPECIAL EQUIPMENT 24 cm (9½ inch) pie dish or foil pie tin about 3 cm (1¼ oz) deep, stand mixer with paddle attachment, food processor, rolling pin, pastry brush, palette knife, lattice cutter (optional)

Cherry jam

200 g (7 oz) frozen or fresh sweet cherries, stones removed
100 g (3½ oz) raw (demerara) sugar
½ vanilla bean, split lengthways and seeds scraped
1 tablespoon lemon juice

Macerated cherries

450 g (1 lb) fresh, tinned or frozen cherries, stones removed
3 tablespoons raw (demerara) sugar
3 tablespoons amaretto

Shortcrust pastry

600 g (1 lb 5 oz) plain (all-purpose) flour, plus extra for dusting
2 pinches of salt
450 g (1 lb) chilled unsalted butter, diced
150 ml (5 fl oz) chilled water
2½ teaspoons lemon juice

This recipe is perfect for a fun time in the kitchen – it's what cherry dreams are made of and is a delicious treat to share with people you love. Just so you know what you're in for: first you will need to make a shortcrust pastry (or you can use bought pastry), as well as a frangipane and cherry jam, then macerate some cherries and line the pie base. Constructing it is the fun and rewarding part. At Cherry Moon, we love dark caramelisation and a lovely crisp pastry – follow our method for the same result.

For the cherry jam, put the cherries in a saucepan and cover with the sugar, vanilla bean and seeds. Cover and leave to macerate for an hour (or overnight in the fridge is also fine).

Once the cherries have let out some of their juice, place the saucepan over low heat and cook slowly until the liquid has reduced and the jam is starting to look thick. Just be careful the jam doesn't go so far as to caramelise. When the jam is ready, add the lemon juice and remove from the heat. Allow to cool, remove the vanilla bean (add it to some sparkling water for a treat) and set aside.

To macerate the cherries, place them in a bowl. Sprinkle the raw sugar and amaretto over them and toss gently. Cover and set aside in the fridge for a few hours or overnight.

For the shortcrust pastry, combine the flour, salt and butter in a food processor (not a blender) and pulse a few times to break down the butter into coarse bits. Add the water and lemon juice and pulse a few more times, taking care not to emulsify them. The dough should look very lumpy. Turn out onto a bench. Using the heel of your hand, push the dough gently away from you to bring it together.

Divide the dough in two, then knead each half very lightly into a ball and press into a disc about 15 cm (6 inches) in diameter. Wrap in baking paper or biodegradable plastic wrap. Refrigerate for 15–20 minutes to firm up, but don't allow the dough to become hard. Dust a work surface lightly with flour and dust a rolling pin. Roll one of the dough pieces into a circle 27–28 cm (10¾–11¼ inches) in diameter.

Prepare a 24 cm (9½ inch) round pie dish or foil pie tin about 3 cm (1¼ inches) deep by spraying with canola oil.

Use the rolling pin to roll up the pastry, then lay it over the tin. Ease the pastry into the sides of the tin. Don't worry about the rustic edges at this point.

Roll the second dough piece, which is for the lattice, into more of a rectangle, the same thickness as the base, and refrigerate to rest for 20 minutes. >

Frangipane
65 g (2¼ oz) almond meal
15 g (½ oz) cake flour
small pinch of salt
65 g (2¼ oz) room-temperature butter, diced
65 g (2¼ oz) raw (demerara) sugar
80 g (2¾ oz) egg (from about 2 eggs)

Egg wash
1 egg
splash of milk

In the meantime, make the frangipane. Sift together the almond meal, flour and salt and set aside. In a stand mixer with the paddle attachment, cream the butter and sugar until light and fluffy. Slowly add the egg a little at a time; by the time you add the last bit it will look like it's about to split, so gently fold through one-third of the dry mix, then add the remaining egg. Make sure all the ingredients are well combined, but don't overwork it.

Remove the lattice pastry from the fridge and lightly dust with flour on both sides. Either cut into 2.5 cm (1 inch) strips if you want to weave your lattice, or if using a lattice cutter; leave a border around the pastry and make sure to cut firmly and then gently separate the lattice. Working with the pastry while it is cool is much easier.

Fill the lined pie dish with the frangipane, spread the cherry jam over, then drain the macerated cherries and scatter them over the top to cover the surface of the pie.

Make an egg wash by whisking the egg and milk together. Using a pastry brush, brush the rim of the pie with egg wash. Gently weave your pastry strips over the top of the pie or lay the lattice-cut pastry over it. Trim any excess pastry from around the edges and gently crimp with a fork or between your thumb and forefinger. Put in the freezer for at least 30 minutes or until ready to bake. Put your feet up – you've had a big day!

When it's time for cherry pie, preheat the oven to 230°C/450°F fan-forced (250°C/500°F conventional) with a flat baking tray on the bottom shelf (important!). While the oven is preheating, pour yourself a drink.

Brush the egg wash gently over the lattice. Turn the oven down to 210°C/400°F fan-forced (230°C/450°F conventional) and quickly place the pie on the hot tray in the oven. Set your timer and cook for 25–30 minutes. Rotate halfway through if you know there's a hot spot in your oven.

Once the pastry is dark golden, turn the temperature down to 170°C/350°F fan-forced (190°C/375°F conventional), and continue cooking to finish crisping the base. Another 10–15 minutes should do it. (Note: I was taught that the colour of caramelisation needs at least 180°C/350°F to occur. This is why it's important to turn your temperature down below this to finish the base without burning the top.)

Use a palette knife or some sort of long, flat utensil to carefully lift the pie slightly from the tin to check the colour and texture of the base. This is probably the hardest part. You are looking for crisp, firm pastry, and an even golden colour on the bottom.

When the base is nicely browned, remove the pie from the oven, and sit it on a window sill to cool slightly. When the neighbours stop by to enquire what that sensational aroma is, take the credit. Your labour of love has really paid off.

Recommended to be served warm or at room temperature with a generous portion of cream or ice cream.

Kimmy Gastmeier

Fig, chocolate and sweet dukkah sundaes

Sophie Hansen
Profiled on page 106

SERVES 4–6
SPECIAL EQUIPMENT food processor or mortar and pestle

Hot chocolate sauce
1 cup (250 ml) pouring cream
40 g (1½ oz) softened unsalted butter
½ cup (110 g) brown sugar
pinch of salt
100 g (3½ oz) dark chocolate, 70%, roughly chopped
¾ cup (80 g) unsweetened cocoa powder
½ teaspoon vanilla extract

Sweet dukkah
½ cup (75 g) hazelnuts or walnuts
⅔ cup (92 g) raw unsalted pistachio nut kernels
⅓ cup (50 g) sesame seeds
½ teaspoon coriander seeds
2 tablespoons poppy seeds
1 teaspoon ground cardamom
1 teaspoon ground cinnamon
½ teaspoon ground nutmeg
2 tablespoons brown sugar
pinch of sea salt

To assemble
quality vanilla ice cream
3–4 fresh figs

What a delicious way to end a summer meal: a little bowl of good vanilla ice cream, fresh figs, a nice dolloping of warm chocolate sauce and a sprinkle of sweet dukkah for crunch and spice. The latter is one of my favourite things, a condiment I'm rarely without, and I love to sprinkle it over porridge, freshly sliced fruit or, in this case, sweet little puddings.

You could replace the figs with any fruit that takes well to chocolate: cherries would be delicious and/or poached pears just for starters. The chocolate sauce is so good it's worth making double. I love to give jars of it to friends as little thank-you presents. It's so delicious.

For the hot chocolate sauce, combine the cream, butter, sugar and salt in a small saucepan over medium heat. Bring to a simmer, then add the chocolate and whisk until it has melted into a smooth sauce. Remove from the heat and whisk in the cocoa and vanilla. Return the pan to low heat and simmer for about 1 minute, until glossy. Serve warm, or refrigerate and reheat when needed.

For the sweet dukkah, preheat the oven to 180°C/350°F fan-forced (200°C/400°F conventional). Spread the hazelnuts or walnuts and the pistachios on a baking tray and toast for 5 minutes. Add the sesame, coriander and poppy seeds, and toast for a further 5 minutes. Remove from the oven.

Tip this mixture into a food processor or mortar and bash with a pestle or blitz until it has a coarse consistency. Transfer to a bowl and stir through the cardamom, cinnamon, nutmeg, sugar and salt. Check the flavour: does it need a little more sugar? Adjust to taste, leave to cool, then store in an airtight jar or container.

To assemble, scoop a little ice cream (or a lot) into bowls, divide the fig pieces between them, pour over the chocolate sauce and finish with the dukkah. Or set up a self-service station so people can make their own.

This recipe makes about 1½ cups (375 ml) of hot chocolate sauce and 1 cup (about 100 g) of sweet dukkah.

Huon apple crumble

Jesse Knierum and Aaron Morgan
Profiled on page 64

SERVES 4–6
SPECIAL EQUIPMENT wide ovenproof frying pan (or bake in a baking dish if you prefer), stand mixer with paddle attachment

Crumble
200 g (7 oz) plain (all-purpose) flour
75 g (2¾ oz) rolled (porridge) oats
75 g (2¾ oz) chopped nuts (almonds, walnuts or hazelnuts)
175 g (6 oz) caster (superfine) sugar
7 g (¼ oz) ground cinnamon
5 g (⅛ oz) ground ginger
pinch of salt
200 g (7 oz) cold diced butter

Apple filling
8 apples (ruby golds, fujis or granny smiths work best)
100 g (3½ oz) caster (superfine) sugar
finely grated zest and juice of 1 lemon, or a splash of apple cider vinegar
7 g (¼ oz) ground cinnamon
5 g (⅛ oz) ground ginger
20 g (¾ oz) unsalted butter

Aaron: One of the first menu items we discussed in the early days of our bakery was based on the importance of using local apples from the many orchards that surround us here in the Huon Valley. My earliest memories are of the aroma of the apple sheds that we visited on a primary school excursion to the valley and the smell of my grandma's freshly baked apple crumble on a Sunday afternoon. Happy times! Here is my re-creation.

For the crumble, mix all the dry ingredients in a stand mixer with the paddle attachment until combined. Slowly, add the butter on low speed, then continue to mix until the mixture has a coarse sandy texture (any more and it will turn into cookie dough).

Preheat the oven to 155°C/300°F fan-forced (175°C/350°F conventional).

For the apple filling, peel, core and roughly dice half the apples. Place in wide ovenproof frying pan with the sugar and lemon zest and juice, and cook over medium heat for about 5 minutes. Meanwhile, peel, core and roughly chop the remaining apples and slowly add to the pan. Stirring regularly to ensure they don't stick to the bottom, cook for a further 5 minutes. (This technique will result in a mixture of contrasting textures.)

Add the spices and butter and stir until the butter is melted.

Cover the apples with the crumble and bake for 45 minutes or until the crumble is nice and golden or the filling is bubbling up and out.

Basque cheesecake

Darren Purchese
Profiled on page 190

SERVES 8
SPECIAL EQUIPMENT 18 cm (7 inch) diameter springform cake tin at least 6 cm (2½ inch) deep, blender

165 g (5¾ oz) egg (from about 3 large eggs)
450 g (1 lb) cream cheese, softened and diced
140 g (5 oz) caster (superfine) sugar
110 g (3¾ oz) mascarpone cheese, at room temperature
65 ml (2¼ fl oz) whipping cream,
1 vanilla bean, split lengthways and seeds scraped
salt, to taste
15 g (½ oz) plain (all-purpose) flour

A Basque cheesecake is such a heavenly dessert, and the aroma that fills your kitchen as you bake it is irresistible. I personally love the cheesecake in all of its stages, but it's best on the day of baking with limited refrigeration. The cheesecake will last up to four days in the fridge, becoming denser as the days progress. Wrap the cheesecake in foil rather than plastic wrap for storage in the fridge.

Pour the egg into a blender and blend on medium speed for 30 seconds. Gradually add the cream cheese and blend again for about a minute. Scrape down the side of the blender with a spatula and mix again for 30 seconds or until smooth. Add the sugar and mix again for 1 minute. Scrape down the side and add the mascarpone, cream, vanilla seeds and salt. Mix again until light and smooth. Finally add the flour and mix again for 1 minute.

Lightly spray an 18 cm (7 inch) diameter springform tin with canola spray and push a 30 cm (12 inch) square sheet of baking paper into the ring (scrunch the paper into a ball first). Push to the edges – you want the paper crinkled, not neat. Lightly spray the inside of the paper with canola spray.

Pour the cheesecake mixture into the prepared tin, then refrigerate for 30 minutes.

Preheat the oven to 200°C/400°F fan-forced (220°C/425°F conventional).

Place the cheesecake in your oven and immediately reduce the temperature to 190°C/375°F fan-forced (210°C/400°F conventional). Bake for 50 minutes.

Cool in the tin for 40 minutes.

The cheesecake will drop as it cools, creating a dip in the surface. Refrigerate for 1 hour, then remove from the tin by releasing the spring and lifting off the ring. Gently pull the paper away from the sides of the cheesecake, being careful not to damage the cake. Lay a large plate over the cheesecake, then invert it and hold the cheesecake in one hand while releasing the base of the tin with the other. Gently remove the entire sheet of paper from the cheesecake and then lay a serving plate on the base of the cheesecake. In one motion, invert the cheesecake once more and remove the first plate. The cheesecake is ready to serve.

To cut, use a sharp non-serrated knife dipped in hot water. Dry the blade with a clean cloth before cutting, and clean, reheat and dry the blade before each cut. Serve each slice on its own, or with lemon curd, fruit compote and pouring cream.

Akira Toyama

Unbaked strawberry cheesecake (opposite)

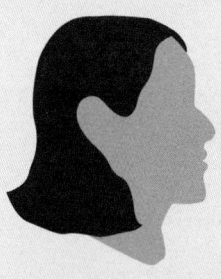

Baker and founder, Only Cheesecake

Melbourne, Vic
Wurundjeri Country

For Akira Toyama, it's always been cheesecake. When Akira was growing up in Aichi, Japan, her mum would take her to the dessert shop on her birthday to choose her cake. It was always cheesecake. 'I've never been as much a fan of spongy cakes or cakes with whipped cream,' says Akira. 'Plus, cheesecakes are so easy to make.' Akira moved to Melbourne in 2016 and swapped a career in fashion design for a different creative expression: baking, with a singular focus on cheesecake. Her pastry career took off during Melbourne's pandemic lockdowns, when she began baking for her partner's cafe, Papirica.

The idea was to deliver something special to cut through the gloomy times – and did it ever. 'At the time, I was really interested in making burnt cheesecake – I loved how creamy and melty it looked on the inside – so I was trying to create my own recipe,' says Akira. 'I think I made over twenty cakes to get it right.' After her baking attracted a cultish following, she launched the aptly named Only Cheesecake.

Akira's work is inspired by the Japanese cheesecakes, with their satisfying form and balance – from burnished Basque-influenced creations infused with the balancing herbal notes of matcha, to airy unbaked cheesecakes with whole strawberry surprises within, and vegan cheesecakes with fresh ingredients such as adzuki beans.

'My inspiration comes from Japanese flavours like yuzu, miso, matcha or hojicha, which is a charcoal-roasted tea,' says Akira. These are balanced with an even sweetness that could convert any so-called savoury tooth and please all 'not-too-sweet' fans. Then there's the satisfaction on the plate. 'It's not just the flavour, it's how it looks on the plate – like a perfect triangle.' And in the time it takes to fork through a slice, it all feels pretty perfect indeed.

ON MAKING PERFECT CHEESECAKES

'Remember that the texture of the cheesecake will be different once you bake it. So mix it for a long time – that means longer than you think – to make sure it's as smooth as can be. I also strain my mixture through a really fine sieve as an extra step. To cut a perfect slice, use a hot, sharp knife – I carefully heat the blade over the flame of a gas stove. Repeat this step before cutting each slice, wiping your knife clean each time.'

Unbaked strawberry cheesecake

SERVES 9
SPECIAL EQUIPMENT 20 cm (8 inch) diameter cake tin, stand mixer with whisk attachment, food processor or blender

Base
130 g (4½ oz) plain sweet biscuits (cookies; e.g. Marie biscuits)
75 g (2¾ oz) unsalted butter, melted

Filling
450 g (1 lb) cream cheese, softened
40 g (1½ oz) sour cream
80 g (2¾ oz) raw (demerara) sugar
50 g (1¾ oz) Greek-style yoghurt
10 g (¼ oz) powdered gelatine
50 ml (1¾ fl oz) water
10 g (¼ oz) lemon juice
360 ml (12 fl oz) whipping cream
15–20 strawberries, hulled

Strawberry sauce
150 g (5½ oz) strawberries, hulled
45 g (1½ oz) raw (demerara) sugar

This type of unbaked cheesecake (it's called 'rare cheesecake' in Japanglish) reminds me of my childhood. It's the kind I would always choose when my mum would take me to the cake shop to buy cakes for our family. With its balance of sweetness and sourness, 'rare cheesecake' is a very common and popular style of cheesecake in Japan. It also has a unique texture: it's rich when you first taste it but so smooth that it quickly melts away in your mouth. My recipe with strawberries makes the cheesecake slightly lighter and gives it added freshness. You can use other fruits – I recommend something seasonal that has some refreshing fruity acidity, such as berries, peaches or apricots.

Line a 20 cm (8 inch) diameter cake tin with a large piece of baking paper that covers the base and side.

For the base, crush the biscuits to the texture of fine sand in a food processor or blender. Transfer to a medium bowl and mix in the melted butter with a spatula.

Press the crumb mixture over the base and side of the tin, making sure you create a flat, compact layer. Refrigerate for 20 minutes to firm.

For the filling, using either a stand mixer with the whisk attachment on medium speed, or whisking by hand, whisk the cream cheese until smooth. Whisk in the sour cream, raw sugar and yoghurt until well combined.

In a small bowl, whisk together the gelatine and water, then heat the mixture in the microwave for 30 seconds.

Add the gelatine mixture to the cheesecake filling and whisk on low speed for 2 minutes, taking care not to overmix.

With the mixer still running on low speed, add the lemon juice and then gradually add the cream. Mix well.

Strain the mixture through a fine-mesh sieve into a large bowl. This will make the cheesecake super smooth and remove any clumps of gelatine and cream.

Halve about half of the strawberries and place them hulled side down around the perimeter of the cheesecake base, side by side, with the cut side flush against the lined cake tin. Arrange the remaining whole strawberries, hulled side down, in two concentric circles on the inside of this ring, about 1 cm (½ inch) apart. Pour the filling over the strawberries, then cover carefully and refrigerate overnight.

To make the strawberry sauce, crush the strawberries in a food processor, add the raw sugar and mix well.

To serve, cut each slice of cheesecake (see opposite for tip) so that a cross-section of strawberry is visible and drizzle with the strawberry sauce.

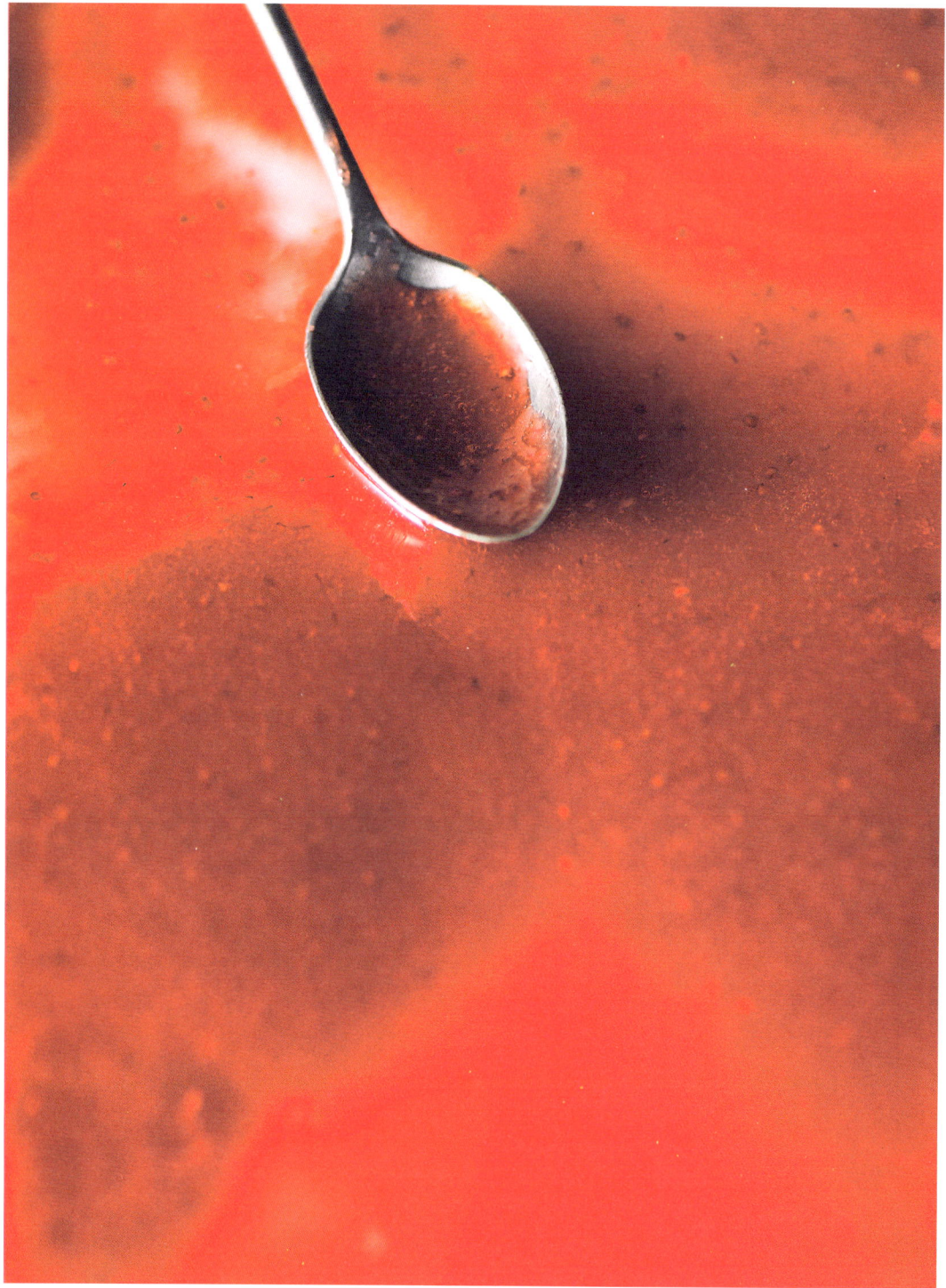

White chocolate and rhubarb pudding with lemon myrtle

Gareth Whitton
Profiled on page 228

SERVES 10

SPECIAL EQUIPMENT 20 cm (8 inch) diameter baking dish, stand mixer with whisk attachment, stick blender, sugar thermometer, kitchen blowtorch

Marinated rhubarb
300 g (10½ oz) rhubarb, cut into 3 cm (1¼ inch) batons
150 g (5½ oz) caster (superfine) sugar
5 g (⅛ oz) citric acid or 10 g (¼ oz) lemon juice

Cake
120 g (4¼ oz) unsalted butter
90 g (3¼ oz) almond meal
45 g (1½ oz) plain (all-purpose) flour
3 g (⅛ oz) baking powder
2 g (1/16 oz) salt
100 g (3½ oz) egg (from about 2 eggs)
120 g (4¼ oz) caster (superfine) sugar

At some point during my career, I made the transition towards being the type of chef who cooks food that is a lot more similar to the food they like to eat themselves. Growing up in fine dining restaurants and being exposed to some of the most concise and elaborate preparations of the time, there was always a disconnect between the food I was cooking at work and the food that I would eat at home.

I still believe that there is a place for innovation in cuisine, but as I became the master of my own destiny, I started to lean towards something that would eventually manifest itself as my own style. This turned out to be something a lot more flavour- and texture-driven, leaning into technique while also emphasising simplicity. I think this dish may even be a move away from that again, but it's so incredibly delicious and easy to execute that, with a little patience and planning, it will steal the show on any occasion.

Preheat the oven to 165°C/325°F fan-forced (185°C/375°F conventional).

For the marinated rhubarb, put the rhubarb in a heatproof bowl with the sugar and citric acid, toss it together and cover with biodegradable plastic wrap. Make a bain-marie by placing the bowl over a saucepan of simmering water, making sure the bowl doesn't touch the water, and leave for about 20 minutes or until the fruit is soft. Gently remove the rhubarb and reserve the syrup (this makes a great cordial for a cocktail or soda water (club soda) – thank me later). Set the marinated rhubarb aside.

To make the cake, melt the butter in a small saucepan over medium heat until it starts to foam. Reduce the heat to low and continue to cook, stirring occasionally, until it stops fizzing and turns mid-brown. Cool slightly, to about 100°C/210°F.

In a medium bowl, stir together the almond meal, flour, baking powder and salt. Using a stand mixer with a whisk attachment on low speed or whisking by hand, slowly combine the egg and sugar until the sugar has dissolved – you don't want to incorporate any air at this stage.

With the mixer still running or while hand-whisking constantly, slowly add the brown butter. Ensure that the mixture is well emulsified, so that the butter doesn't bleed out later and give the cake a greasy texture. Mix in the dry ingredients, making sure there are no lumps.

Pour the batter into a 20 cm (8 inch) diameter baking dish, scatter the rhubarb evenly over the top, and bake for about 25 minutes, or until the crust is golden brown and the centre is firm.

Reduce the oven temperature to 125°C/250°F fan-forced (145°C/300°F conventional).

White chocolate custard

450 g (1 lb) milk
5 g (⅛ oz) lemon myrtle leaves or 2 g (¹⁄₁₆ oz) lemon myrtle powder
2 g (¹⁄₁₆ oz) salt
175 g (6 oz) egg yolk (from about 9 eggs)
20 g (¾ oz) cornflour (cornstarch)
220 g (7¾ oz) white chocolate, roughly chopped

For bruléeing
caster (superfine) sugar

Meanwhile, make the chocolate custard. Bring the milk, lemon myrtle and salt to a simmer in a large saucepan over medium heat. Meanwhile, whisk the egg and cornflour together in a large bowl. Strain the hot milk through a sieve directly into the egg mixture, whisking quickly to combine until there are no lumps. Pour back into the saucepan, return to the heat and, whisking constantly, bring to a simmer. Remove from the heat, then add the chocolate and whisk until combined. Using a stick blender, blend until the mixture is shiny and smooth, keeping the head of the blender fully submerged to ensure no air is incorporated into the mix. Decant into a jug to use straight away – you want to keep it as warm as possible so that it cooks nice and evenly in the next step.

When the rhubarb and almond cake is cooked, leave in the oven and carefully pour the hot custard on top of the cake layer. Bake for 30 minutes or until the custard has a very slight wobble in the centre. Cool completely in the baking dish.

Once cooled, dust the top with a little caster sugar and brulée with a blowtorch until deep golden brown.

This is just as delicious without the caramelised sugar on top, but it adds an amazing textural element that is unmatchable. Take it to another level again by warming slightly and serving with a scoop of any ice cream.

The Baker's Pantry

CHOCOLATE

Cuvée Chocolate, Carrum Downs, Vic
cuveechocolate.com.au
Deniz and Kylie have a real dedication to their product and to using the best single-origin cocoa beans. – GREGORIO MONTALBÁN SÁNCHEZ

Hunted+Gathered, Cremorne, Vic
huntedandgathered.com.au
We have formed a like-minded relationship with Charlie and Harry. Their products and brand really resonate with me.
– NATASHA BROWNFIELD

South Pacific Cacao, Haberfield, NSW
southpacificcacao.com
A social enterprise for chocolate and vanilla.
– MICHAEL JAMES

Valrhona for chocolate and cocoa powder
valrhona.com

Zokoko, Emu Heights, NSW
zokoko.com
Small company that roasts and conches themselves, sourcing ethically grown cacao beans from around the world. – BELINDA JEFFERY

DAIRY

CopperTree Farms, NSW
coppertreefarms.com.au
They use the traditional French method for their butter, which has an 84% fat content, and make the highest-quality cream. – GAD ASSAYAG

Elgaar Farm, Moltema, Tas
elgaarfarm.com.au

Gippsland Jersey, Warragul, Vic
gippslandjersey.com.au

Lard Ass Butter, Ocean Grove, Vic
lardass.com.au
I choose Lard Ass for cream and butter as they're available at farmers' markets regularly.
– GIORGIA McALLISTER FORTE

Stunning cultured butter. – CHARLIE

Pepe Saya, NSW
pepesaya.com.au
The unsalted cultured butter balls have the most perfect consistency as well as quality.
– GARETH WHITTON

Schulz Organic Dairy, Timboon, Vic
schulzorganicdairy.com.au

St David Dairy, Fitzroy, Vic
stdavid.com.au

That's Amore Cheese, Thomastown, Vic
thatsamorecheese.com.au
A favourite producer for all their incredible cheeses including mascarpone.
– DARREN PURCHESE AND CATH CLARINGBOLD

EGGS

Burd Eggs, Goulburn Valley, Vic
burdeggs.com.au

They deliver in Melbourne up to 40 km from the CBD.

Honest Eggs Co., Yandoit, Vic
honesteggsco.com.au

Jessanda Farm Fresh, Yarroweyah, Vic
jessanda.com

Eighty-five birds per hectare. This is proper free range. — ORLANDO ARTAVILLA

FLOUR AND MILLERS

Artisan Grains Australia, Forbes, NSW
@artisangrainsau

Burrum Biodynamics, Wimmera, Vic
burrumbiodynamics.com.au

Oats, wheat and grain by Tania and Steve. — CHARLIE DUFFY

Capital Millers, Miramar, Wellington, NZ
capitalmillers.co.nz

Eden Valley Biodynamic Farm, Dumbleyung, WA
edenvalleybiodynamic.com.au

The Grain Family, Tas
thegrainfamily.com.au

Kialla Pure Organic, Greenmount, Qld
kiallafoods.com.au

Laucke Mills, SA and Vic
laucke.com.au

By far the best range of specialist flours in Australia. They supply the low-protein biscuit flour that we use for all of our shortcrust pastry, but what they're offering extends far beyond. — GARETH WHITTON

Mauri, Australia-wide
mauri.com.au

This is our flour supplier. They have a mill in Northam, one hour east of Perth. — RYAN AND SEREN CHU

Miller + Baker, Perth, WA
millerandbaker.com.au

Milmore Downs, Scargill, NZ
milmoredowns.co.nz

Powlett Hill, Campbelltown, Vic
powletthill.com.au

Rock Paper Flour, Monbulk, Vic
@rockpaperflour

Tuerong Farm, Tuerong, Vic
tuerongfarm.com.au

Whispering Pines Organics, Barrellan, NSW
whisperingpinesorganics.com.au

Wholegrain Milling Co., Gunnedah, NSW
wholegrain.com.au

We get the vast majority of our flours from Wholegrain via Eumarrah. They're family-owned, organic and stoneground. — POOLISH & CO.

Woodstock Flour, Berrigan, NSW/Liliput, Vic
woodstockflour.com.au

The most passionate small flour milling company, just outside of Rutherglen. — ORLANDO ARTAVILLA

Good people growing and milling wheat. — CHARLIE DUFFY

FLOWERS

Petite Ingredient, Wandin North, Vic
petiteingredient.com.au

For edible flowers

Pretty Produce, Canungra, Qld
prettyproduce.com.au

For pressed edible flowers

Wattle Gully Flower Farm, Upper Plenty, Vic
wattlegullyflowerfarm.com.au

Beautiful flowers grown sustainably. Thanisa is usually at the Alphington Farmers' Market on Sundays. – PATCHANIDA CHIMKIRE

The Essential Ingredient, VIC and NSW
essentialingredient.com.au

For dried lavender and liquid natural lavender flavour

FRESH PRODUCE

Berriworx, Yarra Valley, Vic
berriworx.com.au

Vince grows the best berries in Victoria. You can get them fresh when they're in season or frozen all year round. They are frequently at farmers' markets in Victoria. – PATCHANIDA CHIMKIRE

Cane's Orchard, Huon Valley, Tas
eatwelltas.org.au/provider/canes-orchard

A family-owned local institution for beautiful stone fruit and berries. David and Diane are dedicated to caring for the land and producing the best product they can. We love them! – POOLISH & CO.

Carmel Cottage Farm, Bickley, WA
facebook.com/carmelcottagefarm

Independent stone fruit supplier with cherries, apricots, figs, rhubarb, apples and pears.
– NATASHA BROWNFIELD

The Cygnet Garden Larder, Cygnet, Tas
facebook.com/CygnetGardenLarder

We get most of our veg from Bec at The Garden Larder, who works with local, mostly chem-free or organic growers. – POOLISH & CO.

Gippsland Strawberries, Vic
facebook.com/gippslandstrawberries

Delicious red and white strawberries! They are often at Flemington Farmer's Market in Victoria.
– PATCHANIDA CHIMKIRE

Goshen Country, Cape Paterson, Vic
goshencountry.square.site

Mike and Emma stock my bread and pastries at their farm gate and provide their locally grown, chemical-free fruits and vegetables.
– GREGORIO MONTALBÁN SÁNCHEZ

Marlivale farm, Goolmangar, NSW
marlivalefarm.com.au

Pecans and rice grown in the Northern Rivers.
– CHARLIE DUFFY

Morley Growers Market, Malaga, WA
morleygrowers.com.au

This is our fruit and vegetable supplier, whose owners Ryan has known since he was kid! It is a family-run business that supplies the bakery with the highest-quality produce. – SEREN CHU

The Orchard Keepers, Harcourt, Vic
theorchardkeepers.com.au

All the stone fruit imaginable during summer and then onto pears and apples in the winter.
– CHARLIE DUFFY

Spurrel Foraging, Vic
spurrellforaging.com.au

For beautiful lesser known leaves and flowers, alongside some native ingredients and local honey. They also supply my all-time favourite, mountain marigold.
– GIORGIA McALLISTER FORTE

Truelight Farm, Porepunkah, Vic
truelight.farm

For hazelnuts

Wahrina Pistachios, Vic
wahrinapistachios.com.au

For me, the best pistachios in Australia.
— CHARLIE DUFFY

Willow Bridge Farm, Whroo, Vic
facebook.com/willowbridgewalnuts/

For walnuts

HERBS AND SPICES

Cassowary Coast Vanilla, Mourilyan, Qld
@cassowary_coast_vanilla

Divine Vanilla, Cairns, Qld
divinevanilla.com

Gewürzhaus Spice House, Australia-wide
gewurzhaus.com.au

Heilala Vanilla, Tauranga, New Zealand
heilalavanilla.com.au

Sustainably sourced from Tonga

Herbie's Spices, Charmhaven, NSW
herbies.com.au

They really do have the freshest spices ever.
— BELINDA JEFFERY

Luna Vanilla, Melbourne, Vic
lunavanilla.com.au

Sustainably sourced from the Comoros Islands

Mabu Mabu, Melbourne, Vic
mabumabu.com.au

Natural Vanilla Company, O'Connor, WA
naturalvanilla.com.au

I was pleasantly surprised to find someone processing vanilla in Perth. — NATASHA BROWNFIELD

HONEY

Bee Sustainable, Brunswick East, Vic
beesustainable.com.au

MORE PANTRY

Mount Zero, Vic
mountzeroolives.com

Our go-to for olive oil and the olives in our bread.
— ORLANDO ARTAVILLA

The Source Bulk Foods, Australia-wide
thesourcebulkfoods.com.au

It's like an extension of our pantry — we can always find exactly what we need, and we buy in exact quantities so we don't have mountains of leftovers. They stock predominantly Australian products that are beautifully fresh, including dried fruits and nuts, flours, sugars, spices and honey. We take our own containers or use their jars or brown paper bags.
— DARREN PURCHESE AND CATH CLARINGBOLD

TEA AND COFFEE

Little Matcha Girl, Perth, WA
littlematchagirl.com.au

They have a direct relationship with a matcha farm in Kyoto and provide us with premium matcha that gives brilliant taste and colour.
— RYAN CHU

Scullery Made Tea, Barossa Valley, SA
scullerymadetea.com

Seven Seeds Coffee, Melbourne, Vic
sevenseeds.com.au

Local Melbourne legends. — ORLANDO ARTAVILLA

 *Audrey Allard* HOLY SUGAR

 *Anneliese Brancatisano* PEACHES LA CRÈME

 *Alisha Henderson* SWEET BAKES

 *Natalie Paull* BEATRIX BAKES

 *Danielle Alvarez*

 *Natasha Brownfield* TEETER BAKERY

 *Nadine Ingram* FLOUR AND STONE

 *Tilly Pamment* THE PLAIN CAKE APPRECIATION SOCIETY

 *Rosemary Andrews* MIETTA

 *Patchanida Chimkire* MALI BAKES

 *Emelia Jackson*

 *Darren Purchese* STUDIO KITCHEN

 *Orlando Artavilla* CANDIED BAKERY

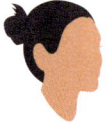 *Ryan and Seren Chu* CHU BAKERY

 *Michael James*

 *Haikal Raji* A1 BAKERY

 *Gad Assayag* BAKER BLEU

 *Marianna Di Bartolo*

 *Belinda Jeffery*

 *Raymond Tan* RAYA BAKERY

 *Jo Barrett* WILDPIE

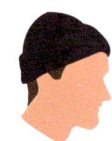 *Charlie Duffy* SMALL BATCH ROASTING CO.

 *Jesse Knierum and Aaron Morgan* POOLISH & CO.

 *Akira Toyama* ONLY CHEESECAKE

 *Gillian Bell*

 *Kimmy Gastmeier* CHERRY MOON GENERAL STORE

 *Giorgia McAllister Forte* MONFORTE VIENNOISERIE

 *Maaryasha Werdiger* ZELDA BAKERY

 *Alice Bennett* MISS TRIXIE DRINKS TEA

 *Sophie Hansen* LOCAL LOVELY

 *Gregorio Montalbán Sánchez* THE INVY BAKER

 *Gareth Whitton* TARTS ANON

 *Nornie Bero* BIG ESSO BY MABU MABU

 *Cherie Hausler* ALL THE THINGS

 *Dougal Muffet* A.P BAKERY

Find the Bakers

Audrey Allard
Holy Sugar
236 High Street, Northcote, Vic
holysugar.com.au
@holysugar__

Danielle Alvarez
daniellemalvarez.com
@daniellemariealvarez

Rosemary Andrews
Mietta
23 Glenferrie Road, Malvern, Vic
miettabyrosemary.com.au
@miettamelbourne
@rosemary___a

Orlando Artavilla
Candied Bakery
136 Hall Street, Spotswood, Vic
candiedbakery.com.au
@candiedbakery

Gad Assayag
Baker Bleu
2 Guilfoyle Avenue, Double Bay, NSW
119–121 Hawthorn Road, Caulfield North, Vic
42 Errol Street, Prahran, Vic
bakerbleu.com.au
@bakerbleu
@bakerbleu.sydney
@gad_assayag

Jo Barrett
Wildpie
wildpie.com.au
@wild.pie
@jobarrett

Gillian Bell
gillianbellcake.com.au
@gillianbellcake

Alice Bennett
Miss Trixie Drinks Tea
misstrixiedrinkstea.com
@misstrixiedrinkstea

Co.Bake Space
239 Swan Street, Richmond, Vic
cobake.com.au
@cobakespace

Nornie Bero
Big Esso by Mabu Mabu
Fed Square, 25/2 Swanston Street,
   Melbourne, Vic
mabumabu.com.au
@mabu_mabu_aus
@norniebero

Anneliese Brancatisano
Peaches la Crème
hipeaches@outlook.com.au
@_peacheslacreme__

Natasha Brownfield
Teeter Bakery
145A Claisebrook Road, Perth, WA
teeterbakery.com
@teeterbakery

Patchanida Chimkire
Mali Bakes
627 High Street, Thornbury, Vic
malibakes.com
@mali_bakes

Ryan and Seren Chu
Chu Bakery
498 William Street, Highgate, WA
@chubakery

Marianna Di Bartolo
Dolcetti Cakes
@dolcetticakes

Charlie Duffy
Small Batch Roasting Co.
3–9 Little Howard Street,
  North Melbourne, Vic
msha.ke/smallbatchroast
@smallbatchroast

Kimmy Gastmeier
Cherry Moon General Store
77A Nelson Street, Annandale, NSW
cherrymoongeneralstore.com.au
@cherrymoongeneralstore

Sophie Hansen
Local is Lovely
local-lovely.com
@locallovely

Cherie Hausler
All The Things
allthethings.com.au
@allthethings_au
@cherie_hausler

Alisha Henderson
Sweet Bakes
@sweetbakes_

Co.Bake Space
239 Swan Street, Richmond, Vic
cobake.com.au
@cobakespace

Nadine Ingram
Flour and Stone
43 and 53 Riley Street,
  Woolloomooloo, NSW
flourandstone.com.au
@flourandstone
@nadineingram

Emelia Jackson
emeliajackson.com
@emelia_jackson

Michael James
Urbanstead
urbanstead.au
@urbanstead.au
@michaeljamesbakes

Belinda Jeffery
belindajeffery.com.au
@belindajefferyfood

Jesse Knierum and Aaron Morgan
Poolish & Co.
26 Mary Street, Cygnet, Tas
@poolishandco

Giorgia McAllister Forte
Monforte Viennoiserie
585A Canning Street, Carlton North, Vic
@monforteviennoiserie
@giorge__

Gregorio Montalbán Sánchez
The Invy Baker
invybaker.com
@theinvybaker

Dougal Muffet
A.P Bakery
80 Commonwealth Street, Surry Hills, NSW
1A Bucknell Street, Newtown, NSW
9 Barrack Street, Sydney, NSW
245 Wilson Street, Eveleigh, NSW
apbakery.com.au
@a.p.bread

Tilly Pamment
tillystable.com.au
@tillys_table

Natalie Paull
Beatrix Bakes
beatrixbakes.com
@beatrixbakes

Darren Purchese & Cath Claringbold
Studio Kitchen
studiokitchen.com.au
@lovestudiokitchen
@darrenpurchese
@cathclaringbold

Haikal Raji
A1 Bakery
643–645 Sydney Road, Brunswick, Vic
122 Station Street, Fairfield, Vic
295 Brunswick Street, Fitzroy, Vic
a1bakery.com.au
@a1bakery
@a1bakeryfoodtruck

Raymond Tan
Raya Bakery
Shop 2, 61 Little Collins Street,
 Melbourne, Vic
rayamelbourne.com
rymondtn.com
@raya.melbourne
@rymondtn

Akira Toyama
Only Cheesecake
onlycheesecake.info
@only.cheese.cake

Maaryasha Werdiger
Zelda Bakery
54 Glen Eira Road, Ripponlea, Vic
zeldabakery.com.au
@z_e_l_d_a_bakery

Gareth Whitton
Tarts Anon
44 Sackville Street, Collingwood, Vic
29A Gwynne Street, Cremorne, Vic
tartsanon.com.au
@tarts_anon
@gareddio

Some of our bakers have generously filmed the recipes they've shared in this book – check out their socials.

The Team

SALLY FRAWLEY, SARAH WATSON, EMELIA JACKSON

MICHAEL JAMES

EMILY O'NEILL

BECI ORPIN

RUBY GOSS

LORAN McDOUGALL

JANE WILLSON

KRISTY ALLEN

ROCHELLE EAGLE, LEE BLAYLOCK

NATALIE PAULL

Thank You

This is for the bakers! Thank you for trusting us with your stories and for sharing your recipes; for giving your time and wisdom, your craft and creativity to this book. Every one of you mentioned what a joy it was to be part of the baking community in Australia. There's something about bakers – a particular generosity – and the fingerprints of this are all over this book, thanks to you. We hope we've done you proud.

Special thank yous to Rosemary Andrews for sparking the idea to hero Australia's bakers and pastry chefs (there's enough talent to fill several books – and rest assured, we wish you were all in these pages!); to Natalie Paull for making our dreams come true and gracing us with the most beautiful opening to this book – a love letter to those who bake; to Michael James for offering guidance and endless enthusiasm, and helping hands on set for a particularly bready day; and to Emelia Jackson, who put her hand up to chef on set and brought delight and finesse in spades.

A huge, huge thank you to Jane Willson for bringing me onto this project and being the ultimate collaborator – always there to offer wisdom, care and excitement, no matter the count on our email threads. Jane is the person you want in your creative corner, and I'm so grateful to have had her in mine. To Loran McDougall – editors hold the entire world of a book in their head – thank you for steering this project with smarts and grace, with eyes on both this biggest of pictures and the finest of its details, and with helpful guidance always at the ready.

To Nicola Young, for having the keenest of eyes and for deftly handling baking queries and narrative alike. Thank you for the balance and precision you've brought to this book.

Thank you to the most brilliant shoot team – six days with you was simply not enough. To the creative duo that is Lee Blaylock and Rochelle Eagle – it was such a treat to watch you dream up the scenes of the book and make them a reality. Your camaraderie is a thing of beauty, and how lucky we are to have it captured in these pages. To Sarah Watson for running the most skilful, seamless and collaborative kitchen – the energy in there was inspiring, and the output works of art. And to Sally Frawley for keeping us smooth-sailing, high-spirited and plied with cake.

Thank you to Kristy Allen for expertly guiding the look and feel of this book. To Emily O'Neill for designing the most beautiful home for it, with its many rooms of wonder. And to Beci Orpin, for illustrations that bring delight and deliciousness. What a treat to have collaborated with you all.

A single book has a whole community behind it – thank you now to mine. To Oli – I love every day with you. For your open ears, wisdom, and cheering-ons, a huge thank you to my butterscotch-pud-partner, my sister Amelia, and to Tom; to the dream duo Francesca and Mireille; and to Tal, Maddy and Ana. To Em for being a magic link. To Mum for making the kitchen table the world. To Dad, Noah and the Kenwrights – I love that food is our favourite language. And to Willa and Delphine, my tiniest, most sparkling bakers.

RUBY GOSS is a writer and editor based in Melbourne/Naarm, on the lands of the Wurundjeri people of the Kulin Nation. Growing up, like most teenagers she spent Saturday mornings in bed reading Nigella Lawson's baking bible *How to Be a Domestic Goddess*, waiting to be old enough to steep rhubarb in vodka. Obsessed as ever by the home kitchen, she has edited cookbooks by notable chefs, written for award-winning publishers and magazines, developed recipes, and worked on food and travel video series in Europe.

Index

A

A1 Bakery 222, 291
A1 pies, three ways 224–5
All Purpose Bakery 132, 390
All The Things 180, 290
Allard, Audrey 238–40, 289
almonds
   almond and emmer sable 122
   almond paste 139, 143
   Burnt butter and pecan cakes 47
   caramelised almond topping 140
   Cherry pie 262–5
   Chocolate, amaretto and sour cherry tart 122–3
   chocolate pastry 243
   Cinnamon braid 142–3
   cinnamon filling 142
   crumble 268
   Dark chocolate, orange and almond crumb-kies 6
   frangipane 107, 134, 264
   Huon apple crumble 268
   Lemon, polenta and raspberry tea cake 127
   Negroni chocolate tart 243
   Pea and feta tart 230–2
   Pear frangipane slab tart 107
   Pistachio amaretti 42
   Plum, frangipane and cream cheese galettes 134–6
   Swedish semlor 139–40
   White chocolate and rhubarb pudding with lemon myrtle 276–7
Alvarez, Danielle 198–203, 289
amaretti, Pistachio 42
amaretto
   Cherry pie 262–5
   Chocolate, amaretto and sour cherry tart 122–3
   chocolate mousse 123
   macerated cherries 262
amaro caramel 255
Amaro crème caramel with salted, caramelised cacao 255–6
Andrews, Rosemary 158–60, 243, 289
A.P Bakery 132, 290
apples
   apple caramel 173
   apple filling 268
   Beetroot and apple cake with wattleseed icing 99
   Hazelnut and apple cake with sour cream frosting and apple caramel 172–3
   Huon apple crumble 268

aquafaba
   Layered rhubarb meringue cake 182–3
   meringue icing 182–3
Artavilla, Orlando 22–5, 90, 289
artichokes *see* Jerusalem artichoke
Assayag, Gad 26–8, 92–3, 289

B

babka, Baker Bleu 92–3
Baker Bleu 26, 289
baking, wood-fired 211
Barrett, Jo 96–9, 204–5, 289
Basque cheesecake 270
Bay gâteau d'émotion 113–14
bay leaves
   Bay gâteau d'émotion 113–14
   bay-infused sugar 113
Beatrix Bakes 4, 290
beer: Ginger and orange blossom cake 115–16
Beetroot and apple cake with wattleseed icing 99
Bell, Gillian 110–16, 289
Bennett, Alice 36–9, 167, 289–8
Bero, Nornie 162–4, 289
berries *see* blackberries, pepperberries, raspberries, strawberries
Big Esso 162, 289
biscuits, Feta and dill, with harissa honey butter 203
blackberries
   blackberry purée 177
   Hibiscus cake 164
   olive oil and blackberry buttercream 177
   Preserved lemon layer cake with blackberry and olive oil buttercream 176–8
blenders, stick 229
braid, Cinnamon 142–3
Brancatisano, Anneliese 244–51, 289
bread
   Baker Bleu babka 92–3
   Burnt fenugreek and sesame loaf 215–16
   Fig-leaf sourdough tin loaf 213–14
   Jerusalem artichoke, chilli greens and goat's cheese focaccias 218–19
   Little Picket potato bread with roasted garlic butter and parsley 204–5
brioche dough 32, 92
brisée pastry 134
brownies, Marshmallow 25
Brownfield, Natasha 170–3, 206–7, 289
bruléeing 277
bundt, Buttermilk, with passionfruit icing 147

buns
   cardamom buns 139
   Cinnamon braid 142–3
   fruit buns 90
   Glazed fruit buns 90
   Little Picket potato bread with roasted garlic butter and parsley 204–5
   Strawberry and matcha maritozzi 32–3
   Swedish semlor 139–40
Burnt butter and pecan cakes 47
Burnt fenugreek and sesame loaf 215–16
butter
   creaming butter and sugar 60
   garlic butter 205
   harissa honey butter 203
buttercream
   olive oil and blackberry buttercream 177
   salted vanilla Swiss meringue buttercream 167
buttermilk 37
   Buttermilk bundt with passionfruit icing 147
   Fluffy buttermilk scones 61–2
butterscotch pecan self-saucing pudding, The 15

C

cacao
   Amaro crème caramel with salted, caramelised cacao 255–6
   Inception cake 160
   London fog castagnole, cacao nib sugar and pots de crème 71
cakes
   almond and emmer sable 122
   Basque cheesecake 270
   Bay gâteau d'émotion 113–14
   Beetroot and apple cake with wattleseed icing 99
   Burnt butter and pecan cakes 47
   Buttermilk bundt with passionfruit icing 147
   chocolate cake 160, 167
   Ginger and orange blossom cake 115–16
   Hazelnut and apple cake with sour cream frosting and apple caramel 172–3
   Hibiscus cake 164
   Inception cake 160
   Layered rhubarb meringue cake 182–3
   Lemon, polenta and raspberry tea cake 127
   Lemon, thyme and honey madeleines 73

Miss Trixie's classic chocolate cake 167-8
pandan chiffon 258
Pandan, coconut and mango chiffon roll 257-9
Pandan drømmekage 148
Peach and sour cream cake 118
perfect cheesecakes 272
Plum streusel cake 150-1
Preserved ha layer cake with blackberry and olive oil buttercream 176-8
rhubarb cake 182
Strawberry, chocolate and balsamic lamington stack 191-2
Unbaked strawberry cheesecake 273
Candied Bakery 22, 289
caramel
  amaro caramel 255
  Amaro crème caramel with salted, caramelised cacao 255-6
  apple caramel 173
caramelised almond topping 140
cardamom
  cardamom buns 139
  Swedish semlor 139-40
cassateddi, Ricotta 100-101
castagnole, London fog, cacao nib sugar and pots de crème 71
cavolo nero *see* kale
chantilly, matcha 33
chantilly cream, vanilla 90
cheese
  A1 pies, three ways 224-5
  Feta and dill biscuits with harissa honey butter 203
  haloumi pies 225
  Jerusalem artichoke, chilli greens and goat's cheese focaccias 218-19
  Pea and feta tart 230-2
  Spinach, leek and smoked cheddar cheese slab pie 199-200
  Tomato, herb and quark tart 206-7
  see also cream cheese, feta, haloumi, mascarpone, ricotta
cheesecakes
  Basque 270
  Unbaked strawberry 273
  perfect 272
cherries
  cherry jam 262
  Cherry pie 262-5
  Chocolate, amaretto and sour cherry tart 122-3
  Chocolate and rye tart with olive oil mascarpone cream 250-1
  Chocolate cherry choux 187-9
  macerated cherries 262
  Miss Trixie's classic chocolate cake 167-8
  morello cherry jam 189
  Pistachio amaretti 42
Cherry Moon General Store 210-11, 290
chiffon, pandan 258
chilli
  Jerusalem artichoke, chilli greens and goat's cheese focaccias 218-19
  see also harissa
Chimkire, Patchanida 174-8, 257-9, 289
chocolate 281
  Baker Bleu babka 92-3
  castagnole 71
  Chocolate, amaretto and sour cherry tart 122-3
  Chocolate and rye tart with olive oil mascarpone cream 250-1
  chocolate cake 160, 167
  Chocolate cherry choux 187-9
  chocolate filling 243, 250
  chocolate glaze 160
  chocolate hazelnut ganache 92
  chocolate mousse 123
  Chocolate rye tahini cookies 28
  cookie dough 51
  dark chocolate whipped ganache 188
  Dark chocolate, orange and almond crumb-kies 6
  Fig, chocolate and sweet dukkah sundaes 267
  hot chocolate sauce 267
  Inception cake 160
  London fog castagnole, cacao nib sugar and pots de crème 71
  Macadamia and wattleseed chocolate chip cookies 59
  Marshmallow brownies 25
  matcha chantilly 33
  Miss Trixie's classic chocolate cake 167-8
  Negroni chocolate tart 243
  pots de crème 71
  Strawberry and matcha maritozzi 32-3
  Strawberry, chocolate and balsamic lamington stack 191-2
  strawberry, chocolate and balsamic vinegar jam 191
  Tiramisukis 51
  White chocolate and rhubarb pudding with lemon myrtle 276-7
  white chocolate custard 277
  white chocolate, vanilla and mascarpone cream 192
  see also cacao, cocoa
choux, Chocolate cherry 187-9
choux pastry 187
Chu Bakery 30, 289
Chu flans 102-3
Chu, Ryan and Seren 30-3, 102-3, 289
cinnamon: Cinnamon braid 142-3
Co.Bake Space 36, 48, 289-90
cocoa
  Baker Bleu babka 92-3
  Beetroot and apple cake with wattleseed icing 99
  cacao nib sugar 71
  Chocolate, amaretto and sour cherry tart 122-3
  chocolate cake 160, 167
  chocolate filling 243
  chocolate glaze 160
  chocolate hazelnut ganache 92
  chocolate pastry 243
  Chocolate rye tahini cookies 28
  chocolate soaking sauce 192
  Fig, chocolate and sweet dukkah sundaes 267
  hot chocolate sauce 267
  Inception cake 160
  London fog castagnole, cacao nib sugar and pots de crème 71
  Miss Trixie's classic chocolate cake 167-8
  Negroni chocolate tart 243
  salted caramelised cacao 256
  Strawberry, chocolate and balsamic lamington stack 191-2
  tiramisu frosting 51
  Tiramisukis 51
coconut
  coconut topping 148
  Ondeh ondeh 79
  Pandan, coconut and mango chiffon roll 257-9
  Pandan drømmekage 148
  Strawberry, chocolate and balsamic lamington stack 191-2
  whipped toasted coconut cream 257
coffee 284
  chocolate cake 167
  cookie dough 51
  Marshmallow brownies 25
  Miss Trixie's classic chocolate cake 167-8
  tiramisu frosting 51
  Tiramisukis 51
cookies
  Chocolate rye tahini cookies 28
  cookie dough 51
  cookie dough base 39
  Dark chocolate, orange and almond crumb-kies 6
  Grapefruit creams 54-5
  Macadamia and wattleseed chocolate chip cookies 59
  Mohn hamantaschen (poppyseed cookies) 83-4

perfectly round cookies 159
Tiramisukis 51
cornflakes
honey joy top 39
Miss Trixie's honey joy slice 39
craquelin 187
cream cheese
Basque cheesecake 270
cream cheese mix 134
Hazelnut and apple cake with sour cream frosting and apple caramel 172-3
Hibiscus cake 164
Pea and feta tart 230-2
pea custard 232
Plum, frangipane and cream cheese galettes 134-6
sour cream frosting 173
strawberry gum cream frosting 164
Unbaked strawberry cheesecake 273
creaming butter and sugar 60
creams
crème anglaise 246-7
crème diplomat 118
crème patissière 103
grapefruit cream 55
matcha chantilly 33
olive oil mascarpone cream 251
pots de crème 71
salted vanilla cream 247
vanilla chantilly cream 90
whipped toasted coconut cream 257
white chocolate, vanilla and mascarpone cream 192
see also sour cream
crème anglaise 246-7
crème caramel, Amaro, with salted, caramelised cacao 255-6
crème diplomat 118
crème patissière 103
croissant dough 102
Crullers 66-7
crumble, Huon apple 268
curds
lemon curd 128, 177
mango curd 257
custards
custard 255
pea custard 232
quiche custard 207
white chocolate custard 277

D

dairy 281
Dark chocolate, orange and almond crumb-kies 6
dark chocolate whipped ganache 188

dates: Fluffy buttermilk scones 61-2
Di Bartolo, Marianna 40-2, 100-101, 290
dill
Feta and dill biscuits with harissa honey butter 203
Pea and feta tart 230-2
pickled zucchini 231
drømmekage, Pandan 148
Duffy, Charlie 44-7, 255-6, 290
dukkah, sweet 267

E

eggs 282
Amaro crème caramel with salted, caramelised cacao 255-6
Basque cheesecake 270
beating egg whites 60
Chocolate cherry choux 187-9
chocolate filling 243
chocolate mousse 123
choux pastry 187
Chu flans 102-3
crème anglaise 246-7
crème diplomat 118
crème patissière 103
custard 255
egg wash 32, 90, 100-101, 107, 139, 200, 205, 239, 264
frangipane 134, 264
heat-and-whip meringues 246
Hibiscus cake 164
lemon curd 128, 177
Lemon curd shortbread tart 128-9
lemon filling 239
Lemon tart 239-40
mango curd 257
meringue 164
Miss Trixie's classic chocolate cake 167-8
Negroni chocolate tart 243
olive oil and blackberry buttercream 177
Pandan, coconut and mango chiffon roll 257-9
pea custard 232
Peaches and cream meringue tower 246-7
Preserved lemon layer cake with blackberry and olive oil buttercream 176-8
quiche custard 207
salted vanilla Swiss meringue buttercream 167
Tomato, herb and quark tart 206-7
White chocolate and rhubarb pudding with lemon myrtle 276-7
white chocolate custard 277

F

fennel seeds: Plum, frangipane and cream cheese galettes 134-6
fenugreek seeds: Burnt fenugreek and sesame loaf 215-16
ferment 204
feta
Feta and dill biscuits with harissa honey butter 203
Pea and feta tart 230-2
pea cake 232
figs
Fig, chocolate and sweet dukkah sundaes 267
Fig-leaf sourdough tin loaf 213-14
Hibiscus cake 164
fillings
apple filling 268
chocolate filling 243, 250
cinnamon filling 142
cream cheese mix 134
frangipane filling 107
Jerusalem artichoke, chilli greens and goat's cheese filling 218
lemon filling 239
poppyseed filling 83
quark, herb and tomato filling 207
ricotta filling 100-101
spinach, leek and smoked cheddar filling 200
strawberry and cream cheese filling 273
flaky pastry 206
flans, Chu 102-3
flatbread see manouche
Flour and Stone 120, 290
flours 17, 282
flowers 282-3
see also hibiscus, lavender
Fluffy buttermilk scones 61-2
focaccia: Jerusalem artichoke, chilli greens and goat's cheese focaccias 218-19
frangipane 107, 134, 264
frostings
sour cream frosting 173
strawberry gum cream frosting 164
tiramisu frosting 51
see also icings
fruit and nuts 247
fruit buns 90

G

galettes, Plum, frangipane and cream cheese 134-6
ganache
chocolate hazelnut ganache 92
dark chocolate whipped ganache 188
garlic butter 205
Gastmeier, Kimmy 210-14, 262-5, 290

gel, strawberry 33
Ginger and orange blossom cake 115–16
Glazed fruit buns 90
glazes
    chocolate glaze 160
    sour cream glaze 67
Grainz 56, 80, 290
grapefruit: Grapefruit creams 54–5

H

haloumi: haloumi pies 225
hamantaschen dough 83–4
stick blenders 229
Hansen, Sophie 106–7, 267, 290
harissa
    Feta and dill biscuits with harissa honey butter 203
    harissa honey butter 203
Hausler, Cherie 180–3, 290
hazelnuts
    Baker Bleu babka 92–3
    chocolate hazelnut ganache 92
    crumble 268
    Fig, chocolate and sweet dukkah sundaes 267
    Hazelnut and apple cake with sour cream frosting and apple caramel 172–3
    Huon apple crumble 268
    sweet dukkah 267
heat-and-whip meringues 246
Henderson, Alisha 48–51, 118, 290
herbs 284
    Tomato, herb and quark tart 206–7
    za'atar manouche 224
    see also bay leaves, dill, lemon myrtle, lemon thyme, oregano, parsley, strawberry gum
hibiscus: Hibiscus cake 164
Holy Sugar 238, 289
honey 284
    A1 pies, three ways 224–5
    Feta and dill biscuits with harissa honey butter 203
    harissa honey butter 203
    honey joy top 39
    Jerusalem artichoke, chilli greens and goat's cheese focaccias 218–19
    Lemon, thyme and honey madeleines 73
    Miss Trixie's honey joy slice 39
    Mohn hamantaschen (poppyseed cookies) 83–4
    poppyseed filling 83
hot chocolate sauce 267
Huon apple crumble 268

I

ice cream: Fig, chocolate and sweet dukkah sundaes 267
icings
    meringue icing 182–3
    passionfruit icing 147
    raspberry icing 127
    wattleseed icing 99
    see also frostings
Inception cake 160
Ingram, Nadine 120–3, 290
Invy Baker, The 138, 290

J

Jackson, Emelia 52–5, 187–9, 290
jams
    cherry jam 262
    morello cherry jam 189
    strawberry, chocolate and balsamic vinegar jam 191
James, Michael 56–9, 127, 290
Jeffery, Belinda 60–2, 128–9, 290
Jerusalem artichoke, chilli greens and goat's cheese focaccias 218–19
juice, pandan 148, 258

K

kafta manouche 225
Kahlua: Tiramisukis 51
kale: Jerusalem artichoke, chilli greens and goat's cheese focaccias 218–19
kefir: Fluffy buttermilk scones 61–2
Knierum, Jesse 64–7, 268, 290

L

lamb
    A1 pies, three ways 224–5
    kafta manouche 225
lamington stack, Strawberry, chocolate and balsamic 191–2
lavender: London fog castagnole, cacao nib sugar and pots de crème 71
Layered rhubarb meringue cake 182–3
leeks
    Pea and feta tart 230–2
    pea cake 232
    Spinach, leek and smoked cheddar cheese slab pie 199–200
lemons
    apple filling 268
    blackberry purée 177
    castagnole 71
    cherry jam 262
    Cherry pie 262–5
    Chocolate cherry choux 187–9
    Hazelnut and apple cake with sour cream frosting and apple caramel 172–3
    Hibiscus cake 164
    Huon apple crumble 268
    Jerusalem artichoke, chilli greens and goat's cheese focaccias 218–19
    Layered rhubarb meringue cake 182–3
    lemon curd 128, 177
    Lemon curd shortbread tart 128–9
    lemon filling 239
    Lemon, polenta and raspberry tea cake 127
    Lemon tart 239–40
    Lemon, thyme and honey madeleines 73
    lemon zest 238
    London fog castagnole, cacao nib sugar and pots de crème 71
    mango curd 257
    marinated rhubarb 276
    morello cherry jam 189
    olive oil and blackberry buttercream 177
    Pandan, coconut and mango chiffon roll 257–9
    Pea and feta tart 230–2
    Preserved lemon layer cake with blackberry and olive oil buttercream 176–8
    raspberry icing 127
    rhubarb cake 182
    Ricotta cassateddi 100–101
    shortcrust pastry 262
    Unbaked strawberry cheesecake 273
    White chocolate and rhubarb pudding with lemon myrtle 276–7
lemon myrtle
    White chocolate and rhubarb pudding with lemon myrtle 276–7
    white chocolate custard 277
lemon thyme: Lemon, thyme and honey madeleines 73
Little Picket potato bread with roasted garlic butter and parsley 204–5
loaves see bread
London fog castagnole, cacao nib sugar and pots de crème 71
lye water 79

M

Mabu Mabu 162, 289
macadamias: Macadamia and wattleseed chocolate chip cookies 59

macerated cherries 262
madeleines, Lemon, thyme and honey 73
Mali Bakes 174, 289
mangos
   mango curd 257
   Pandan, coconut and mango chiffon roll 257-9
   whipped toasted coconut cream 257
manouche
   kafta manouche 225
   za'atar manouche 224
marinated rhubarb 276
maritozzi, Strawberry and matcha 32-3
marsala
   castagnole 71
   London fog castagnole, cacao nib sugar and pots de crème 71
Marshmallow brownies 25
mascarpone
   Basque cheesecake 270
   Chocolate and rye tart with olive oil mascarpone cream 250-1
   cookie dough 51
   olive oil mascarpone cream 251
   Strawberry, chocolate and balsamic lamington stack 191-2
   tiramisu frosting 51
   Tiramisukis 51
   white chocolate, vanilla and mascarpone cream 192
matcha
   matcha chantilly 33
   Strawberry and matcha maritozzi 32-3
McAllister Forte, Giorgia 68-71, 218-19, 290
meringue 164
   meringue icing 182-3
   meringue tower, Peaches and cream 246-7
   meringues, heat-and-whip meringues 246
Mietta 158, 289
millers 282
Miss Trixie's classic chocolate cake 167-8
Miss Trixie Drinks Tea 36, 289
Miss Trixie's honey joy slice 39
Mohn hamantaschen (poppyseed cookies) 83-4
Monforte Viennoiserie 68, 290
Montalbán Sánchez, Gregorio 138-43, 290
morello cherry jam 189
Morgan, Aaron 64-7, 268, 290
mousse, chocolate 123
Muffet, Dougal 132-6, 215-16, 290

N
Negroni chocolate tart 243
nuts *see* almonds, hazelnuts, macadamias, pecans, pistachios, walnuts

O
oats
   crumble 268
   Huon apple crumble 268
olive oil and blackberry buttercream 177
olive oil mascarpone cream 251
Ondeh ondeh 79
Only Cheesecake 272, 291
orange blossom water: Ginger and orange blossom cake 115-16
oranges
   Crullers 66-7
   Dark chocolate, orange and almond crumb-kies 6
   fruit buns 90
   Glazed fruit buns 90
   hamantaschen dough 83-4
   Mohn hamantaschen (poppyseed cookies) 83-4
   Plum streusel cake 150-1
   sour cream glaze 67
   Strawberry, chocolate and balsamic lamington stack 191-2
   white chocolate, vanilla and mascarpone cream 192
oregano: za'atar manouche 224

P
Pamment, Tilly 72-3, 147, 290
pandan 258
   Ondeh ondeh 79
   pandan chiffon 258
   Pandan drømmekage 148
   pandan juice 148, 258
   Pandan, coconut and mango chiffon roll 257-9
parsley
   A1 pies, three ways 224-5
   garlic butter 205
   Little Picket potato bread with roasted garlic butter and parsley 204-5
passionfruit
   Buttermilk bundt with passionfruit icing 147
   passionfruit icing 147
pastes
   almond paste 139, 143
   praline pastes 52
pastries
   brisée pastry 134
   chocolate pastry 243

   choux pastry 187
   croissant dough 102
   flaky pastry 206
   pie pastry 200
   rye pastry 250
   shortbread pastry 128
   shortcrust pastry 231, 262
   tart pastry 107
Paull, Natalie 4-6, 290
peaches
   Peach and sour cream cake 118
   Peaches and cream meringue tower 246-7
Peaches la Crème 244, 289
pear
   Pear frangipane slab tart 107
   poached pears 107
peas
   Pea and feta tart 230-2
   pea cake 232
   pea custard 232
pecans
   Burnt butter and pecan cakes 47
   The legendary butterscotch pecan self-saucing pudding 15
pepperberries 163
   Hibiscus cake 164
   strawberry gum cream frosting 164
pickled zucchini 231
pies
   A1 pies, three ways 224-5
   Cherry pie 262-5
   haloumi pies 225
   kafta manouche 225
   Spinach, leek and smoked cheddar cheese slab pie 199-200
   za'atar manouche 224
piping 48, 175
pistachios
   Fig, chocolate and sweet dukkah sundaes 267
   Peaches and cream meringue tower 246-7
   Pistachio amaretti 42
   sweet dukkah 267
plums
   Plum, frangipane and cream cheese galettes 134-6
   Plum streusel cake 150-1
poached pears 107
polenta
   Dark chocolate, orange and almond crumb-kies 6
   Lemon, polenta and raspberry tea cake 127
poolish 102
Poolish & Co. 64, 290
poppyseeds
   Fig, chocolate and sweet dukkah sundaes 267
   Mohn hamantaschen (poppyseed cookies) 83-4

poppyseed filling 83
sweet dukkah 267
potatoes: Little Picket potato bread with roasted garlic butter and parsley 204-5
pots de crème 71
praline pastes 52
Preserved lemon layer cake with blackberry and olive oil buttercream 176-8
produce, fresh 282
pudding, The legendary butterscotch pecan self-saucing 15
Purchese, Darren 190-2, 270, 291
purée, blackberry 177

Q
quiche custard 207

R
Raji, Haikal 222-5, 291
raspberries
Lemon, polenta and raspberry tea cake 127
raspberry icing 127
Raya Bakery 76, 291
refrigeration 245
rhubarb
Layered rhubarb meringue cake 182-3
marinated rhubarb 276
rhubarb cake 182
White chocolate and rhubarb pudding with lemon myrtle 276-7
rice cake balls: Ondeh ondeh 79
ricotta
castagnole 71
London fog castagnole, cacao nib sugar and pots de crème 71
Ricotta cassateddi 100-101
ricotta filling 100-101
roll, Pandan, coconut and mango chiffon 257-9
Russell, Mike 26-7
rye pastry 250

S
sable, almond and emmer 122
salted caramelised cacao 256
salted vanilla cream 247
salted vanilla Swiss meringue buttercream 167
sauces
chocolate soaking sauce 192
hot chocolate sauce 267
strawberry sauce 273
scones, Fluffy buttermilk 61-2

seeds see fennel seeds, fenugreek seeds, poppyseeds, sesame seeds, wattleseeds
semlor, Swedish 139-40
sesame seeds
A1 pies, three ways 224-5
Burnt fenugreek and sesame loaf 215-16
Chocolate rye tahini cookies 28
Fig, chocolate and sweet dukkah sundaes 267
Spinach, leek and smoked cheddar cheese slab pie 199-200
sweet dukkah 267
za'atar manouche 224
shortbread pastry 128
shortcrust pastry 231, 262
slice, Miss Trixie's honey joy 39
Small Batch Roasting Co. 44, 290
sour cream 37
Baker Bleu babka 92-3
brioche dough 92
chocolate cake 167
Crullers 66-7
Hazelnut and apple cake with sour cream frosting and apple caramel 172-3
Miss Trixie's classic chocolate cake 167-8
Peach and sour cream cake 118
Peaches and cream meringue tower 246-7
Plum streusel cake 150-1
salted vanilla cream 247
sour cream frosting 173
sour cream glaze 67
Unbaked strawberry cheesecake 273
sourdough, Fig-leaf, tin loaf 213-14
spices 284
Spinach, leek and smoked cheddar cheese slab pie 199-200
stick blenders 229
strawberries
Strawberry and matcha maritozzi 32-3
Strawberry, chocolate and balsamic lamington stack 191-2
strawberry, chocolate and balsamic vinegar jam 191
strawberry gel 33
strawberry sauce 273
Unbaked strawberry cheesecake 273
strawberry gum
Hibiscus cake 164
strawberry gum cream frosting 164
streusel 150
Studio Kitchen 190, 291
sugar
bay-infused sugar 113

cacao nib sugar 71
creaming butter and sugar 60
sugar syrup 90, 93
sultanas
Fluffy buttermilk scones 61-2
fruit buns 90
Glazed fruit buns 90
sundaes, Fig, chocolate and sweet dukkah 267
suppliers 281-4
Swedish semlor 139-40
Sweet Bakes 48, 290
sweet dukkah 267
sweet potato: Ondeh ondeh 79
syrups
sugar syrup 90, 93
vanilla syrup 142

T
tahini: Chocolate rye tahini cookies 28
Tan, Raymond 76-9, 148, 291
tarts
Chocolate, amaretto and sour cherry tart 122-3
Chocolate and rye tart with olive oil mascarpone cream 250-1
Chu flans 102-3
Lemon curd shortbread tart 128-9
Lemon tart 239-40
Negroni chocolate tart 243
Pea and feta tart 230-2
Pear frangipane slab tart 107
tart base 239
Tomato, herb and quark tart 206-7
Tarts Anon 228, 291
tea 284
castagnole 71
London fog castagnole, cacao nib sugar and pots de crème 71
pots de crème 71
Teeter Bakery 170, 289
texture 97, 223
The legendary butterscotch pecan self-saucing pudding 15
thyme see lemon thyme
tiramisu frosting 51
Tiramisukis 51
Tivoli Road Bakery 44, 56, 96
Tomato, herb and quark tart 206-7
toppings
caramelised almond topping 140
coconut topping 148
honey joy top 39
Toyama, Akira 272-3, 291

U
Unbaked strawberry cheesecake 273
Urbanstead 56, 290

V

vanilla
  Basque cheesecake 270
  crème anglaise 246–7
  crème diplomat 118
  crème patissière 103
  Peaches and cream meringue
      tower 246–7
  salted vanilla cream 247
  salted vanilla Swiss meringue
      buttercream 167
  vanilla chantilly cream 90
  vanilla syrup 142
  white chocolate, vanilla and
      mascarpone cream 192

W

walnuts
  crumble 268
  Fig, chocolate and sweet dukkah
      sundaes 267
  Huon apple crumble 268
  sweet dukkah 267
wattleseeds 163
  Beetroot and apple cake with
      wattleseed icing 99
  chocolate glaze 160
  Inception cake 160
  Macadamia and wattleseed
      chocolate chip cookies 59
  wattleseed icing 99
Werdiger, Maaryasha 80–4,
  150–1, 291
whipped toasted coconut cream 257
White chocolate and rhubarb pudding
  with lemon myrtle 276–7
white chocolate custard 277
white chocolate, vanilla and
  mascarpone cream 192
Whitton, Gareth 228–32, 276–7, 291
Wildpie 96, 289
wood-fired baking 211

Y

yoghurt
  Preserved lemon layer cake
      with blackberry and olive oil
      buttercream 176–8
  Unbaked strawberry
      cheesecake 273

Z

za'atar manouche 224
Zelda Bakery 80, 291
zucchini
  Pea and feta tart 230–2
  pea cake 232
  pickled zucchini 231

Index

Published in 2025 by Murdoch Books,
an imprint of Allen & Unwin

Murdoch Books Australia
Cammeraygal Country
83 Alexander Street
Crows Nest NSW 2065
Phone: +61 (0)2 8425 0100
murdochbooks.com.au
info@murdochbooks.com.au

Murdoch Books UK
Ormond House
26–27 Boswell Street
London WC1N 3JZ
Phone: +44 (0) 20 8785 5995
murdochbooks.co.uk
info@murdochbooks.co.uk

For corporate orders and custom publishing, contact our business development team at salesenquiries@murdochbooks.com.au

Publisher: Jane Willson
Editorial manager: Loran McDougall
Design manager: Kristy Allen
Editor: Nicola Young
Designer: Emily O'Neill
Illustrator: Beci Orpin
Photographer: Rochelle Eagle
Stylist: Lee Blaylock
Photoshoot chefs: Sarah Watson, Emelia Jackson, Michael James
Production director: Natalie Crouch

With special thanks to Sage and Clare for the linen (pp. 24, 67, 94, 95, 125, 153, 153, 185, 193, 217, 261, 288) and to Listen to the Flowers (pp. 91, 135, 263) for the plates.

Text © individual contributors 2025
The moral right of the authors has been asserted.
Design © Murdoch Books 2025
Photography © Rochelle Eagle 2025

Murdoch Books acknowledges the Traditional Owners of the Country on which we live and work. We pay our respects to all Aboriginal and Torres Strait Islander Elders, past and present.

All rights reserved. No part of this publication may be reproduced, stored in a retrieval system or transmitted in any form or by any means, electronic, mechanical, photocopying, recording or otherwise, without the prior written permission of the publisher.

ISBN 978 1 76150 026 8

A catalogue record for this book is available from the National Library of Australia

A catalogue record for this book is available from the British Library

Colour reproduction by Splitting Image Colour Studio Pty Ltd, Wantirna, Victoria

Printed by 1010 Printing International Limited, China

10 9 8 7 6 5 4 3 2 1

TABLESPOON MEASURES: We have used 20 ml (4 teaspoon) tablespoon measures. If you are using a 15 ml (3 teaspoon) tablespoon, add an extra teaspoon of the ingredient for each tablespoon specified.

CUP MEASURES: We have used 250 ml (9 fl oz) cups. If you are using a US cup measure (approximately 235 ml/8 fl oz), be generous with your cup measurements. However, for best results, we recommend following the weights in these recipes.

MIX
Paper | Supporting responsible forestry
FSC® C016973